OXFORD
UNIVERSITY PRESS

geog.2

teacher's resource file

◆ photocopiable materials   ◆ assessment package, including assessment
for learning, with editable files on CD-ROM   ◆ worksheets and enquiries

1/1

25-08-11

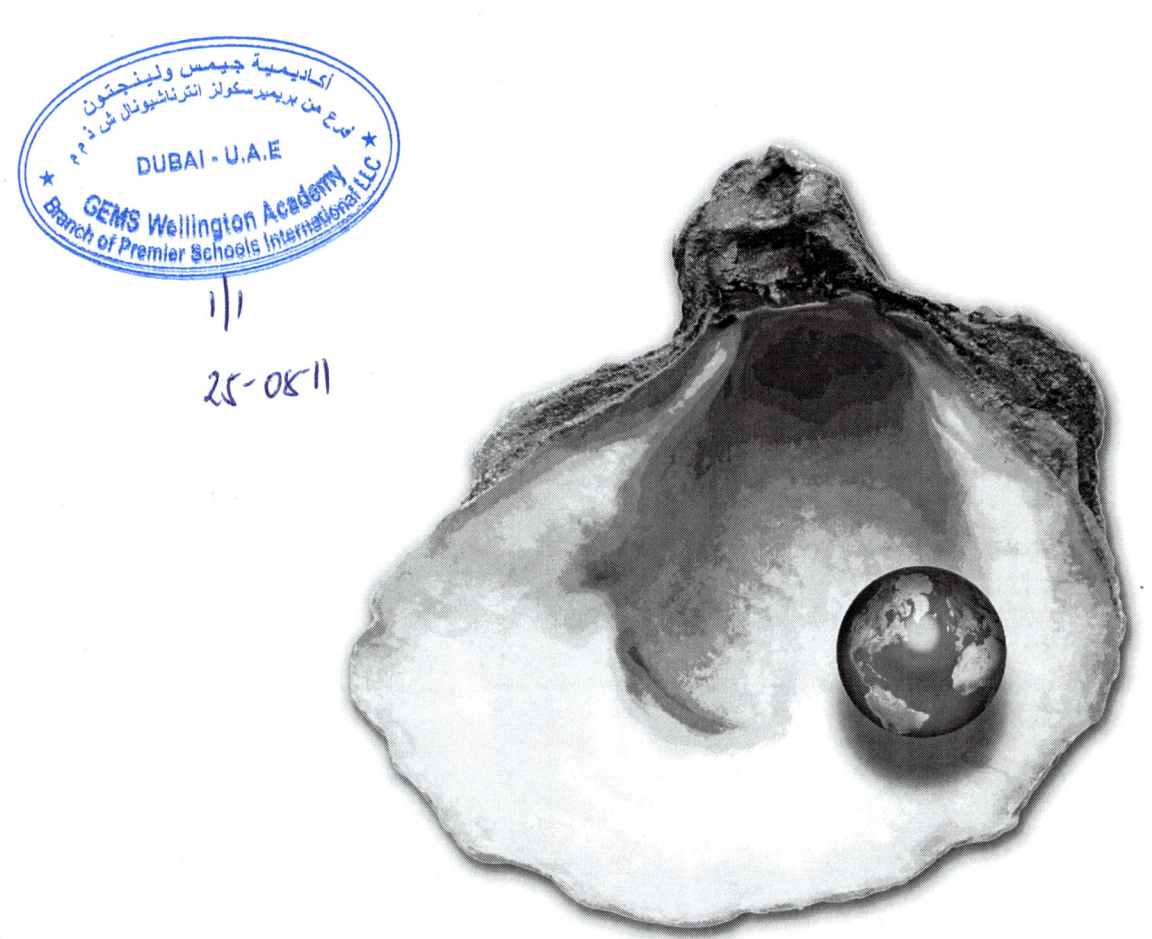

< rosemarie gallagher >< john edwards >< chris stevens >< anna king >
< phyl gallagher >< rosemary grenyer >
< hazel wright >

OXFORD
UNIVERSITY PRESS

Great Clarendon Street, Oxford OX2 6DP

Oxford University Press is a department of the University of Oxford.
It furthers the University's objective of excellence in research,
scholarship, and education by publishing worldwide in

Oxford   New York

Auckland   Cape Town   Dar es Salaam   Hong Kong   Karachi
Kuala Lumpur   Madrid   Melbourne   Mexico City   Nairobi
New Delhi   Shanghai   Taipei   Toronto

With offices in

Argentina   Austria   Brazil   Chile   Czech Republic   France   Greece
Guatemala   Hungary   Italy   Japan   Poland   Portugal   Singapore
South Korea   Switzerland   Thailand   Turkey   Ukraine   Vietnam

Oxford is a registered trade mark of Oxford University Press
in the UK and in certain other countries

© RoseMarie Gallagher, John Edwards, Chris Stevens, Anna King, Phyl Gallagher,
Rosemary Grenyer, Hazel Wright 2005

The moral rights of the author have been asserted

Database right Oxford University Press (maker)

First published 2005

British Library Cataloguing in Publication Data

Data available

ISBN: 978-0-19-913453-3

10 9 8 7 6 5

Printed in the United Kingdom by Bell and Bain Ltd. Glasgow

Cover photo: Getty Images and Hemera

Certain materials in this title were first published in *geog.2 teacher's book*, Oxford
University Press, 2001, or *geog.2 teacher's CD-ROM*, Oxford University Press, 2002.

Contents

geog.2 is the second book of *geog.123* – the complete geography course for KS3. The course covers the KS3 Programme of Study, and provides material for the QCA Scheme of Work and the prior learning this requires. It offers excellent support for FS/TLF.

The course components

The course consists of:

For pupils
- three pupils' books
- the course website

For teachers
- three handbooks
- three resource files, each with a CD-ROM
- three *basics* books
- three *challenges* books
- the course website

Find out more about the course components by looking at these panels.

The pupils' books
- Three books for the course
- Chapters divided into two-page units
- Chapter openers give the big picture – the big ideas behind the chapter – and the goals for the chapter
- Aims of unit given in pupil-friendly language at the start of each unit
- 'Your turn' questions at the end of each unit

The teacher's resource files
- One for each pupils' book
- Assessment package containing level-marked assessments, success criteria, and feedback and self-assessment forms – with editable files on the CD-ROM
- Scored tests, with mark schemes
- Photocopiable worksheets, with answers
- Photocopiable enquiries, decision-making exercises, role-plays, fieldwork, games, and thinking skills activities – with opportunities for pair and group work
- Outline maps
- Management and planning aids
  – course, theme, and lesson planners
  – pupil profile sheet
- All material on CD-ROM; assessment materials and management aids provided as editable Word files

The teacher's handbooks
- One for each pupils' book
- Chapter overviews
- Help at a glance for each unit
- Ideas for starters and plenaries for each unit
- Outcomes for each unit
- Answers for 'Your turn' questions
- Further suggestions for class and homework

The course website

- Interactive material for every chapter in the pupils' books
- *geog aid*: interactive skills lessons, scrapbook, interactive glossary, hotlinks
- On-screen activities
- Interactive country data section
- Ideal for individual study
- Can be accessed by teachers and pupils, in school and at home
- Teacher's notes throughout the site
- *Teacher zone* containing extra support material
- Ideal for whole-class use via an interactive whiteboard or projector

geog.123 provides a wide range of materials. The pupils' books are the core of the course. They combine a rigorous approach to content with a uniquely engaging style.

You can decide how to use the wealth of support materials, but notes in the teacher's handbooks will point you towards appropriate material in the teacher's resource files, in the *basics* and *challenges* books, and on *geog.world*. The result is a truly comprehensive and flexible geography course – which we hope you will enjoy using.

The *basics* teacher's books

- Materials for lower-ability pupils
- One for each pupils' book
- Chapter overviews
- Help at a glance for each unit
- Specially differentiated 'Your turn' questions, with answers
- Photocopiable worksheets, with answers

The *challenges* teacher's books

- Materials for higher-ability pupils
- One for each pupils' book
- Chapter overviews
- Extended 'Your turn' questions, with answers
- Further challenges
- Photocopiable extension activities, with answers

Using this resource file

This resource file contains vital support material for *geog.2* pupils' book, to help you plan and deliver an exciting geography course.

- It offers a wide range of photocopiable worksheets, learning activities, and assessments, as well as course, theme, and lesson planning documents.
- All materials are also provided on the accompanying CD-ROM.
- Selected assessment materials and forms, and the management and planning documents, are also provided as Word files, so that you can adapt them.

[PDF] indicates material provided in PDF format on the CD-ROM.
[W] indicates material provided as editable Word files.

Worksheets [PDF]

There are photocopiable worksheets for each chapter. Some provide revision, and some are extension material. They have been graded *, **, or *** according to level of difficulty. (* is easiest.) Answers are given where appropriate.

We would like to acknowledge *Thinking through Geography*, edited by David Leat, as inspiration for some of the worksheets.

Learning activities [PDF]

There's a collection of learning activities for each chapter – enquiries, decision-making exercises, role-plays, fieldwork, games, and thinking skills activities.

Some of these activities are quite short. Others will take pupils several hours to complete. Some are for individual work, while others provide opportunities for pupils to work in pairs or small groups.

Like the worksheets, they have been graded *, **, or *** according to level of difficulty.

There are teacher's notes for each activity, giving the aims of the activity, and advice on how to set up and run it.

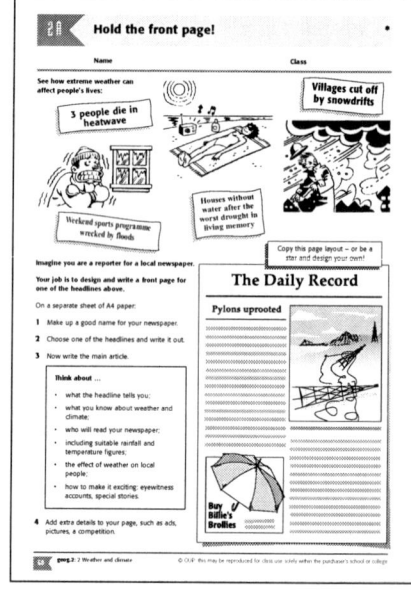

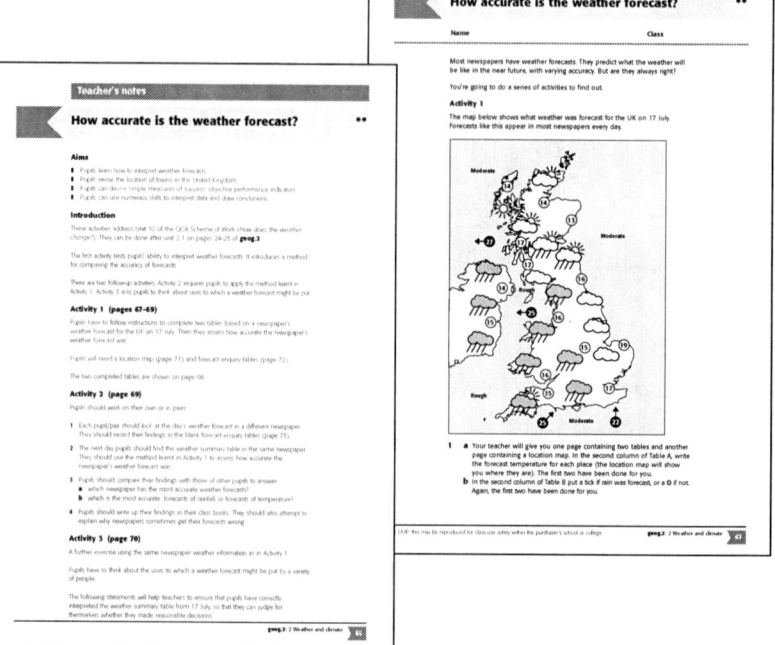

Assessment package [PDF] [W]

There are four types of assessment material on the file and accompanying CD-ROM:

1 assessment overviews
2 level-marked assessments, with feedback forms
3 scored tests
4 forms for recording overall performance – the pupil profile sheet, and self-assessment forms.

There's more about the assessment package on pages 8-9.

Outline maps [PDF]

Photocopiable maps of Brazil (blank), Brazil (regions), South America (political), the British Isles, Europe (political), the World (political) and the World (regions to know) are provided.

Management and planning documents [PDF] [W]

The course, theme, and lesson planning documents are all provided as Word files to help you plan and record your own schemes of work.

To save you time, the theme planning document for each chapter contains editable details of unit objectives and outcomes, skills practised, and vocabulary. It also sets the chapter in its Key Stage 3 Programme of Study and QCA Scheme of Work context.

The management and planning documents are provided as templates on the CD-ROM, for you to use and adapt. They are provided only on the CD-ROM; hard copy versions are not reproduced on this file.

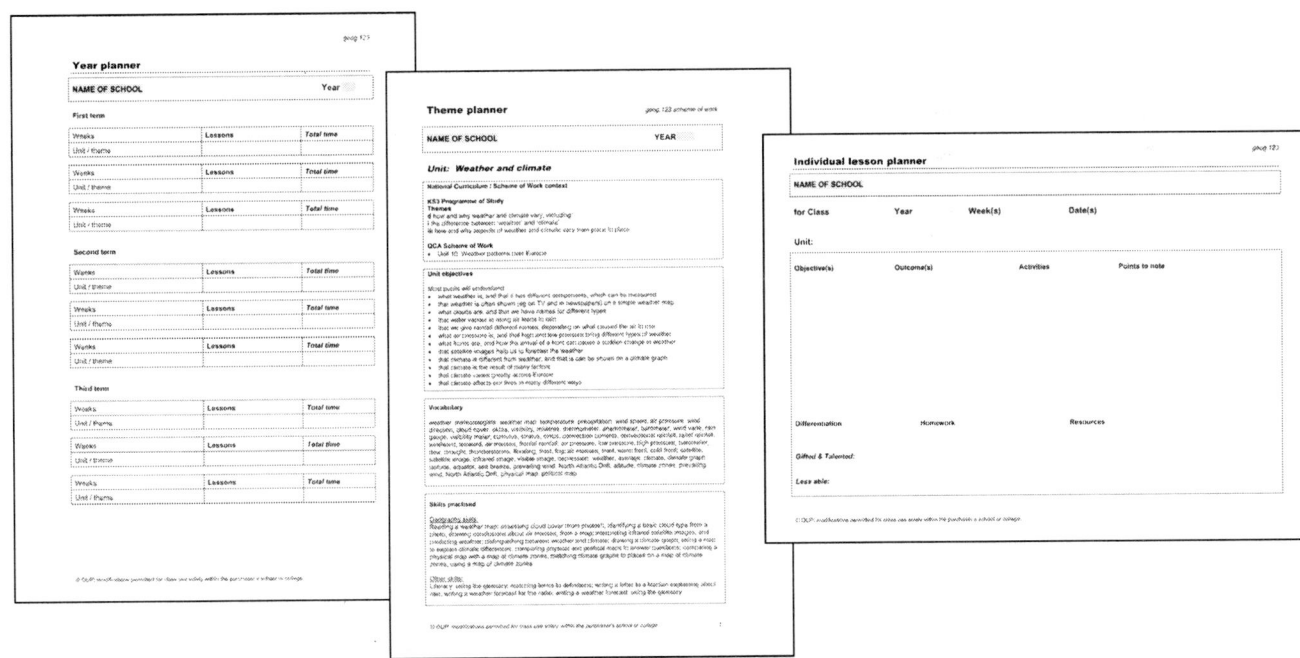

More about the assessment package

This resource file provides a wide range of assessment materials to help you deliver a varied and effective assessment programme.

There are four types of assessment material on the file and accompanying CD-ROM:
1 assessment overviews
2 level-marked assessments, with feedback forms
3 scored tests
4 forms for recording overall performance – the pupil profile sheet, and self-assessment forms.

[PDF] indicates material provided in PDF format on the CD-ROM.
[W] indicates material provided as editable Word files.

1 Assessment overviews [PDF] [W]

The formal assessment material for each chapter begins with an assessment overview – useful notes about the level-marked assessment, and suggestions for 'interim assessments' using other materials and activities in this file, the teacher's handbook, and on *geog.world*.

2 Level-marked assessments [PDF] [W]

There's a level-marked assessment for each chapter, with easy-to-use success criteria written in pupil-friendly language.

You can discuss with pupils their target levels for the assessment, and there's space to record this at the start of the assessment. So each pupil sets out with a clear idea of what he or she is aiming for, and why.

Because the success criteria are included in the level-marked assessment, pupils can check what they have to do to achieve – and improve upon – their target level.

The assessments are varied and interesting, and cover a range of activity types and skills.

Most pupils should be able to complete the assessments in under two hours, although some may need a little longer.

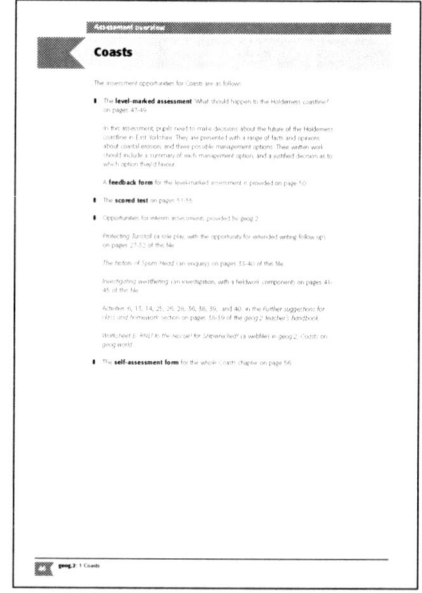

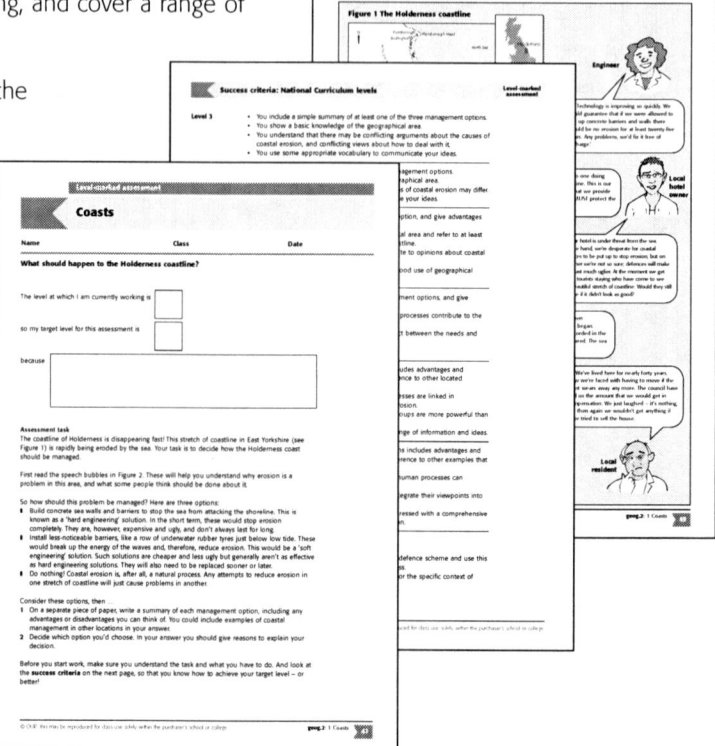

More about the assessment package

Assessment feedback forms [PDF] [W]
Each level-marked assessment has a feedback form, designed to be used with individual pupils. It allows you to record the level achieved, to comment, and to identify areas for improvement. It also allows the pupil take part in this process.

The feedback form can then form part of the pupil's assessment portfolio.

You can amend the success criteria sheet and the feedback form so that they can be used in peer assessment.

3 Scored tests [PDF]

There's a scored test for each chapter. Each is marked out of 50, with the marks for each question indicated. Answers are provided.

These tests can be used at any time you choose. They are not designed to produce levelled results. But they will help to provide a varied and flexible approach to tracking your pupils' progress.

4 Forms for recording performance

Pupil profile sheet [PDF] [W]
Designed to be used with individual pupils, it allows you to create and maintain an overall record of their performance in the level-marked assessments and scored tests.

You can adapt the sheet to include details of any interim assessments, or any other information relating to the pupil's performance and progress.

At the end of the year or course, it can then form part of the pupil's assessment portfolio.

The profile sheet is provided as a template, for you to use and adapt to suit your assessment programme. It is provided only on the CD-ROM; a hard copy version is not reproduced on this file.

Self-assessment forms [PDF] [W]
There's a self-assessment form for each chapter. Designed to be used at the end of the chapter, it allows individual pupils to review and analyse their own work.

The table relates to the text 'Your goals for this chapter' laid out at the start of each chapter in the pupils' book.

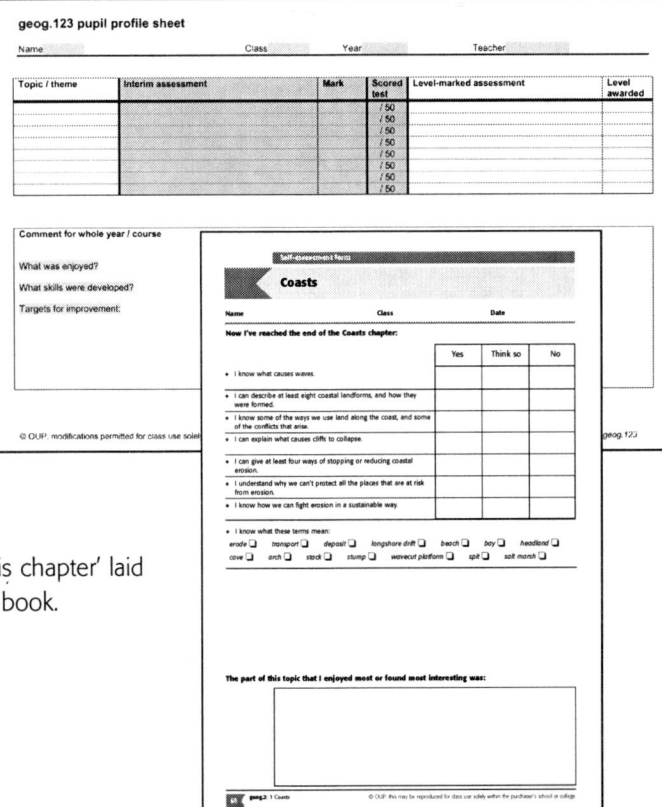

About the teacher's handbook

The *geog.2 teacher's handbook* aims to save you time and effort! It offers full support for *geog.2* students' book, and will help you prepare detailed course and lesson plans.

What it provides

For each chapter of the students' book, the teacher's handbook provides:
1. a chapter overview
2. help at a glance for each unit, including answers for 'Your turn'
3. further suggestions for class and homework.

It also has a glossary at the back, covering the geographical terms the students will meet.

Find out more about the three main components, below.

1   The chapter overview

This is your introduction to the corresponding students' chapter. Look at its sections.

Shows how the students' chapter relates to the KS3 Programme of Study and QCA Scheme of Work.

Sets out the objectives and outcomes for the chapter, and the corresponding unit numbers.

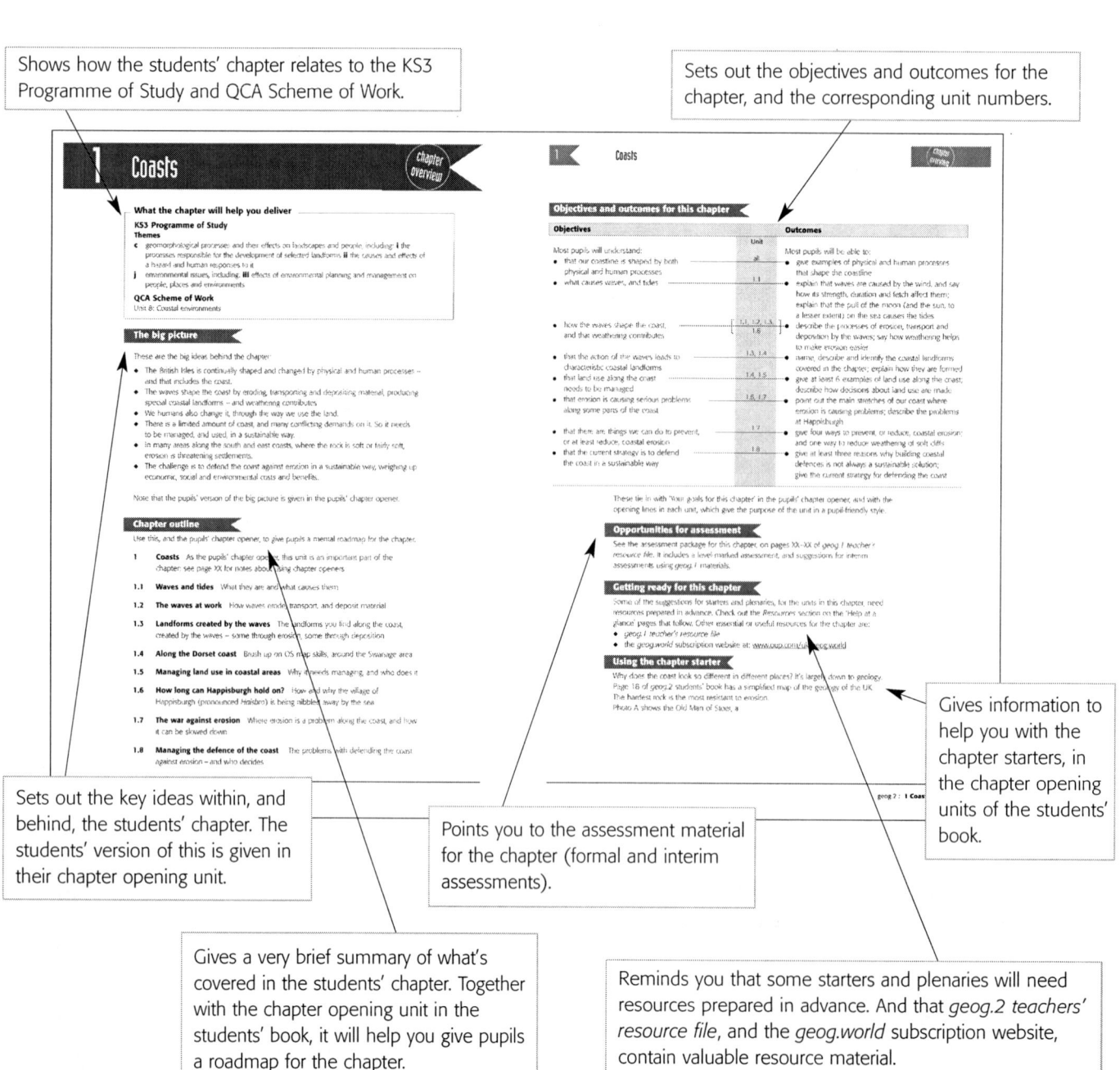

Gives information to help you with the chapter starters, in the chapter opening units of the students' book.

Sets out the key ideas within, and behind, the students' chapter. The students' version of this is given in their chapter opening unit.

Points you to the assessment material for the chapter (formal and interim assessments).

Gives a very brief summary of what's covered in the students' chapter. Together with the chapter opening unit in the students' book, it will help you give pupils a roadmap for the chapter.

Reminds you that some starters and plenaries will need resources prepared in advance. And that *geog.2 teachers' resource file*, and the *geog.world* subscription website, contain valuable resource material.

2 Help at a glance for each unit

These pages give comprehensive help for each unit of *geog.2* students' book.

Starts with a brief walk through the unit, to show you how it develops.

Summarises ideas covered in the unit, plus underlying ideas where appropriate.

Suggests plenaries for throughout the lesson, not just at the end.

New vocabulary introduced in the unit. See the glossary at the back of this book.

A breakdown of the skills practised. It will help you identify where pupils may need extra support.

Expected outcomes for the unit. They tie in with the expected outcomes for the chapter.

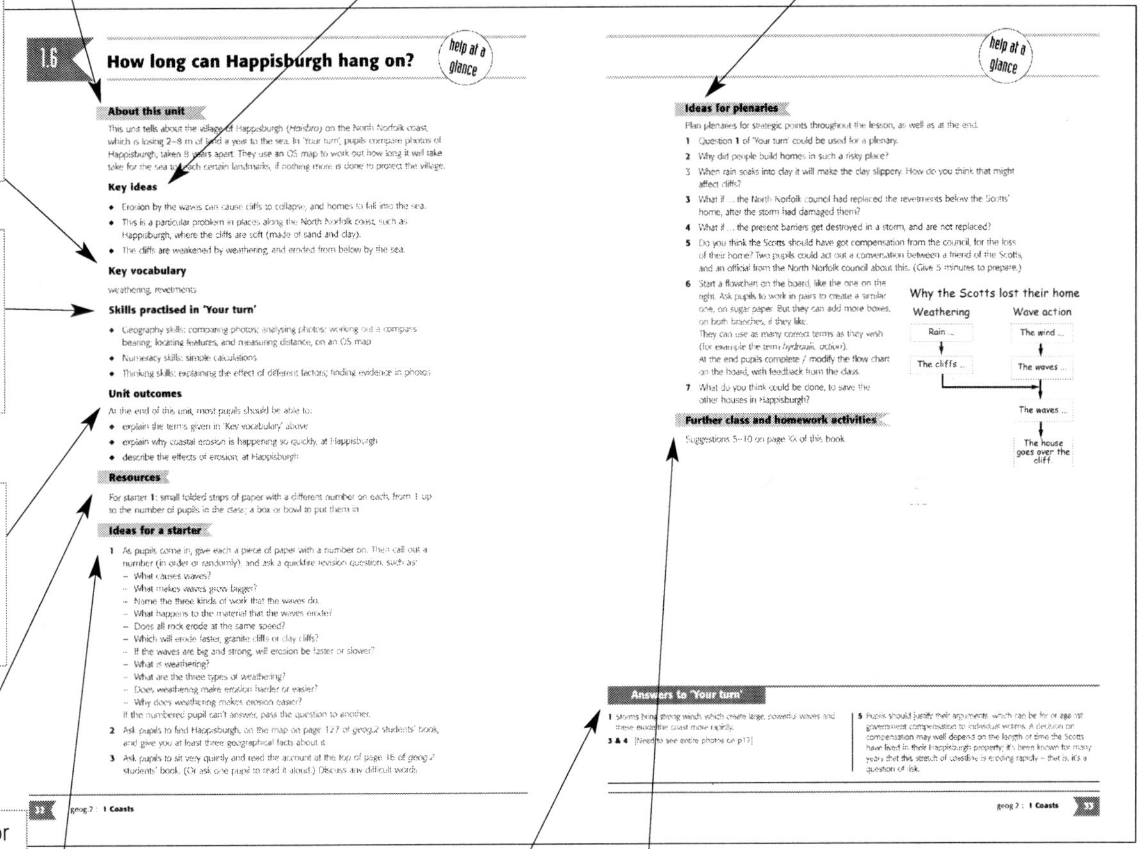

Resources needed for some of the suggested starters and plenaries.

Suggestions for starters.

Full answers to the 'Your turn' questions in the students' book, to save you time.

Points you to related material, including worksheets, homework ideas, assessment opportunities, and activities on *geog.world*.

3 Further suggestions for class and homework

These pages give a wealth of further suggestions for class and homework.
Many are based on suggestions in the QCA Scheme of Work.
They have been graded *, ** or *** according to level of difficulty.
Some are suitable for all levels, and differentiated by outcome.

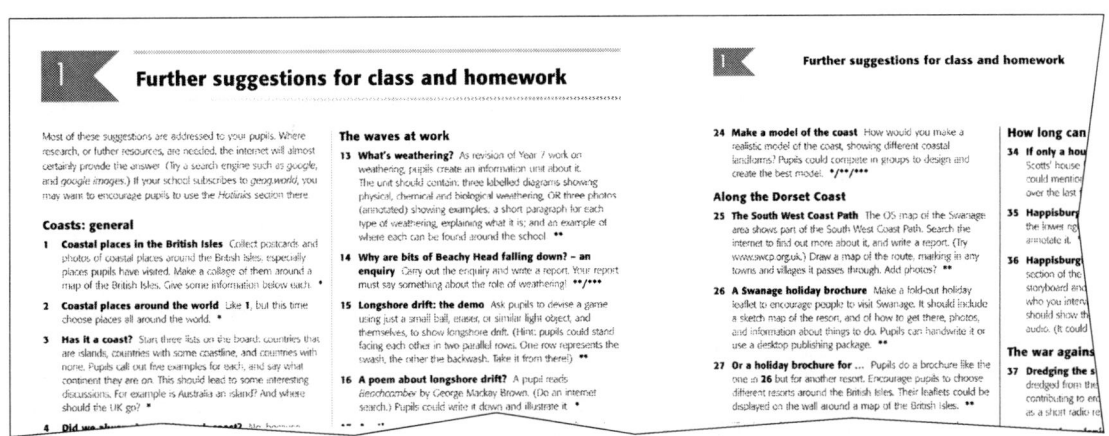

Planning your lessons around *geog.2*

Planning for high-quality lessons

Well-planned and well-structured lessons are a key requirement, for delivering high-quality teaching and learning in any subject, at any level. The *geog.123* course aims to make it easy to plan, structure, and deliver, high-quality lessons for KS3 geography.

Structure of a typical lesson

You will already be familiar with the guidelines on structuring lessons, promoted as part of the FS strand of the KS3 strategy. This shows a typical lesson structure, as recommended in those guidelines:

STARTER

Purpose: To capture pupils' attention and focus the class. Use it as the lesson hook, or to find out what pupils know already about a new topic, or for quick revision of earlier work.

INTRODUCTION

Purpose: To prepare pupils for the activities ahead.

- If this is a new topic, tell pupils the topic objectives. Write these on the board.
- If it's a continuation of a topic, you can refer back to an objective as appropriate.

ACTIVITIES

This is the main body of the lesson.

Purpose: To achieve one or more of the topic objectives.

- Emphasis on exploration and investigation.
- Provide for practice in different types of skill: geographical, literacy, numeracy, thinking, listening, speaking, teamworking, and ICT skills.
- Choose from a variety of activities: reading, answering questions, enquiries, role play, game playing, fieldwork, and ICT.

Plenaries: note that plenaries can be used as staging posts throughout the activities, to gain feedback, check understanding, link to earlier work, and encourage reflection on what is being learnt, and how.

FINAL PLENARY

Purpose: To round off and review what has been done, and to assess what has been achieved against the topic objectives. This is where you help pupils to:

- check, and crystallise, their understanding
- generalise, for example from an individual case study
- set work in context, and make links to work already done, or to be done in the future
- reflect on how they have learned, as well as what
- check how well they have achieved the topic objectives (self-assessment).

HOMEWORK

Purpose: To confirm, give practice in, and extend, what has been learnt in the lesson.

- The homework can lead on from the final plenary, and be the basis for a starter for the next lesson.

Planning around *geog.2*

Now see how the components of *geog.2* provide material for each part of your lesson.

STARTERS

- The *Help at a glance* pages in the teacher's handbook have suggestions for lesson starters.
- See further notes about starters, and resources for them, in the teacher's handbook.

OBJECTIVES

- The opening lines of each unit in the students' book give the purpose of the unit, in pupil-friendly language. The goals for each chapter are given in its opening unit.
- See also the objectives and outcomes given in the teacher's handbook.

ACTIVITIES

Using the students' books

- The text in the students' books provides the core information students need. Some lends itself to reading aloud, but try 'quiet time' too.
- You can let pupils work through the text uninterrupted, or break it up with 'Your turn' questions. (These generally follow the order of the text.)
- The questions give practice in literacy, numeracy, thinking, and geography skills.
- Some are ideal as whole-class questions with verbal response. Others can be worked through by pupils working alone, in pairs or in small groups. The final 'Your turn' questions are usually open questions that challenge pupils to show what they can do.
- For pupils who finish early, check out *Further suggestions for class and homework* at the end of each chapter in the teacher's handbook. Or select a *worksheet* from this file.

Using the *basics* and *challenges* books

- The *basics teacher's books* contain simplified 'Your turn' questions, and worksheets, for pupils working at lower attainment levels.
- The *challenges teacher's books* contain more stretching questions, and extended activities, for pupils working at higher attainment levels.

Using this file

- This file has a wide range of activities you can base lessons on, including role plays, enquiries and fieldwork.

Using *geog.world*

- The *geog.world* subscription website has many activities you can base lessons on. These include interactive lessons with scored questions, skills lessons, and webfiles with onscreen worksheets, giving plenty of ICT practice.
- Much of the material is suitable for whole-class teaching using an interactive whiteboard or projector, and offers scope for very effective lessons.

PLENARIES

- The *Help at a glance* pages in the teacher's handbook give suggestions for plenaries, for throughout the lesson as well as at the end.
- See further notes about plenaries, and resources for them, in the teacher's handbook.

HOMEWORK

- *Further suggestions for class and homework* at the end of each chapter in the teacher's handbook offer lots of ideas. Or select a *worksheet* from this file.
- If your school is a *geog.world* subscriber, pupils can access the site from home too.

About the *geog.world* website

ICT for *geog.123*

The ICT component for *geog.123* is provided by *geog.world*, the subscription website at www.oup.com/uk/geog.world.

geog.world contains a wealth of interactive material, with something for every chapter of the *geog.123* students' books. It offers lots of opportunity for your pupils to practice ICT skills, and other skills. Most of the material is aimed directly at pupils. But there is also a *Teacher zone*, and teacher notes throughout the site, which are invisible to your pupils.

Material continues to be added to *geog.world*. The latest contents list is provided in the *Teacher zone*, or can be obtained by emailing geog.worldfeedback@oup.com.

Access to *geog.world*

If your school already subscribes to *geog.world* you will know that:

*   subscribing gives 24-hour access to you and your pupils, from school and home
*   all pupils at the school use the same user name and password, to avoid confusion
*   teachers also share a user name and password, which gives access to the teacher's material
*   subscription can be purchased using e-learning credits.

Why go online?

Providing the ICT materials on a website rather than a CD-ROM has many advantages:

*   pupils can treat the site as a personal geography resource to 'take home'
*   new material can easily be added
*   material can easily be updated; for example *Hot topics* are regularly replaced
*   interactive whiteboards, with online access from classrooms, are making it easier to incorporate online material into everyday lessons.

How can *geog.world* be used?

You can use *geog.world* in many different ways.

*   Much of the material is suitable for whole-class teaching in the classroom, using an interactive whiteboard or projector. This can make for some very exciting lessons. See for example:
    - the interactive lessons such as: *Volcano!* and *How shopping has changed*. These have scored questions at the end, in which the whole class can participate.
    - walkthroughs such as *How settlements grow* and *Land use in towns and cities*, which are ideal for topic starters, and/or topic reviews.
    - skills lessons such as *How to draw a field sketch* or *Hat thinking*.
*   All material is suitable for pupils working alone, or in small groups, in the IT room.
*   You can set some for homework, to be done outside the classroom, whether at school or home. Many of the webfiles (interactive magazine articles, with worksheets) are ideal for this. Check out the *Hot topics* too.
*   The scrapbook provides images that can be used in a variety of ways.
*   The *Teacher zone* has a range of materials that you can adapt for your pupils.

The *Help at a glance* pages in the teacher's handbooks indicate where there is relevant *geog.world* material. However, more material is being added to the website. So you also need to check out the latest contents list. (See above.)

geog.world can help you deliver exciting and high-quality geography teaching. Everyone will have their own ideas about how to use it. But the first essential step is to become familiar with its content, by sitting down and working through every corner of the site.

Some typical content

geog.world offers material for each chapter of the students' books. For example here is the topic menu for the *Coasts* topic for *geog.2*:

All menus are set in context, with a clearly written introduction and a photo. So there's less chance of pupils feeling lost.

A webfile about erosion around our coastline, which complements the material in the student's book.

For this worksheet, pupils write a letter advising against building on a clifftop. It can be completed onscreen.

A webfile about shipwrecks, with two worksheets. This could be classwork or homework.

For this worksheet, pupils identify wrecks using a series of clues. They can complete it onscreen.

For this worksheet, pupils use Excel to draw a graph showing RNLI launches for one year, and then analyse it.

No scrolling means menus and other material are easier are to use; pupils won't feel overwhelmed.

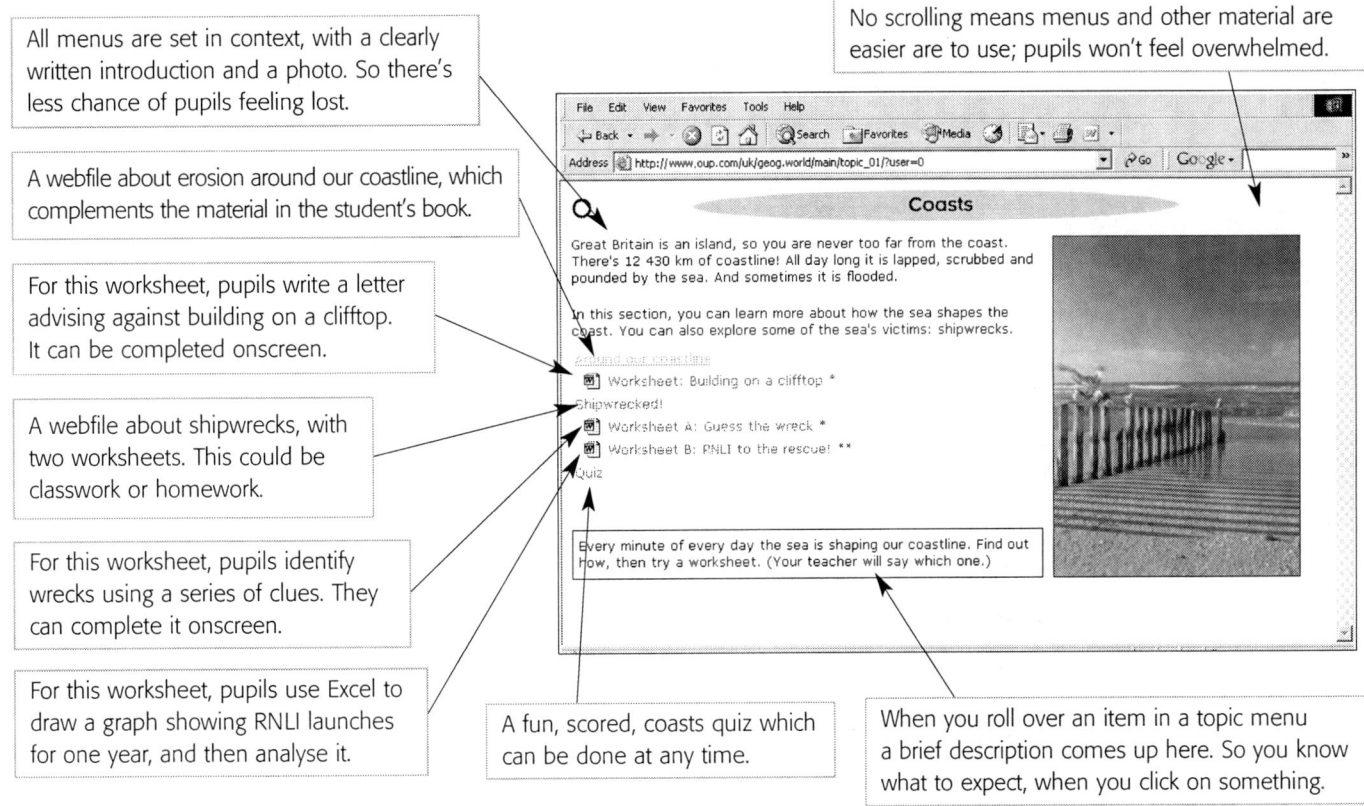

A fun, scored, coasts quiz which can be done at any time.

When you roll over an item in a topic menu a brief description comes up here. So you know what to expect, when you click on something.

The different types of content

There's a wide variety of content on *geog.world*. This table gives the different types:

Type of material	What does it do?
Topic work	
Interactive topic lesson	Focuses on a specific theme or Scheme of Work topic; ends with scored questions
Interactive walkthrough	Explains concepts and processes; ideal as a topic starter, and/or for a final review
Webfile	Like a magazine article, with worksheets; the worksheets give practice in a wide range of skills, including desk-top publishing and use of Excel; many can be completed on-screen
Scored topic quizzes	Useful for revision, and fun at any time; drawn from a question bank
End-of-topic scored test	This has more focused questions, drawn from a question bank
Hot topic	News story with a link to geography, with graded activities to choose from
Map work	
Mapping (*a country*)	Explores a country through interactive maps; a great way to get to grips with the geography of a country – with a quiz at the end
Countries at a glance	Shows where different countries are, on a world map; a click of a button gives a data card for a country; worksheets let pupils compare countries
Make your own data tables	Pupils can create their own data tables for a range of 30 countries, large and small, rich and poor; worksheets give lots of practice in using Excel
Mapping data	Pupils map development data around the world; worksheets encourage them to look for patterns and correlations (and you can print the maps out for OHTs)
geog aid	A range of resources that can be used throughout KS3; see next page for more
Teacher zone	Information and resources for you; see page 17 for more

geog aid

This section of *geog.world* has four components that will be useful right across your school's KS3 geography programme.

1 Skills kit

This is a set of interactive lessons for a range of skills, including geographical, thinking and study skills. These lessons are great for introducing new skills or brushing up on old ones. They are ideal for whole-class teaching using an interactive whiteboard or projector.

Bright attractive graphics.

Clear step-by-step instructions.

When pupils have worked through the instructions, they put them into practice – and then assess how they've done.

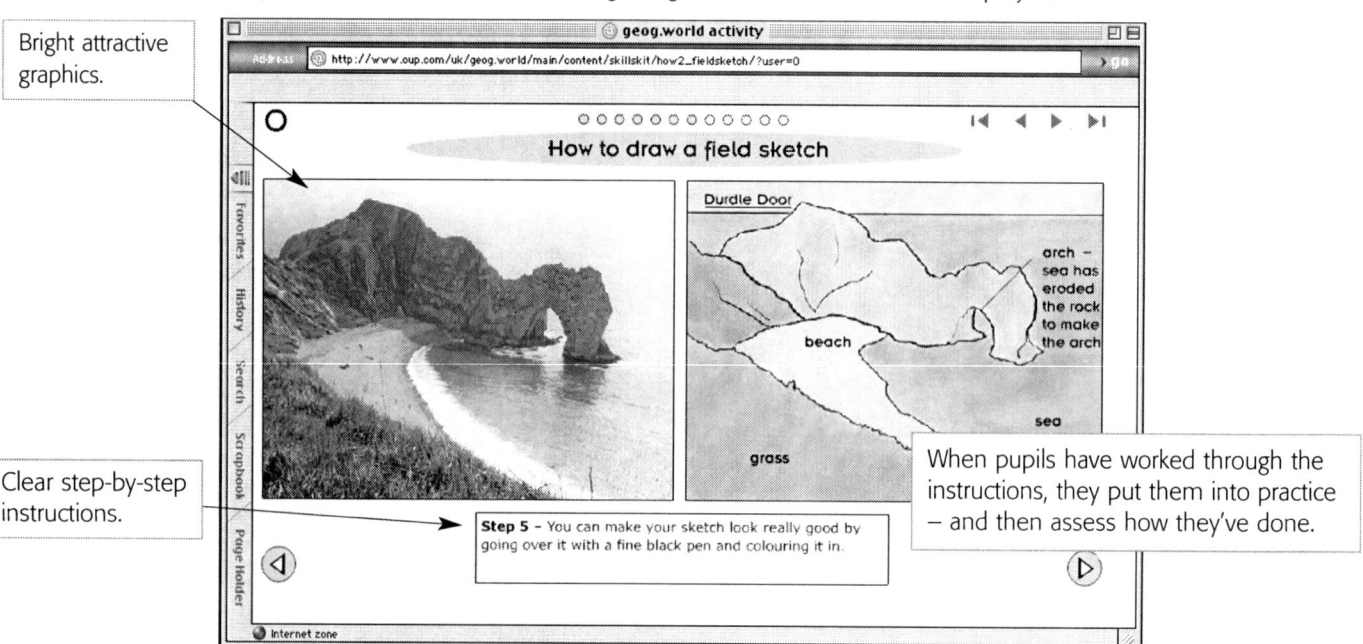

2 Scrapbook

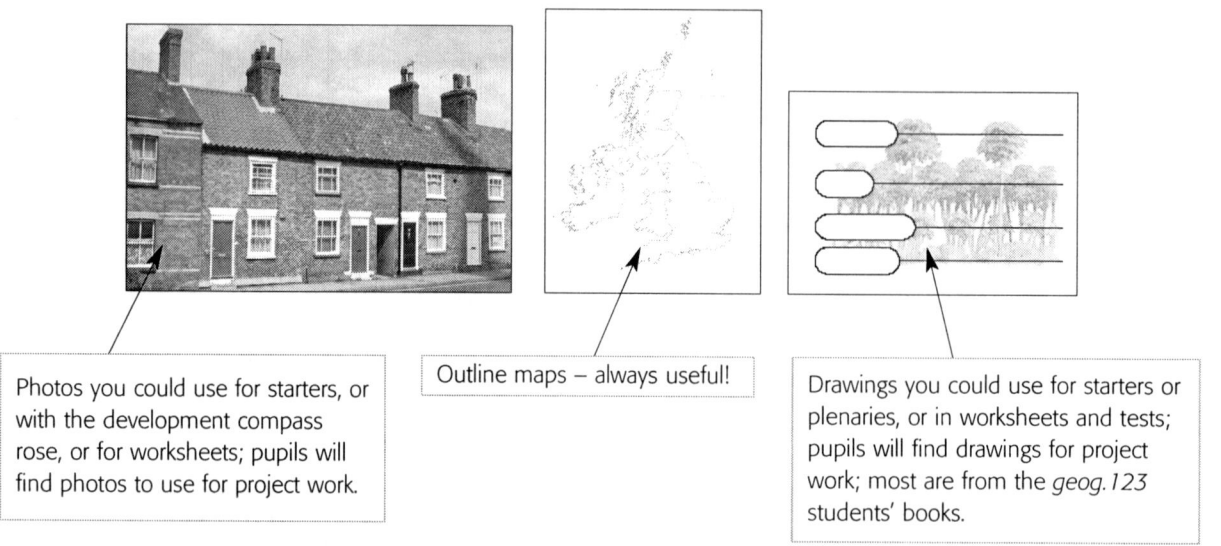

Photos you could use for starters, or with the development compass rose, or for worksheets; pupils will find photos to use for project work.

Outline maps – always useful!

Drawings you could use for starters or plenaries, or in worksheets and tests; pupils will find drawings for project work; most are from the *geog.123* students' books.

3 Interactive glossary

The glossary contains more than 600 key geographical words and their definitions. A bonus is that pupils can copy and paste definitions to make a glossary of their own.

4 Hotlinks

This has hotlinks for every topic, to other suitable sites. Great for enquiries! Each is graded according to its level of difficulty. The hotlinks are regularly checked.

Teacher materials

Using the teacher's username, you can enter the site in teacher mode, and access the teacher's notes and *Teacher zone*.

Teacher's notes

This shows how the *Coasts* menu from page 15 looks, when you're in teacher mode.

A T-button shows where there are teacher's notes. Click on it to access them.

The teacher's notes include suggestions about using the material, and for further work.

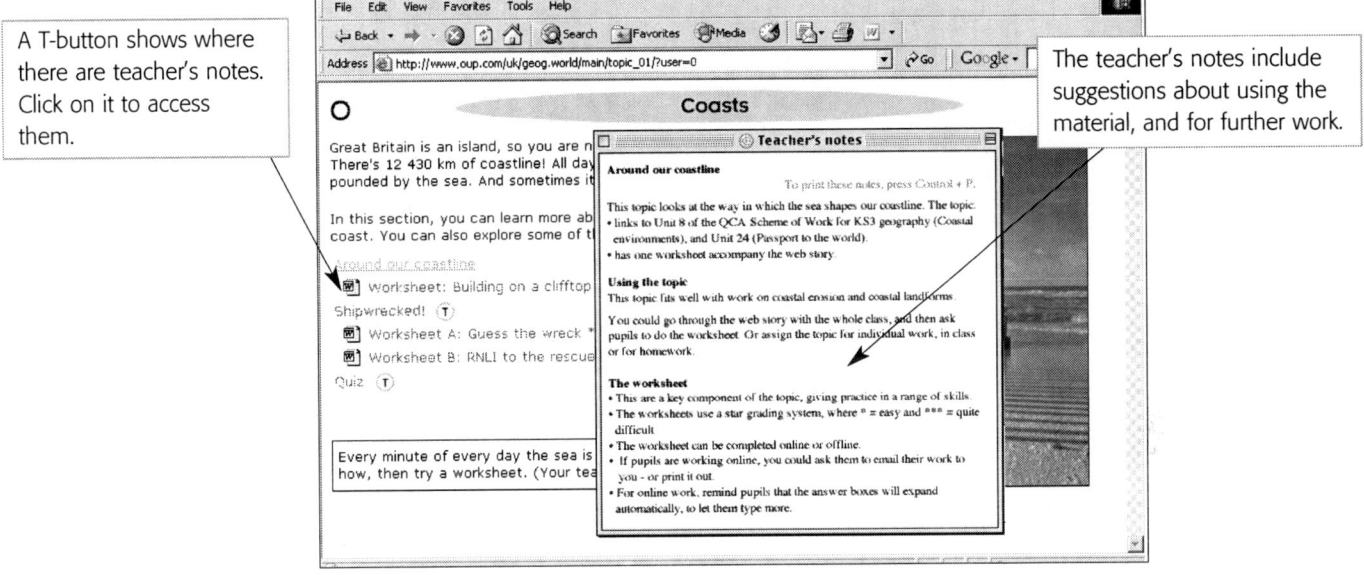

The *Teacher zone*

The *Teacher zone* provides information on *geog.world* itself, as well as a range of support materials. Look at its sections.

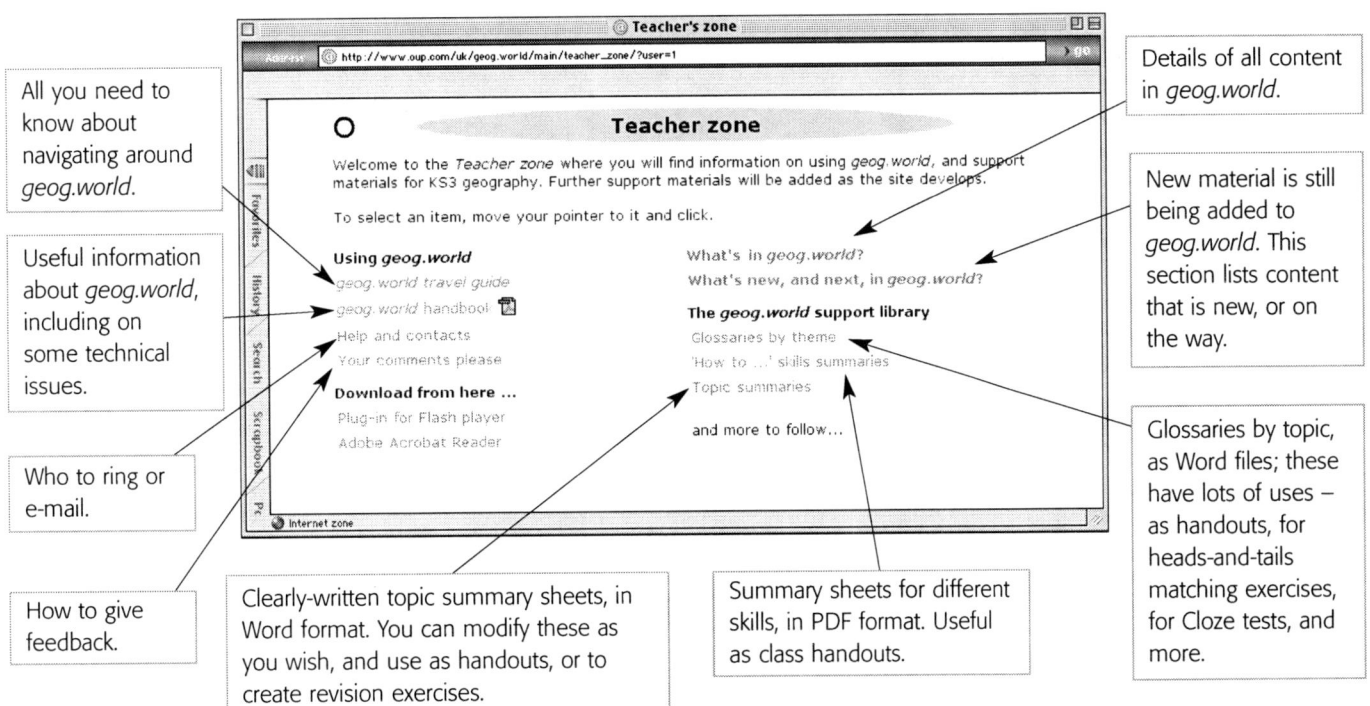

All you need to know about navigating around *geog.world*.

Useful information about *geog.world*, including on some technical issues.

Who to ring or e-mail.

How to give feedback.

Clearly-written topic summary sheets, in Word format. You can modify these as you wish, and use as handouts, or to create revision exercises.

Summary sheets for different skills, in PDF format. Useful as class handouts.

Details of all content in *geog.world*.

New material is still being added to *geog.world*. This section lists content that is new, or on the way.

Glossaries by topic, as Word files; these have lots of uses – as handouts, for heads-and-tails matching exercises, for Cloze tests, and more.

More material will be added to *Teacher zone*, as *geog.world* grows.

Coasts

1

Photocopiable worksheets

Learning activities

Assessment materials

[W] indicates material provided as editable Word files, as well as in PDF format, on the CD-ROM.

On the CD-ROM: pupil profile sheet; course theme, and lesson planning documents.

Name _____   **Class** _____

Ports
Belfast ❑
Dublin ❑
Liverpool ❑
London ❑
Newcastle ❑
Southampton ❑

Seaside resorts
Blackpool ❑
Bournemouth ❑
Brighton ❑
Great Yarmouth ❑

Islands
Anglesey ❑
Isle of Man ❑
Isle of Wight ❑
Orkneys ❑
Outer Hebrides ❑
Skye ❑

Seas
Atlantic Ocean ❑
Celtic Sea ❑
Irish Sea ❑
North Sea ❑

Sea channels
Bristol Channel ❑
English Channel ❑
North Channel ❑
St George's Channel ❑

Bays / inlets
Cardigan Bay ❑
Donegal Bay ❑
Lyme Bay ❑
Firth of Forth ❑
Humber ❑
Moray Firth ❑
Solway Firth ❑
The Wash ❑

Headlands
Flamborough Head ❑
Land's End ❑
Malin Head ❑
Spurn Head ❑
St David's Head ❑

1 Use an atlas to find each place in the list. Mark it on the map above, and label it. Keep your writing small and neat! Tick each box when you finish with it.

2 Now, using the map to help you, see if you can explain in your own words:
  a what a headland is   **b** what the Scottish word 'Firth' means
  c the difference between a firth and a bay
  d the difference between an ocean, a sea and a sea channel.
  Write your answers on the back of this sheet.

Wearing the coastline away

**

Name   Class

**All around the British Isles the coastline is being weathered.
In many places it's being eroded too.**

1 See if you can complete the paragraph below about weathering, using words from the box.

clays   pieces   weathering   chemical   physical   bedrock   water   organic   reacts   biological

_____ is the process that breaks rock down. In _____ and _____

weathering, the rock just gets broken into _____ . But in _____ weathering it

_____ with air and water and is changed into sand and _____ .

2 This drawing shows how the coastline gets eroded by the waves.

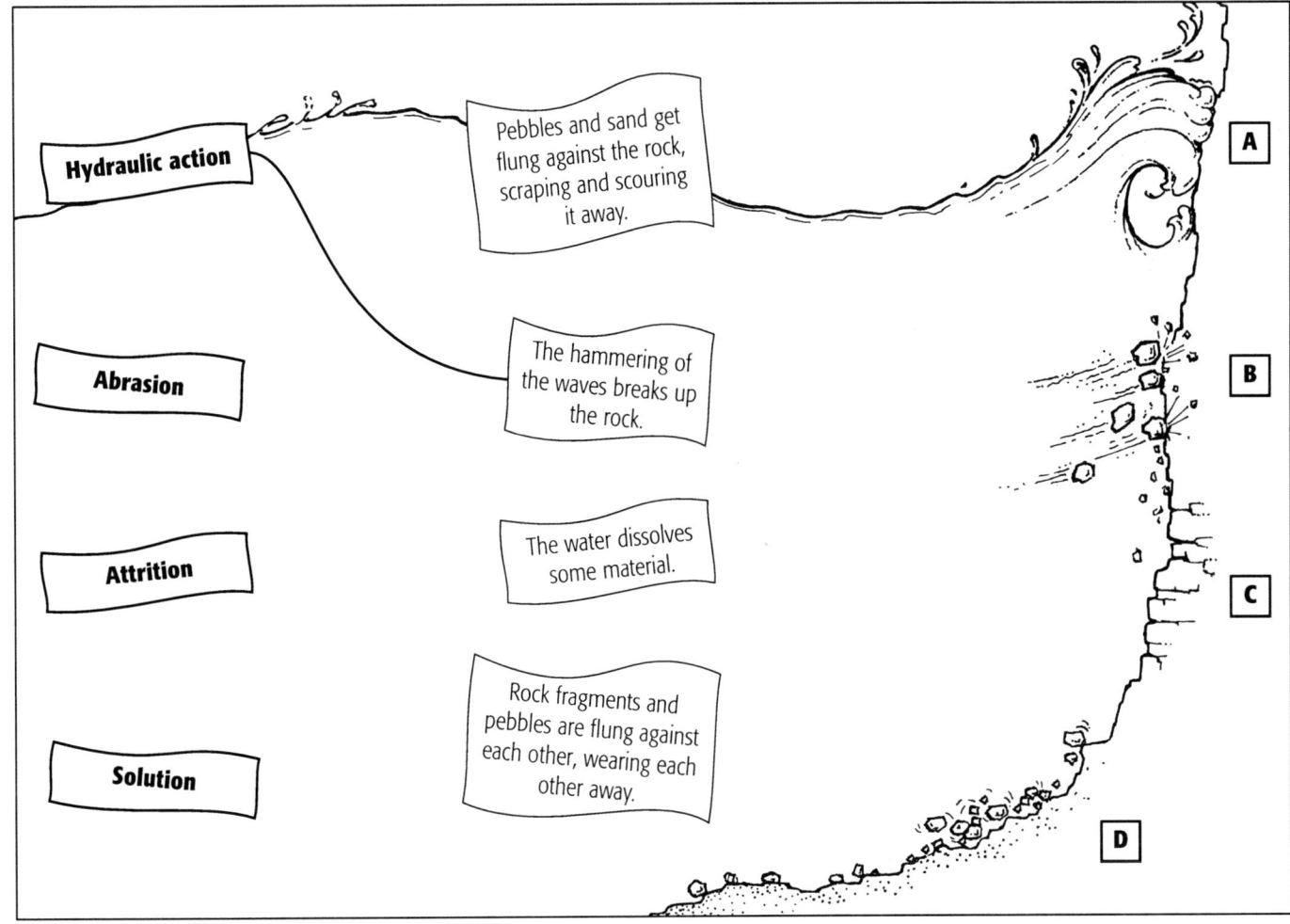

This is what you have to do.

a First, draw a line joining the name of each erosion process to its definition.
(One has been done for you.)

b Then join each definition to the correct label on the drawing (A, B, C or D).

c Next colour in each joined group of boxes. Use a different colour for each group.

d Now colour in the rest of the drawing.

geog.2: 1 Coasts

These 12 pictures belong to 4 different sequences.

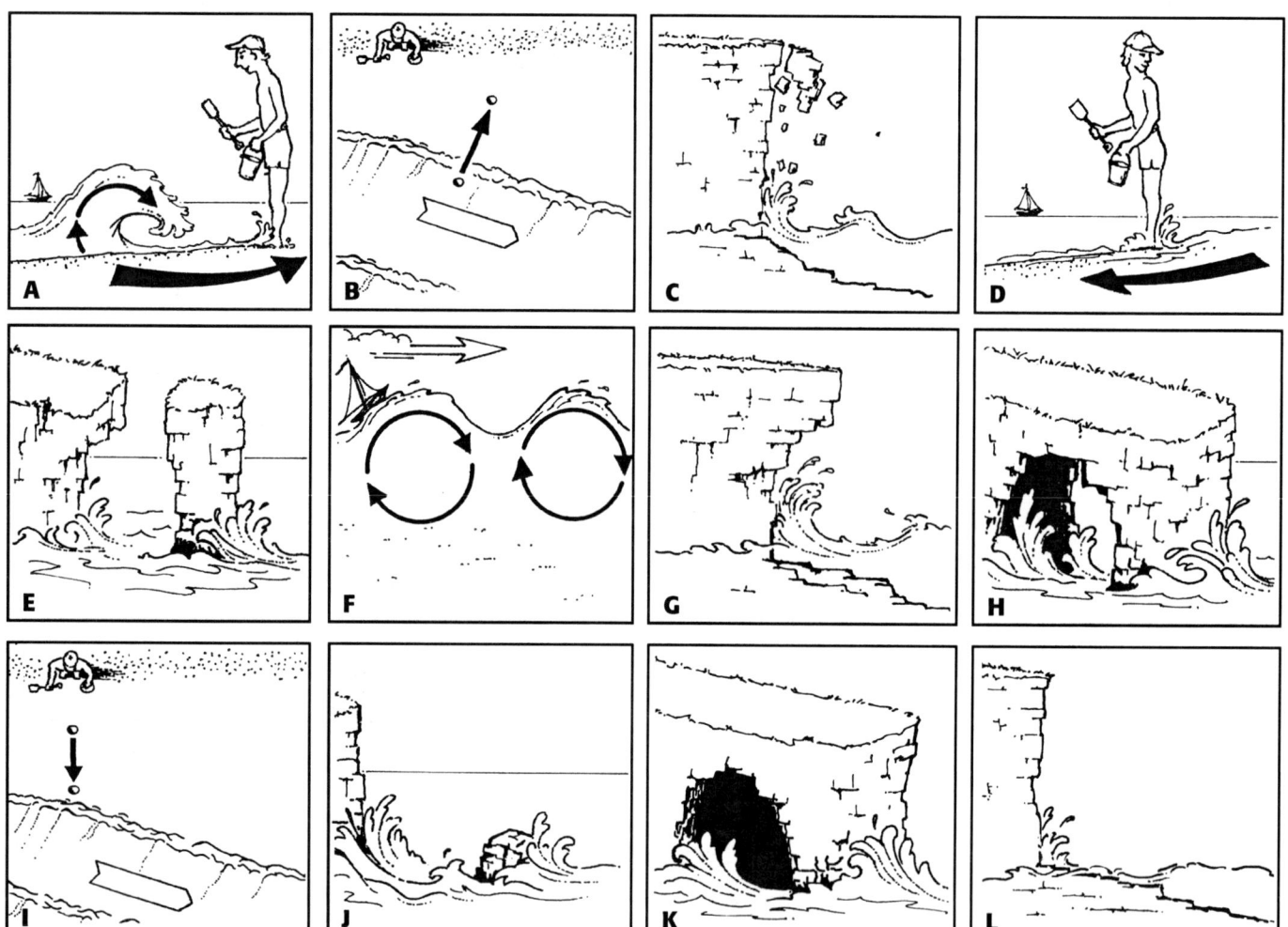

Your job is to sort them and put them in order.

1 Write the correct letters in the boxes, in the correct order.

Stages in forming a stump

Stages in forming a wave-cut platform

Stages of a wave breaking on the beach

Stages in longshore drift

Now, in your exercise book:

2 Copy each 'Stages' heading, leaving enough depth for a row of pictures below each heading.

3 Cut out the pictures. Stick them, in order, under the correct headings. Colour them in.

Name   Class

Look at the three maps a, b and c. They show three areas of coastline, marked D, E and F on this outline map of the British Isles.

1 See if you can match the maps to the right areas.

   a is at _____   **b** is at _____   **c** is at _____

2 Study each map, and decide where you'd be most likely to:

Walk the pier ___ *b*

Sunbathe on a beach ___

Rock climb with ropes ___

Squelch through marshes ___

Swim in the pool ___

Visit the lighthouse ___

Hire a boat ___

Find many salt-loving plants ___

Take a donkey ride ___

Clamber over rocks ___

Buy an ice-cream ___

See birds' nests in the reeds ___

Explore rockpools ___

Hire a deckchair ___

Collect seashells ___

Visit an amusement arcade ___

Explore sand banks ___

Find barnacles ___

Walk along the promenade ___

Get mud on your shoes ___

Watch seagulls nesting ___

Look out for seals ___

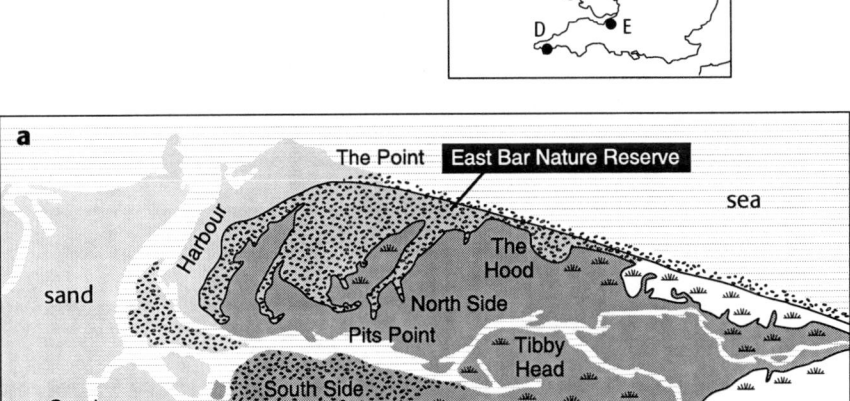

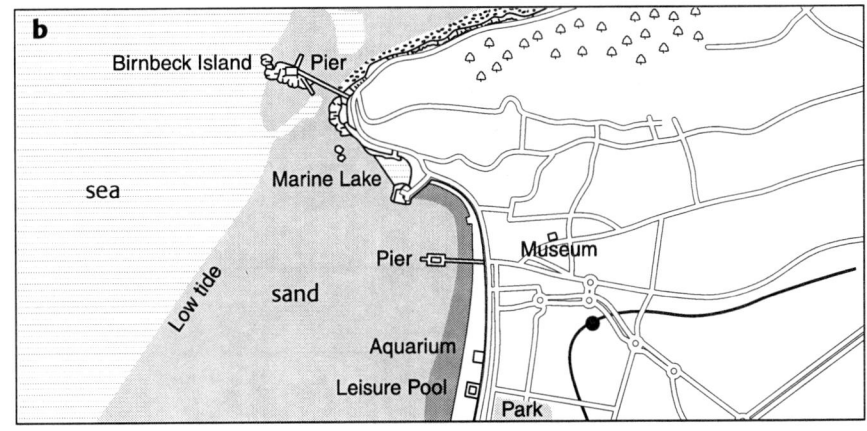

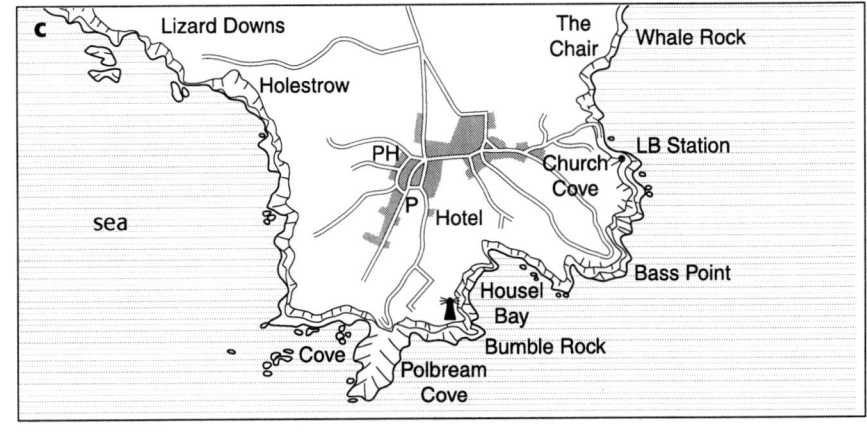

3 Which map area would you most like to visit? Explain why on the back of this sheet.

Name | Class

Every so often, somewhere along the coast, there's a landslip.
Cliffs topple into the sea. Houses, roads and cars may go with them.
People may get killed or injured.

1 Complete these sentences about why coastal landslips occur.

a The sea plays a part because the waves _____
_____

b Weathering plays a part because it _____
_____

c It depends on the rock type too. Clay cliffs are more vulnerable than granite cliffs because
_____
_____

d Heavy rain can bring on a landslip because _____
_____

Where people are in danger from landslips, engineers try to prevent them.

2 The diagram below shows what they can do to make an unstable clay cliff safe.
But the labels are missing! Use the words in bold to label it correctly.

A Permeable **geotextile bags filled with clay** are packed against the slope.

B **Rock armour** is cemented into a trench to reduce erosion at the foot of the cliff.

C **Salt-resistant vegetation** is planted to stabilise the cliff top.

D **Drainage pipes** are dug into the cliff to let rainwater drain away.

E The **angle of slope is altered** – the flatter it is, the less likely it is to give way.

F An infill of **small rocks** allows rainwater to pass through.

G **Geotextile sheets** help to stabilise the clay.

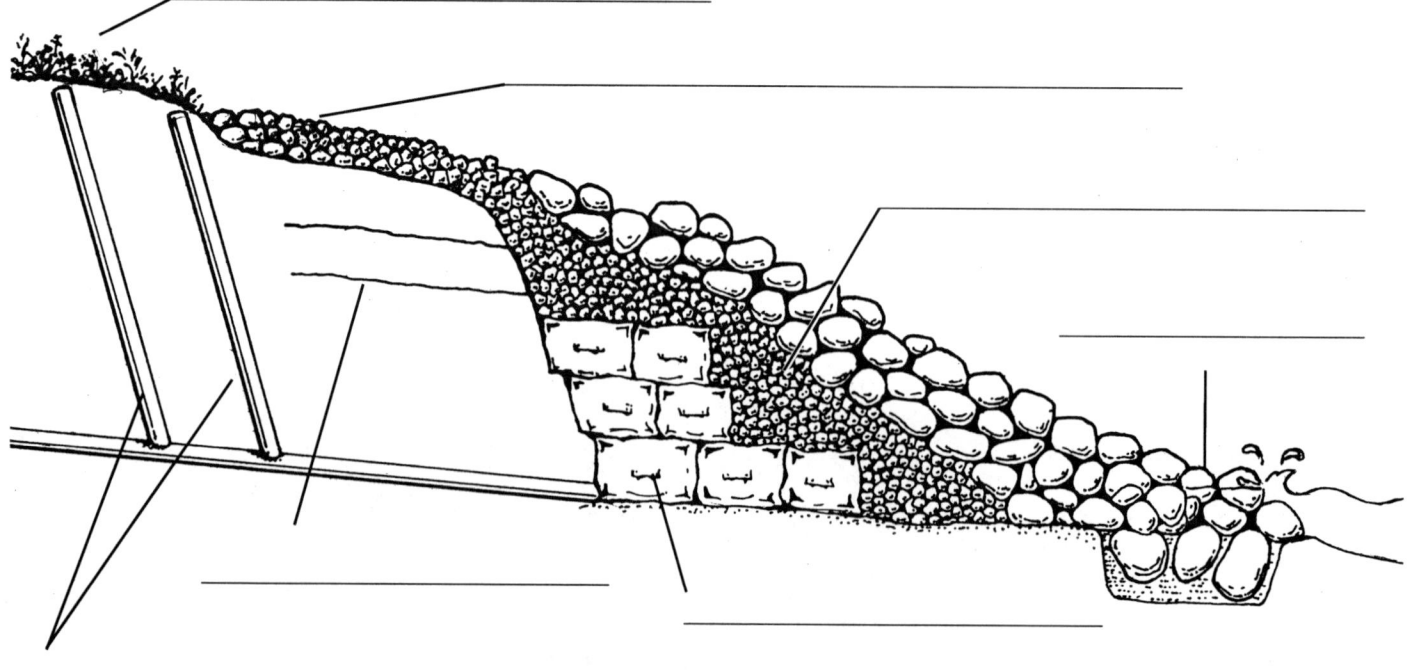

© OUP: this may be reproduced for class use solely within the purchaser's school or college

Name   Class

1   Use the clues to complete the crossword.

2   Find the coastal process hidden in the shaded boxes.

3   On the back of this sheet, draw a labelled diagram to explain how the hidden process works.

Clues

1	Clay cliffs may do this after heavy rain	**8**	Made from large rocks, and protects the base of cliffs
2	The ultimate fate of eroded material	**9**	The cause of low and high water marks
3	A wave-cut platform starts with this	**10**	All the structures built to protect the coast (2 words)
4	Some beaches are made of this	**11**	When a cave has eroded all the way through
5	It's rising as the world warms up (2 words)	**12**	People can object to plans at this (2 words)
6	Water from a wave, rushing up the beach	**13**	Length of water over which the wind has blown
7	The shape of the coastline depends on this	**14**	An arm of sand building up in the sea

1A Check out the coastline **

You may find it helpful to enlarge this activity sheet a little, before copying, to give pupils more room for labelling. The places and features should be easy to locate in an atlas.

1B Wearing the coastline away **

1 **Weathering** is the process that breaks rock down. In **physical** and **biological** weathering, the rock just gets broken into **pieces**. But in **chemical** weathering it **reacts** with air and water and is changed into sand and **clays**.

2 Hydraulic action → The hammering ... → A
   Abrasion → Pebbles and sand ... → B
   Attrition → Rock fragments ... → D
   Solution → The water ... → C

1C Sort out the seaside muddle! *

1 Stump: **K, H, E, J**

   Platform: **G, C, L**

   Wave: **F, A, D**

   Longshore drift: **I, B**

1D All kinds of seaside? **

a is at **F** – it is an area of saltmarsh at Morston in Norfolk. The map shows marshes, sand banks and mudflats, and you'd expect to find birds' nests in the reeds, and a variety of salt-loving plants – and get mud on your shoes. (Wear wellies!)

b is at **E** – it is Weston-super-Mare, a traditional seaside resort with a pier, beach, pool, boats for hire, donkeys, ice-creams, deckchairs, arcade, promenade.

c is at **D** – it is Lizard Point in Cornwall; there are steep cliffs for rock climbing, the famous Lizard lighthouse, rocks to climb over, rockpools with barnacles, limpets and so on; seashells among the shingle, seals offshore and seagulls nesting on the clifftops.

1E No more landslips! **

1 Pupils' answers should be along these lines:
   a because the waves erode the base of a cliff, making it weaker
   b because it weakens cliffs and makes cracks for the rain to get in
   c because clay is softer than granite and it weathers and erodes more easily
   d because it soaks into the cliffs, making them heavier and more unstable. It also makes clay slippery.

2 This shows the correct labelling:

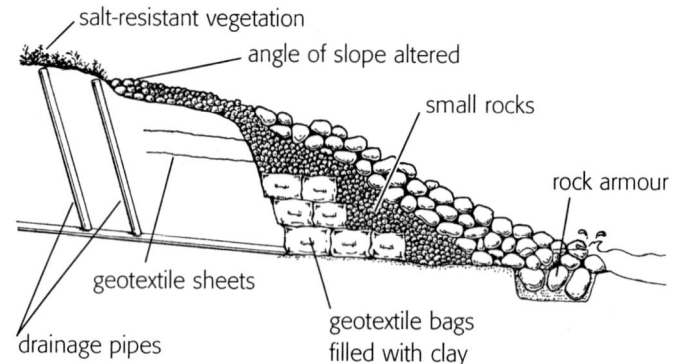

salt-resistant vegetation
angle of slope altered
small rocks
rock armour
geotextile sheets
drainage pipes
geotextile bags filled with clay

1F Coastal crossword **

1 Answers to crossword are: 1 Collapse   2 Deposition
   3 Notch   4 Shingle   5 Sea level   6 Swash
   7 Geology   8 Armour   9 Tides   10 Sea defences
   11 Arch   12 Public enquiry   13 Fetch   14 Spit

2 The hidden process is **longshore drift**

3 For longshore drift diagram see page 9 of geog.2 pupil's book.

Protecting Tunstall

**

Aims

■ Pupils understand the complexities of issues relating to coastal protection
■ Pupils understand the viewpoints of different groups
■ Pupils are able to understand, deliver, and argue a case in a public enquiry
■ Pupils are able to make and justify decisions

Introduction

This activity addresses Unit 8 of the QCA Scheme of Work (*How can coastal areas be managed? What are the effects of environmental planning and management on coastal landscapes and the people who use them?*). It can be done after unit 1.8 on pages 20-21 of **geog.2**.

The activity is set in the area of Tunstall, north of Spurn Head in Yorkshire. Pupils should hold a public enquiry into whether a coastal protection scheme, proposed by Tunstall Parish Council, should go ahead along the shore at Tunstall between Mappleton and Withernsea. It should be made clear that there are, in fact, no current proposals for such a scheme. It is an example of the kind of situation that arises when controversial schemes are proposed. You can never please everyone!

Activity

1 Divide pupils into eight groups to represent the:
   ■ manager of Easington Gas Plant, south east of Withernsea;
   ■ caravan site owner at Kiln House, Tunstall;
   ■ farmer at Higher Ball, Tunstall;
   ■ farmer at Cliff Top Farm, south east of Tunstall;
   ■ owner of the Mill House Hotel and Restaurant, Tunstall;
   ■ vicar of Tunstall*;
   ■ Ramblers' Association, defending the rights of footpath walkers*;
   ■ Holderness Council.
   (asterisks denote the more difficult roles)

2 Issue each group with the pupils' notes (page 28), the map of the area (page 29), and the role card for their particular group (pages 30-31).

3 Give the groups time to read the role cards, consult the map, and prepare their case.

4 Hold the public enquiry with spokespersons from each group. Allow each group to speak uninterrupted, then let the other groups ask them questions.

5 At the end, invite pupils to vote for or against the scheme. They should do this out of role, as themselves.

Follow-up work

The work could be written up as a newspaper article using either the headline **'TUNSTALL SCHEME TO GO AHEAD'** or **'TUNSTALL COASTAL SCHEME REJECTED'**.

Alternatively, pupils could evaluate the public enquiry using the writing frame provided on page 32.

Name   **Class**

Coastal erosion can have a really big impact on the lives of people living in coastal areas. You are going to find out how different people might feel about coastal erosion and what they might think about protecting the coast.

The class has been divided into groups. Each group has been given these information notes, a role card and a map of the area.

Each group will be either **for** or **against** the coastal protection scheme.

Each group will give its argument to the Chief Inspector of the public enquiry.

Background information for the public enquiry in Tunstall

★ Tunstall is a small village on the Holderness coast. Like all the settlements along this stretch of coast, Tunstall is in danger of sliding into the sea.

★ Holderness Council has planned what it is going to do to this coastline in the future. It does not intend to protect the whole coast. Tunstall is one of the areas that the council doesn't plan to protect.

★ Tunstall Parish Council doesn't think this is good enough. It thinks coastal defences should be put in to protect the village.

★ Not everyone will agree with this suggestion.

---

1 Read your group's role card and look at the map. Decide how your group will present the point of view on the card.

2 Between you, prepare a speech to defend your group's point of view. You'll need to choose a spokesperson from your group to speak at the enquiry.

Top Tips for the spokesperson

★ Introduce yourself politely to the Chief Inspector of the enquiry. You could start with 'Madam Inspector, I represent the ...'

★ Say clearly whether you OPPOSE or SUPPORT the coastal protection scheme.

★ Give several reasons for your point of view. Explain each reason in as much detail as you can.

★ Asking the Inspector questions is a good trick. For example, the owner of Mill House Hotel and Restaurant might say, "Do you want this area to lose all its visitors?"

★ Listen to other people's arguments carefully. Don't interrupt. You can ask them questions later.

★ Show you care – be passionate!

---

3 After all the speeches it's time to vote! Do you think the coastal protection scheme for Tunstall is a good or bad idea? Vote as yourself, not in role.

Protecting Tunstall

Name   **Class**

Map of the Tunstall coastline

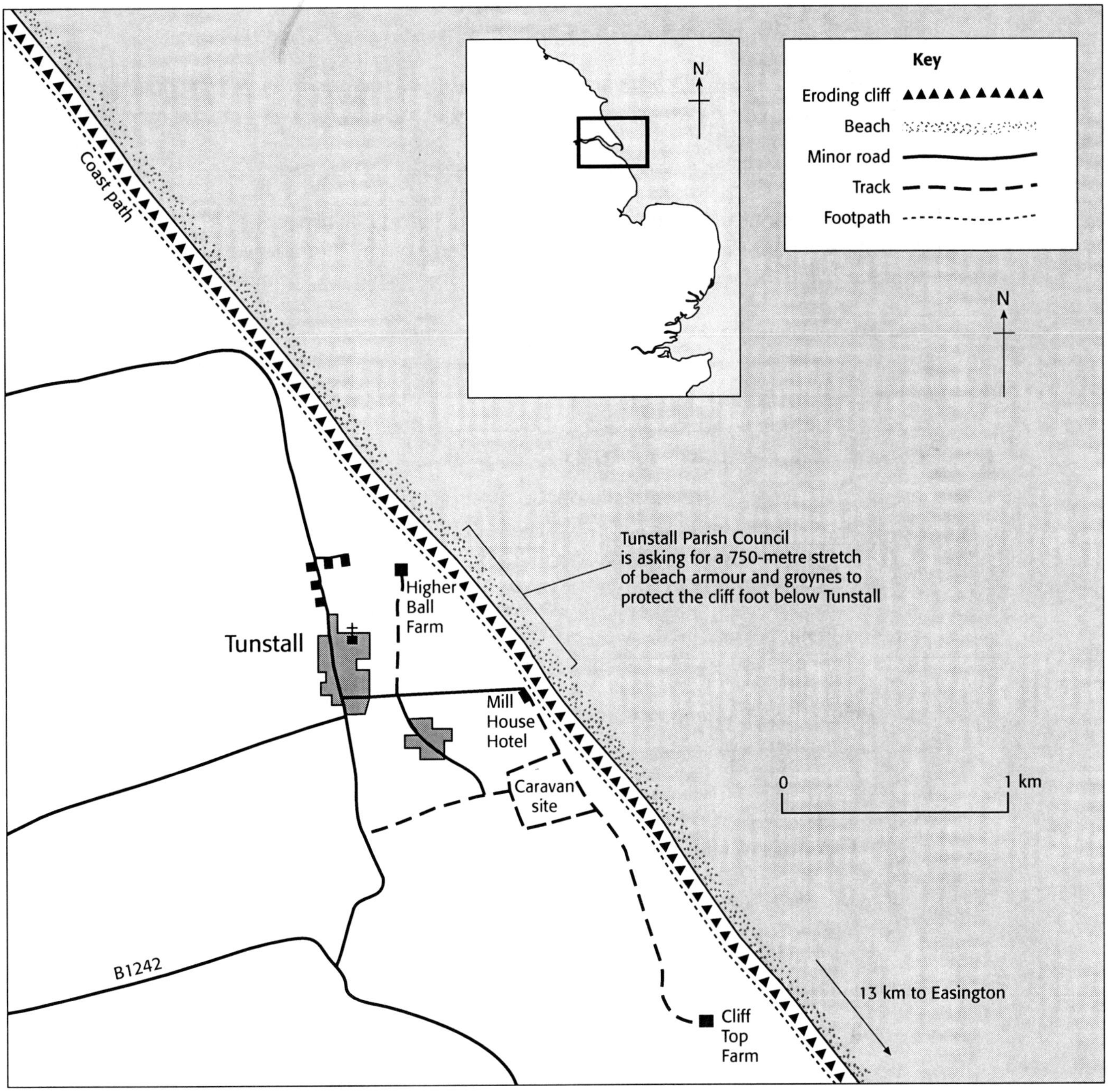

Key

Eroding cliff	▲▲▲▲▲▲▲▲▲▲
Beach	░░░░░░░░░░
Minor road	———
Track	– – –
Footpath	········

Coast path

Tunstall

Higher Ball Farm

Mill House Hotel

Caravan site

B1242

Cliff Top Farm

Tunstall Parish Council is asking for a 750-metre stretch of beach armour and groynes to protect the cliff foot below Tunstall

N

0   1 km

13 km to Easington

Name   Class

Group role cards

Manager of the Easington Gas Plant, south east of Withernsea

You're in charge of a multi-million pound gas works at Easington. Your gas plant pumps in gas from the North Sea, and checks it for impurities. Then it pumps the gas into the mains pipeline.

Holderness Council has a policy to protect Easington by rock armour.

If the coast is protected at Tunstall, it might cut off the supply of sand to the beach below the cliffs at Easington. This could cause erosion. This erosion might damage the foundations of your gas plant. To move your plant would cost many millions of pounds.

★   You OPPOSE the proposed protection work at Tunstall.

Caravan site owner at Kiln House, Tunstall

You are the owner of a caravan site on the coast near Tunstall. Erosion is already causing problems, and caravans have to be kept away from the cliffs. You worry that campers might be in danger if they go too near to the edge of the unstable cliffs. If anything goes wrong your customers could sue you.

If the erosion is allowed to carry on, there will be no field left for campers to use. If there is no field for campers to use, you will lose your income.

★   You OPPOSE the proposal unless it is extended down the coast to include your field.

Farmer at Higher Ball Farm, Tunstall

Your fields are being reduced by coastal erosion. If this continues you won't be able to afford to run your farm. Use of heavy modern tractors and farm equipment is very dangerous near the unstable cliffs. Without coastal protection your farm will disappear. Any land that is left will be worthless; you certainly wouldn't be able to sell it.

★   You strongly SUPPORT the proposal for beach protection below your farm.

Farmer's family at Cliff Top Farm, south east of Tunstall

At present the fields along the cliff top are being slowly eroded. You are worried that protecting the coast at Tunstall will starve the beach below your cliffs of material. This will dramatically increase the rate of erosion because the waves will be able to reach the foot of the cliffs. You will then lose your living much more quickly.

★   You OPPOSE the works up the coast, as this will starve the beach at the foot of your cliffs.

Name   Class

Owner of Mill House Hotel and Restaurant in Tunstall above the cliffs

You have invested your life savings in this business and are very worried that it could all be washed into the sea. Without coastal protection it is very difficult to get house insurance and you wouldn't get any compensation. The guests at your hotel and the tourists that come to your restaurant bring lots of money into the area. All this benefit could be washed away without coastal protection.

★   You SUPPORT the coastal protection plan for Tunstall very strongly, and so do your staff.

Vicar of Tunstall

Most of your parishioners live along the coast in farms or in the village. At the moment the church is safe, it's 0.5 km from the sea. If, however, the coast continues to disappear at a rate of 8 metres a year, it could soon be under threat. But before then it will be at risk because there will be few parishioners left – all their houses will have fallen into the sea!

The church is an old building worth protecting. The church and its graveyard are on consecrated ground, meaning it is sacred, so should be protected.

★   You SUPPORT the coastal protection plan for Tunstall.

Ramblers' Association

This association tries to protect the rights of people to use footpaths, and to do so safely. The coastal path at Tunstall links Flamborough Head and Spurn Head. The cliffs are between 12 and 17 metres high. They provide stunning views over the North Sea and of the rural country inland. But these cliffs are dangerous; footpaths often have to be closed because of rock falls.

★   Until some arrangement can be made to divert footpaths to a safer route, you SUPPORT the coastal protection scheme.

Holderness Council

Tunstall lies about half way between Mappleton and Withernsea. The council does not intend to protect the whole coast. It will protect the coast at Bridlington, Hornsea (including the stretch near the gas plant), Mappleton, Withernsea, and Easington. But at Tunstall the policy is to do nothing, for the eroding cliffs will provide material for the beach to protect Withernsea and Easington down the coast.

★   You OPPOSE the use of beach armour and groynes at Tunstall.

Protecting Tunstall

**

Name _____   **Class** _____

Writing frame for coastal enquiry

Some people think that Tunstall's coast should be protected

They include _____ and _____

They say _____

and _____

_____

Other people are against the scheme.

They include _____ and _____

They say _____

and _____

_____

I think the scheme should go ahead/be rejected because _____

_____

_____

_____

_____

_____

_____

_____

_____

_____

_____

Signed _____

Date _____

The history of Spurn Head   **

Aims

▪ Pupils learn that the spit has a history of growth, breaching, and erosion
▪ Pupils can relate this to historical events with which they are familiar, and so have a concept of timescale
▪ Pupils can appreciate that there is a pattern to the history of the spit as a cycle repeated over the centuries

Introduction

This activity addresses Unit 8 of the QCA Scheme of Work (*How is the coast shaped by wave action?* and *How to do erosion and deposition create coastal landforms?*). It is an exercise that pupils can do in pairs after unit 1.8 on pages 20-21 of **geog.2**.

Activity

The pupils' notes are on pages 35-36.

1   The pairs should begin by drawing a long time-line. It should start at 600 AD and be labelled at intervals of a hundred years. It should stretch up to the present day.

2   Each pair should then be issued with a set of 15 map cards (pages 37-40) showing the spit at different dates.

3   The pairs should divide their map cards into groups showing similar shapes, and make a note of the dates in each group.

4   Then they should arrange all their map cards into date order, and put them in place on the time-line.

5   They should note what happens to the spit in 850, 1100, 1360, 1610, and 1850. Then they should note what happens to the length of the spit between these dates.

6   The pairs could write down their conclusions or join the heads and tails.

The time-line will show a regular cycle of spit growth, breaching, and being washed away, as detected by the geographer, George de Boer in 1964. The 1850 breach was repaired but the road along the spit was breached again as recently as 1991.

Time-line for growth of Spurn Head

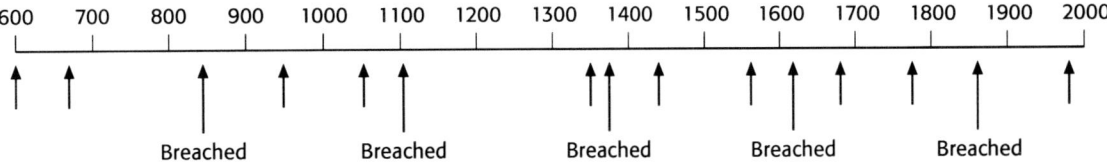

| 600 | 700 | 800 | 900 | 1000 | 1100 | 1200 | 1300 | 1400 | 1500 | 1600 | 1700 | 1800 | 1900 | 2000 |

Breached   Breached   Breached   Breached   Breached

The history of Spurn Head   **

How do we know the spit developed along these lines?

In case anyone asks:

1991 AD   The position is clear from OS maps, and newspapers at the time record the breach.

1850 AD   OS maps record the position of the spit. In 1849 a breach occurred and it is still shown on the 1852 First Edition of the OS map.

1776 AD   The engineer John Smeaton's charts record the position of his lighthouse and of the end of the spit. He was called in because the previous lighthouse had been washed away.

1674 AD   Pilot books record the position of Justinian Angell's lighthouse.

1610 AD   British Museum charts for 1608 and 1623 show the situation.

1360 AD   The population of Ravenser Odd, a port on the spit, appealed to the King for a reduction to their taxes when the port was washed away.

1100 AD   Domesday Book records villages in the area.

1066 AD   Just before the Battle of Hastings, Harald Hardrada and King Harold fought at the Battle of Stamford Bridge which Harold of England won. The defeated army sailed from Hrafnceyrr (Ravenser on Spurn Head) back to where they came from.

950 AD   An Icelandic saga tells how Egil was wrecked on the Stony Binks, a long shoal arching away from the tip of Spurn Head. This bank is still shown on John Smeaton's maps, and on modern charts. On a chart dated 1671 they are shown as 'Stone Banks'.

Extension work

Tell pupils to measure the distance along the top margin of their map cards between the north-west corner and the east coast, and to fill in the empty table accordingly.

These distances should then be plotted on the blank graph using the time-line as the X-axis.

This graph seems to show that the rate of coastal retreat is generally steady, but that the increases in the erosion after each breach of the spit have become less severe over the years.

The title of the graph should show their conclusions.

The history of Spurn Head

Name   **Class**

You will be given 15 small map cards showing Spurn Head at various dates in the past.

Activity

1   Draw a time-line from 600 to 2000 which is big enough for the cards to be placed along it. Label it at intervals of 100 years.

2   Sort the map cards into groups that show roughly the same shape.

3   Make a note of the dates in each group.

4   Sort all the map cards again, this time into date order.

5   Put them in place on the time-line.

6   What do you notice about these dates - 850, 1100, 1360, 1610, and 1850?

7   What happens to the length of the spit between these dates?

Now …

8   Write your conclusion or join the following heads and tails to make logical sentences:

Heads	Tails
1 The sea erodes the coast …	**a** … it is broken or breached.
2 Sand and shingle are carried down the coast …	**b** … north of Spurn Head.
3 When longshore drift is interrupted …	**c** … once every 250 years or so.
4 The spit grows longer until …	**d** … by longshore drift.
5 When a breach occurs, the sea end …	**e** … material is deposited and a spit forms.
6 The breaches seem to have happened …	**f** … no longer receives any sand or gravel.

Name   **Class**

Extension exercise

1   On each of your map cards measure along the top margin from the top left-hand corner (north-west corner) to the east coast and fill in the table below.

Date	Distance	Date	Distance
600		1428	
670		1580	
850		1610	
950		1674	
1066		1776	
1100		1850	
1350		1991	
1360			

2   Now plot these figures on the graph below.

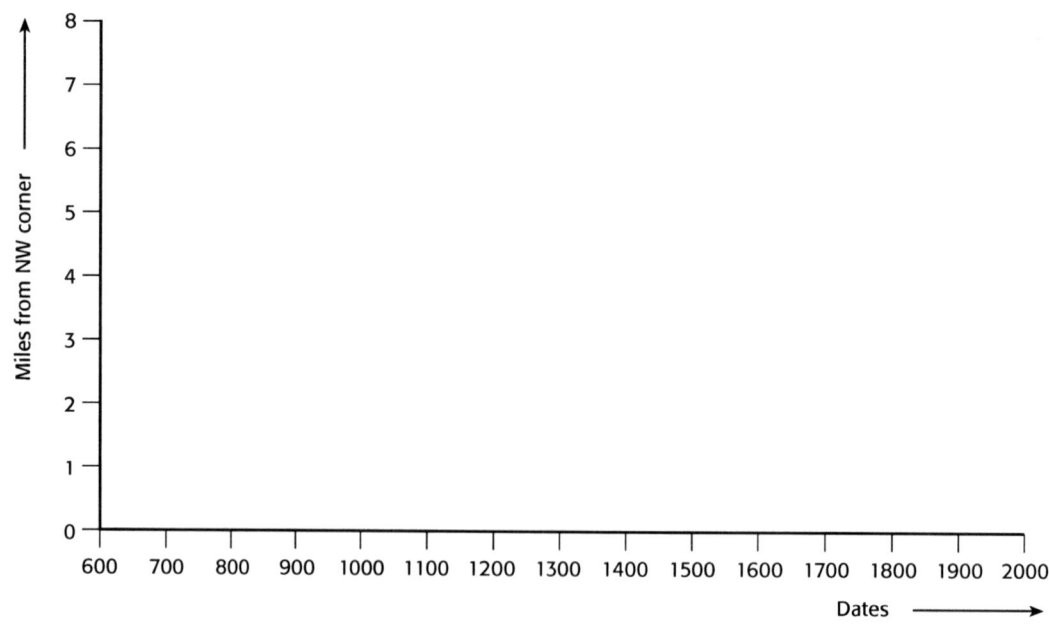

3   Do you think that the graph shows that the rate of erosion of the Holderness coast is:

a   getting faster?

b   slowing down?

c   staying the same?

4   Give your graph a title that shows what you think.

Name

Class

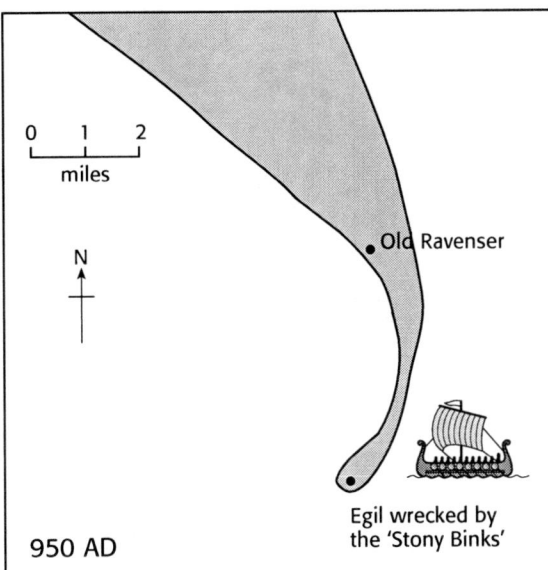

0 1 2
miles

N

• Old Ravenser

Egil wrecked by
the 'Stony Binks'

950 AD

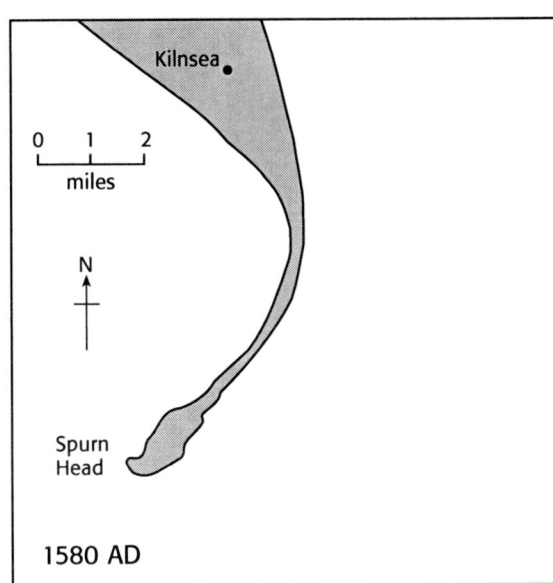

0 1 2
miles

N

Kilnsea •

Spurn
Head •

1580 AD

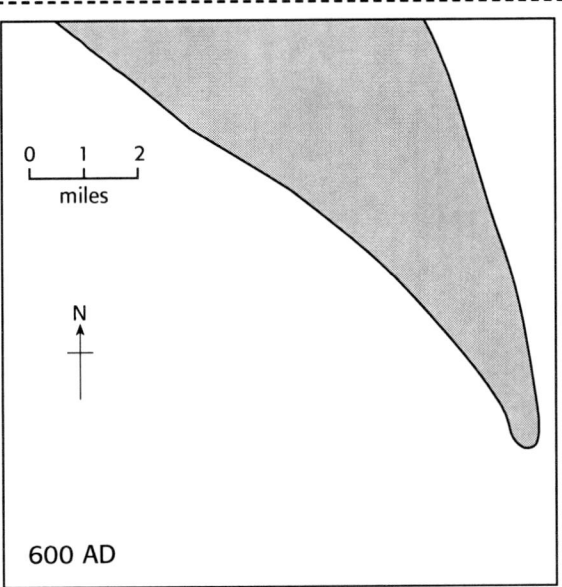

0 1 2
miles

N

600 AD

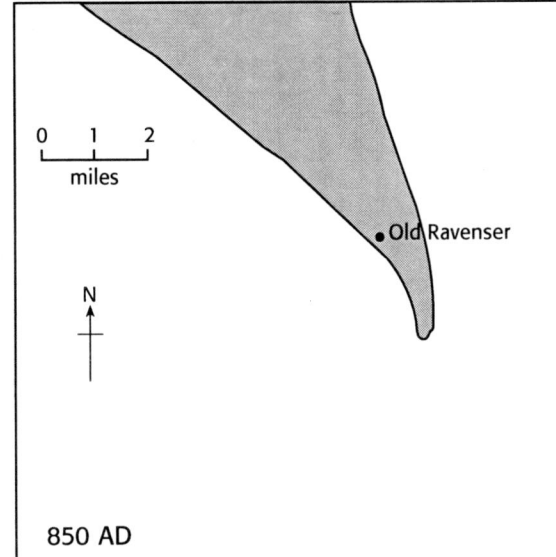

0 1 2
miles

N

• Old Ravenser

850 AD

The history of Spurn Head

Name   Class

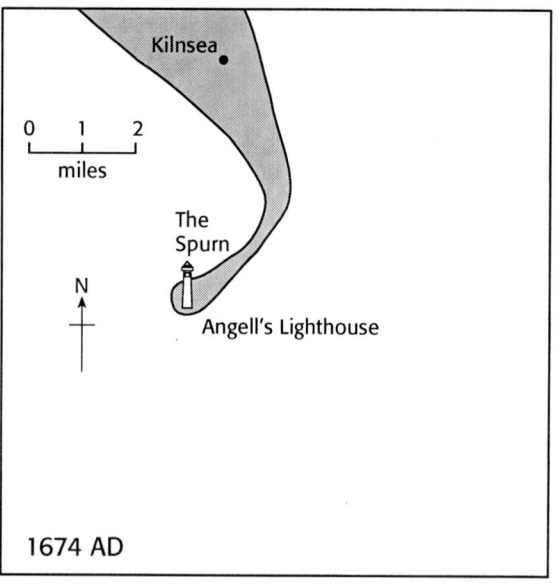

1674 AD

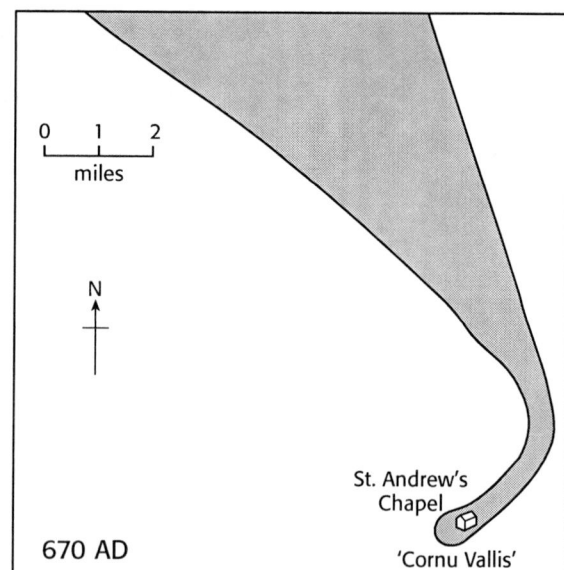

670 AD

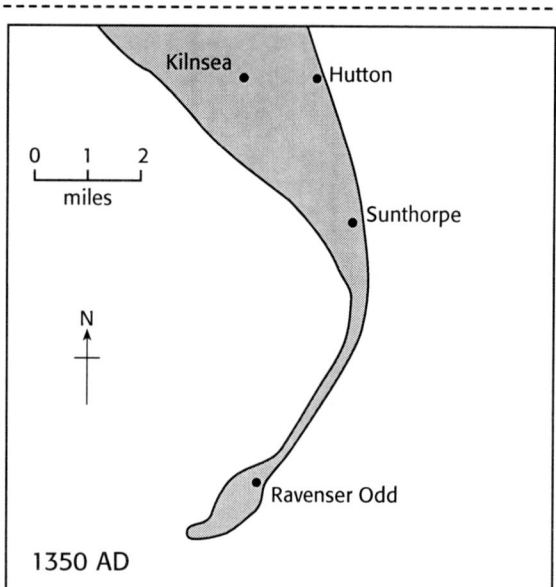

1350 AD

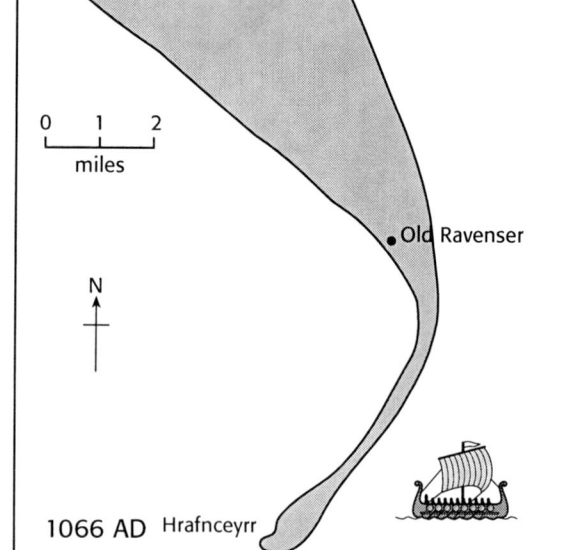

1066 AD Hrafnceyrr

Name   **Class**

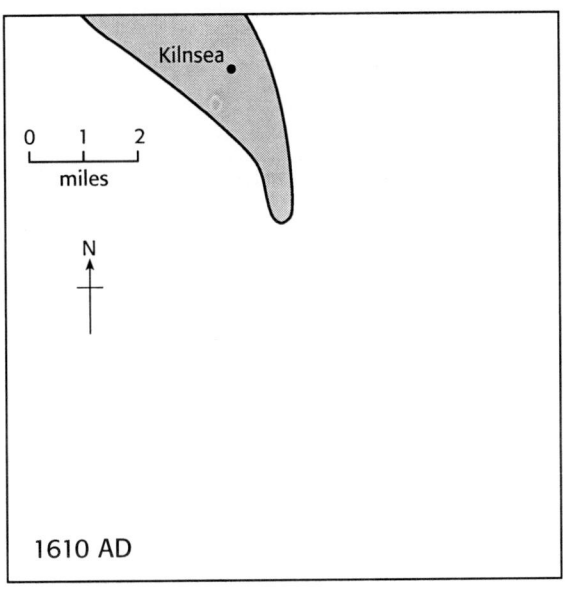

1610 AD

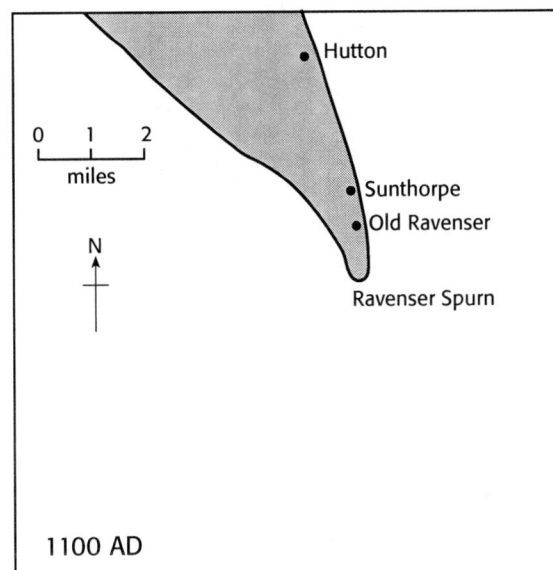

1100 AD

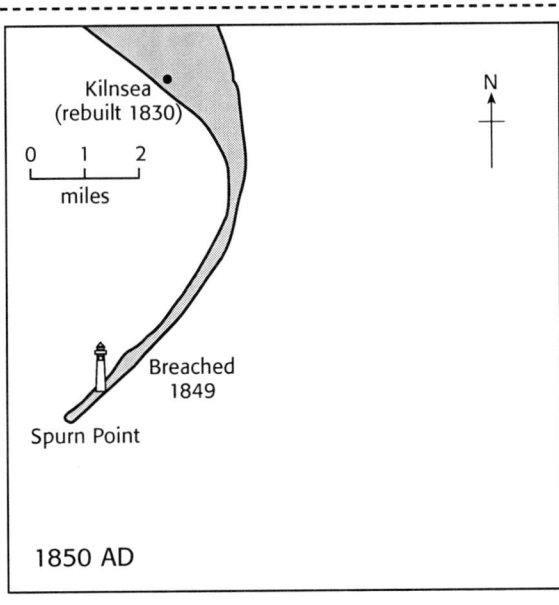

1850 AD

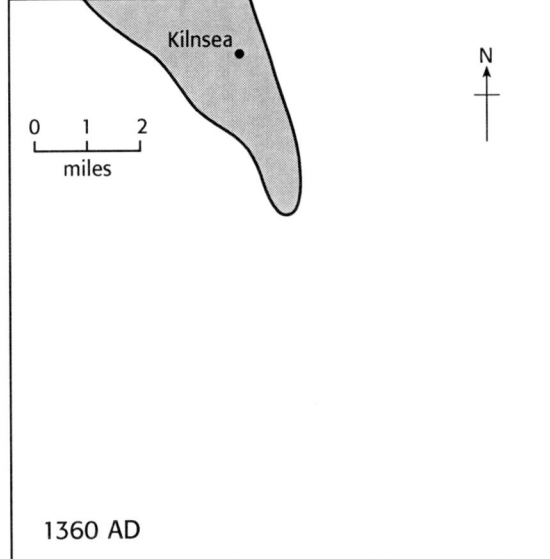

1360 AD

Name   **Class**

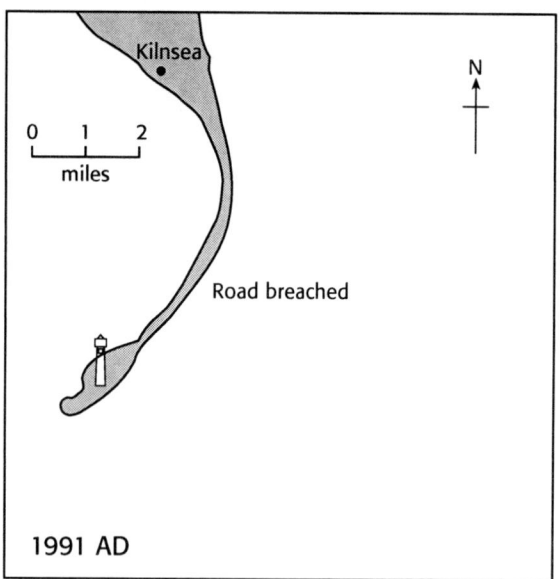

1991 AD

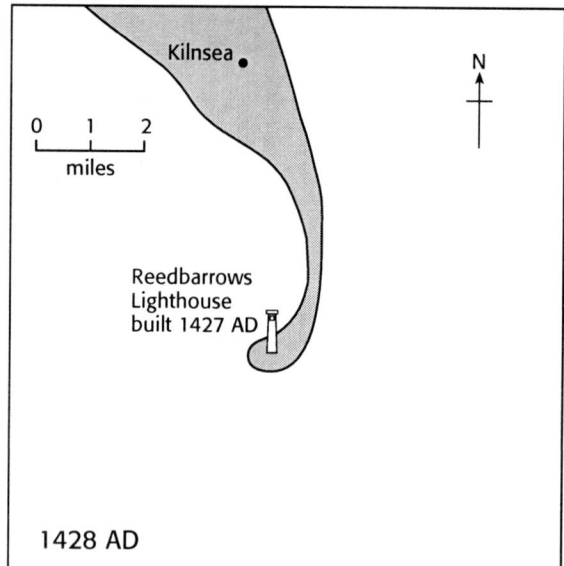

1428 AD

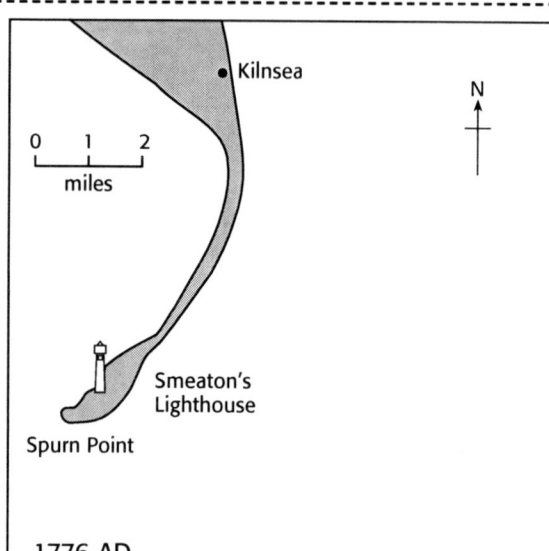

1776 AD

Investigating weathering

***

This activity also appears in the geog.1 teacher's resource file as 'Weathering in the local area'. It is repeated here as it addresses specific learning objectives identified in Unit 8 of the QCA Scheme of Work (*What is weathering? How does weathering affect different types of rock?*).

Aims

- Pupils know the main types of weathering
- Pupils understand the difference between weathering and erosion
- Pupils are able to carry out an enquiry into weathering

Introduction

These activities support the prior learning required for Units 7, 8, and 13 of the QCA Scheme of Work.
The first activity quickly tests knowledge and understanding of weathering.
The second activity requires pupils to carry out an enquiry into weathering in the school grounds.

Activity 1 Revising weathering (page 42)
Pupils should complete the table of weathering by putting the causes in the correct place. Here are the expected answers:

Less weathering	Causes of weathering	More weathering
inland air	salt crystals grow in cracks in rocks	salty, seaside air
dry air	moist air helps chemical reactions	damp air
clean air	airborne sulphur causes acid rain	polluted air
cool climate	warmth speeds up chemical changes	warm climate
steady temperature	heated rocks expand at different rates	changing temperature
always very cold	ice crystals help push cracks apart	freezing and thawing
no plants	rotting plants corrode rocks	lichen, algae, and plant roots
no roots	roots force cracks further open	plant roots

Activity 2 Weathering survey (pages 43-44)
1 Pupils should complete the table 'Where will weathering happen?' to show where they think weathering takes place in and around the school.

2 They should then complete the table 'What are the causes of weathering?' to show how likely different causes of weathering are.

3 Finally, they should carry out their investigation. They could use the planning sheet (page 45) to help them.

Pupils could take photographs of examples of weathering around the school, which, along with their reports, could form a display.

Name   Class

In these activities you will learn more about weathering.
You will carry out your own investigation into weathering around your school.

Activity 1 Revising weathering

Look at the table below. It shows the conditions causing **more** or **less** weathering.
But the middle column has got in a muddle. The causes of weathering are all in the wrong order. Complete the table below, writing the **causes of weathering** in the correct places.

Less weathering	Causes of weathering	More weathering
inland air	rotting plants corrode rocks	salty, seaside air
dry air	roots force cracks further open	damp air
clean air	heated rocks expand at different rates	polluted air
cool climate	ice crystals help push cracks apart	warm climate
steady temperature	salt crystals grow in cracks in rocks	changing temperature
always very cold	moist air helps chemical reactions	freezing and thawing
no plants	airborne sulphur causes acid rain	lichen, algae, and plant roots
no roots	warmth speeds up chemical changes	plant roots

Less weathering	Causes of weathering	More weathering
inland air		salty, seaside air
dry air		damp air
clean air		polluted air
cool climate		warm climate
steady temperature		changing temperature
always very cold		freezing and thawing
no plants		lichen, algae, and plant roots
no roots		plant roots

Name   Class

Activity 2 weathering survey

You are now going to do an investigation into weathering around your school.

1   First, you are going to make some **predictions** about weathering around
    your school.
    Look at the table below. It shows the conditions for more or less weathering.
    Tick the conditions you think you will find in your school.
    Write down where you think you will find them - think about the school
    buildings and the school grounds.

Where will weathering happen?

	Tick if you think you can find this condition around your school	Where will this condition be found in your school?
Less weathering		
inland air		
dry air		
clean air		
cool climate		
steady temperature		
always very cold		
no plants		
no roots		
More weathering		
salty, seaside air		
damp air		
polluted air		
warm climate		
changing temperature		
freezing and thawing		
lichen, algae, and plant roots		
plant roots		

Name   **Class**

2   Now think about the causes of weathering.
        Look at the table below.
        For each cause, tick if you think it is very likely, quite likely, or not likely to
        happen around your school.

What are the causes of weathering?

Causes of weathering	Very likely	Quite likely	Not likely
salt crystals grow in cracks in rocks			
moist air helps chemical reactions			
airborne sulphur causes acid rain			
warmth speeds up chemical changes			
heated rocks expand at different rates			
ice crystals help push cracks apart			
rotting plants corrode rocks			
roots force cracks further open			

3   Now you are ready to carry out your investigation.
        Use the planning sheet to help you.

        Write up your investigation.
        Include maps and sketches (or photographs if possible).

Investigating weathering

Name   Class

An investigation into weathering – planning sheet

Name of school: _____   Name: _____

Location: _____   Date: _____

Aim

I   To find out where and why weathering happens around my school.

Method

I   I will make some predictions about weathering around my school.
I   How many sites will I investigate? (This table gives room for 10.)
I   I will look for evidence of rocks peeling, rocks cracking and features wearing away.
     I will describe this evidence carefully.
I   How will I record my results? (This table gives room for brief descriptions.)
I   I will draw a map to show the school grounds and the sites I investigated.

Results

Site number	Location	Evidence of weathering
1		
2		
3		
4		
5		
6		
7		
8		
9		
10		

Conclusions

I   Is there much evidence of weathering around the school? What? Where?
I   Were my predictions correct? Why? Why not?
I   Is there more weathering on one side of the school than the other? Why?
I   Is there more or less weathering high up on the buildings? Why?
I   What types of weathering are the most common?

Evaluation

I   How could I have improved on my investigation? If I did this again what would I do
     differently? Why?

Coasts

The assessment opportunities for Coasts are as follows:

■ The **level-marked assessment** 'What should happen to the Holderness coastline?' on pages 47-49.

In this assessment, pupils need to make decisions about the future of the Holderness coastline in East Yorkshire. They are presented with a range of facts and opinions about coastal erosion, and three possible management options. Their written work should include a summary of each management option, and a justified decision as to which option they'd favour.

A **feedback form** for the level-marked assessment is provided on page 50.

■ The **scored test** on pages 51-55.

■ Opportunities for interim assessments provided by **geog.2**:

Protecting Tunstall (a role play, with the opportunity for extended writing follow up) on pages 27-32 of this file.

The history of Spurn Head (an enquiry) on pages 33-40 of this file.

Investigating weathering (an investigation, with a fieldwork component) on pages 41-45 of this file.

Activities 6, 13, 14, 25, 26, 28, 36, 38, 39, and 40 in the *Further suggestions for class and homework* section on pages 38-39 of the *geog.2 teacher's handbook.*

Worksheet B: RNLI to the rescue! for Shipwrecked! (a webfile) in *geog.2, Coasts* on *geog.world.*

■ The **self-assessment form** for the whole Coasts chapter on page 56.

Coasts

Name	Class	Date

What should happen to the Holderness coastline?

The level at which I am currently working is [ ]

so my target level for this assessment is [ ]

because [   ]

Assessment task

The coastline of Holderness is disappearing fast! This stretch of coastline in East Yorkshire (see Figure 1) is rapidly being eroded by the sea. Your task is to decide how the Holderness coast should be managed.

First read the speech bubbles in Figure 2. These will help you understand why erosion is a problem in this area, and what some people think should be done about it.

So how should this problem be managed? Here are three options:

■ Build concrete sea walls and barriers to stop the sea from attacking the shoreline. This is known as a 'hard engineering' solution. In the short term, these would stop erosion completely. They are, however, expensive and ugly, and don't always last for long.
■ Install less-noticeable barriers, like a row of underwater rubber tyres just below low tide. These would break up the energy of the waves and, therefore, reduce erosion. This would be a 'soft engineering' solution. Such solutions are cheaper and less ugly but generally aren't as effective as hard engineering solutions. They will also need to be replaced sooner or later.
■ Do nothing! Coastal erosion is, after all, a natural process. Any attempts to reduce erosion in one stretch of coastline will just cause problems in another.

Consider these options, then …

1 On a separate piece of paper, write a summary of each management option, including any advantages or disadvantages you can think of. You could include examples of coastal management in other locations in your answer.
2 Decide which option you'd choose. In your answer you should give reasons to explain your decision.

Before you start work, make sure you understand the task and what you have to do. And look at the **success criteria** on the next page, so that you know how to achieve your target level – or better!

Level 3
- You include a simple summary of at least one of the three management options.
- You show a basic knowledge of the geographical area.
- You understand that there may be conflicting arguments about the causes of coastal erosion, and conflicting views about how to deal with it.
- You use some appropriate vocabulary to communicate your ideas.

Level 4
- You include a simple summary of all three management options.
- You show an adequate knowledge of the geographical area.
- You understand that opinions about the problems of coastal erosion may differ.
- You use appropriate vocabulary to communicate your ideas.

Level 5
- You include a summary of each management option, and give advantages and disadvantages for at least one.
- You show a good knowledge of the geographical area and refer to at least one human and one natural feature of the coastline.
- You understand that a range of factors contribute to opinions about coastal erosion.
- Your work is presented effectively and makes good use of geographical vocabulary.

Level 6
- You include a summary of each of the management options, and give advantages and disadvantages for all three.
- You understand that both human and physical processes contribute to the issues surrounding coastal erosion.
- You understand that there may be direct conflict between the needs and viewpoints of different groups.
- You use geographical vocabulary correctly.

Level 7
- Your summary of the management options includes advantages and disadvantages for each, and makes some reference to other located examples.
- You understand how human and physical processes are linked in contributing to the issue surrounding coastal erosion.
- You understand that the viewpoints of some groups are more powerful than others, and are able to explain this.
- Your work is clearly written with a very good range of information and ideas.

Level 8
- Your summary of the three management options includes advantages and disadvantages of each, and makes detailed reference to other examples that link clearly to a named solution.
- You show how the interaction of physical and human processes can contribute to the processes of coastal erosion.
- You evaluate the nature of the opinions and integrate their viewpoints into your suggested solution to minimise conflict.
- Your work is fully explained and coherently expressed with a comprehensive range of ideas to support your choice of solution.

Exceptional performance

In addition to Level 8...
- You evaluate at least one other named coastal defence scheme and use this information to inform your choice for Holderness.
- You adapt and customise the chosen solution for the specific context of Holderness.

geog.2: 1 Coasts

Figure 1 The Holderness coastline

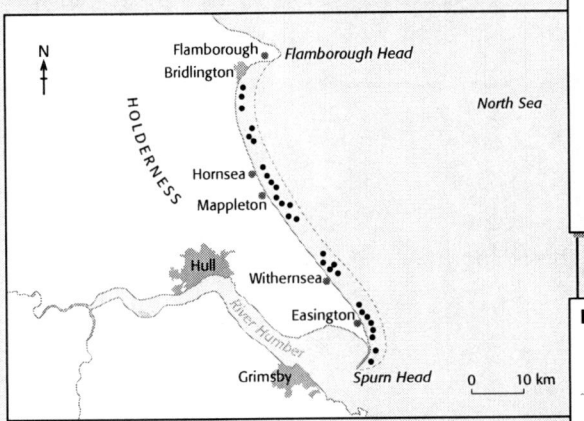
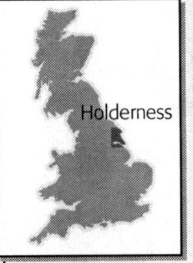

Key
- lost village
- - - - the coastline 2000 years ago

0   10 km

Figure 2 What should happen to the coastline?

Engineer

'Technology is improving so quickly. We could guarantee that if we were allowed to put up concrete barriers and walls there would be no erosion for at least twenty-five years. Any problems, we'd fix it free of charge.'

Local farmer

'This is madness! Why is no-one doing anything to protect the coastline. This is our livelihood, and don't forget that we provide food for people as well! We MUST protect the coast at all cost.'

Local hotel owner

'Our hotel is under threat from the sea. On one hand, we're desperate for coastal defences to be put up to stop erosion, but on the other we're not so sure; defences will make the coast much uglier. At the moment we get lots of tourists staying who have come to see this beautiful stretch of coastline. Would they still come if it didn't look as good?'

Geologist

'Much of this stretch of coastline is formed of boulder clay. This is material deposited by moving ice during the Ice Ages. It has not had time to form into solid rock, and so is very easily worn away by the sea.'

Local historian

'The Holderness coast has been wearing away since our records began. Dozens of villages that were recorded in the Middle Ages have now disappeared. The sea has simply worn them away.'

Government representative

'It's simply too costly to put central government money into saving this part of the coastline. On balance, people should allow nature to take its course. We will help with removal costs.'

Local resident

'We've lived here for nearly forty years. Now we're faced with having to move if the coast wears away any more. The council have told us the amount that we would get in compensation. We just laughed – it's nothing, but then again we wouldn't get anything if we tried to sell the house.'

Local councillor

Environmentalist

'Coastal erosion is a natural process; we shouldn't interfere. Anyway, the plant and animal life copes with the retreating coast, and they have as much right to it as we have. We should leave it alone.'

'Protecting the coast is possible, and, of course, it is important for the people who live there. But we must remember that we're responsible for all our residents, most of whom do not live near the coast. The more money spent on protecting the coast, the less there is for other things.'

Coasts

Name	Class	Date

What should happen to the Holderness coastline?

Assessment task
A written evaluation of three management options proposed for the Holderness coastline, including a justified decision over which to choose.

Level awarded:

Teacher's comments:

Targets for improvement:

- Describe ideas in greater detail. ❏
- Suggest more reasons/processes to explain geographical ideas. ❏
- Try to use more geographical words and terms in your writing. ❏
- Try to support your writing with further, researched ideas. ❏
- Improve accuracy and/or presentation skills. ❏
- Use a greater range of presentation styles/techniques in your work. ❏
- Improve personal organisation and homework to raise your achievement level. ❏
- Ask for help about ideas you don't understand. ❏

Student's comments:

Coasts Test

Name   **Class**   **Date**

Read these instructions carefully before you start:
✓ Write your name, class, and the date in the spaces above.
✓ Your teacher will tell you how long you have to complete this test.
✓ Start time _____ End time _____
✓ Read the questions through before you start.
✓ Check your answers at the end.

1   In the UK most of us live near to the **coast**, but what does the word coast mean? Put a tick in the right box.

The coast is …

❑ the bottom of cliffs

❑ where the land and sea meet

❑ where the waves break   *[1 mark]*

2   a   Many people go to the coast for holidays or days out. Write down FOUR things that people can do at the coast.   *[4 marks]*

_____

_____

_____

_____

   b   Why do you think tourists might not like industries along the coast?   *[2 marks]*

_____

_____

   c   If a company wanted to build a leisure complex by the sea, people would have different opinions about it.
      i   Suggest one person who would be happy about it, and explain why they would like it.

   Person = _____

_____

_____

_____ *[3 marks]*

      ii   Suggest one person who would not like it, and explain their opinion on the next page.

   Person = _____

_____

_____

_____ *[3 marks]*

3 **a** Tides make the sea level change during the day. Use the words below to fill in the gaps in the box. Be careful! You don't need all the words. *[2 marks]*

Moon   **Sun**   **Earth** $12\frac{1}{2}$ $24\frac{1}{2}$

Tides are caused by the pull of the _____ on the water in

the sea. High tides happen about every _____ hours.

b The paragraph below is about waves. In the brackets there are two choices, one of which is wrong. Cross out the WRONG word(s) in each bracket. *[5 marks]*

Waves can be strong or weak. Strong waves can do (**lots of/little**) damage. Waves are strong when the wind is (**strong/gentle**), and the distance of sea they have travelled over is (**long/short**). When waves break, the water going up the beach is called the (**swash/backwash**) and the water going back down the beach is called the (**swash/backwash**).

4 **a** Waves carry out THREE important jobs. Unscramble these words to help you fill in the flow diagram about these jobs.

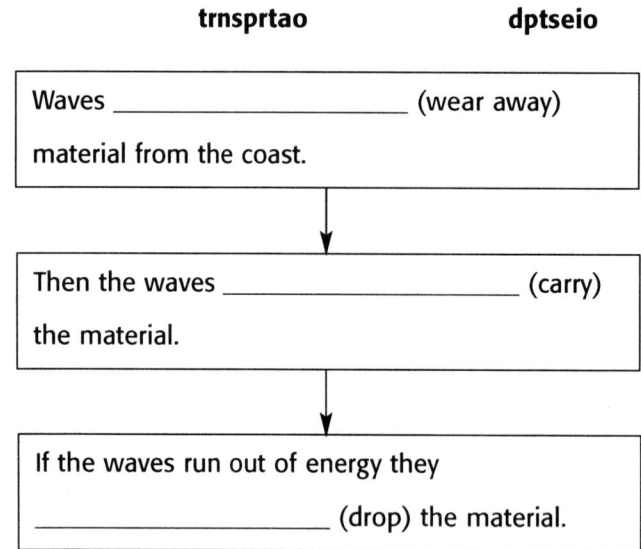

eeord   **trnsprtao**   **dptseio**

Waves _____ (wear away)
material from the coast.

Then the waves _____ (carry)
the material.

If the waves run out of energy they
_____ (drop) the material.

[3 marks]

b There are FOUR processes that waves can use to erode the coast. Match up the process with the definition by drawing a line. One has been done for you.

solution   *water is forced into the cracks in the rock*

attrition   *sand and pebbles scrape at the rock and wear it away*

hydraulic action   *pebbles bang into each other and break bits off each other*

abrasion   *sea water dissolves rocks*   *[3 marks]*

5 Longshore drift is the movement of material along the beach. This diagram shows how it works.

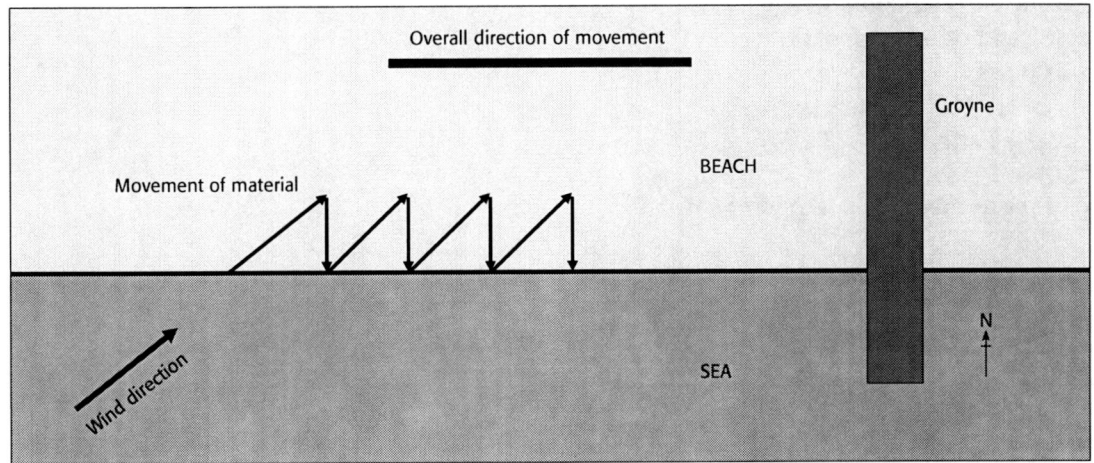

a Draw an arrow on the line on the diagram to show the overall direction of movement of material along the beach. *[1 mark]*

b A groyne (wooden barrier) has been built across the beach, as shown on the diagram. What will happen to the sand on the western side of the groyne? *[2 marks]*

_____

_____

c What will happen to the beach on the eastern side of the groyne? *[2 marks]*

_____

_____

6 If a headland is eroded, arches and stacks can form. This paragraph tells you about what happens.

> Some rocks have cracks in them and the cracks can be eroded easily. When the <u>crack</u> is eroded, it turns into a <u>cave</u>. The cave can be worn straight through the headland and this makes an <u>arch</u>. If the roof of the arch collapses, it makes a <u>stack</u>. If the stack is worn down, it makes a <u>stump</u>.

Read the paragraph. Then use the underlined words to draw and label a diagram of what has happened. Draw your diagram here. *[7 marks]*

7 Sometimes cliffs can collapse because of the effects of the weather and the waves. Councils can try to protect the cliffs by doing things like:
- planting grasses and other vegetation
- using drainage pipes
- making layers of large rocks (rock armour)
- making the slopes flatter

a Choose one of these methods and describe it.   [2 marks]

_____

_____

_____

b Explain how it works.   [4 marks]

_____

_____

_____

c People will have different opinions about the methods used to protect the cliffs. Explain why some people will be in favour and some against using the method you have described and explained.   [6 marks]

_____

_____

_____

_____

_____

_____

_____

_____

_____

Total marks: 50 **Total score:**	**/50**

1 The coast is where the land and sea meet (1 mark).

2 a 1 mark for each sensible activity up to 4 marks.
 b Either 1 mark each for two reasons OR 1 mark for one reason and second mark for expansion.
 c i 1 mark for naming a person (e.g. local child, leisure centre owner). 2 marks for two sensible reasons OR 1 mark for one reason and second mark for expansion.
 ii 1 mark for naming a person (e.g. local child, leisure centre owner). 2 marks for two sensible reasons OR 1 mark for one reason and second mark for expansion.

> Tides are caused by the pull of the <u>Moon</u> on the water in the sea. High tides happen about every $12\frac{1}{2}$ hours.

3 a 1 mark for each correct word placement.
 b 1 mark for each correct crossing out.

> Waves can be strong or weak. Strong waves can do (lots of/~~little~~) damage. Waves are strong when the wind is (strong/~~gentle~~) and the distance of sea they have travelled over is (long/~~short~~). When waves break, the water going up the beach is called the (swash/~~backwash~~) and the water going back down the beach is called the (~~swash~~/backwash).

4 a 1 mark for each correct word

> Waves <u>erode</u> (wear away) material from the coast.

↓

> Then the waves <u>transport</u> (carry) the material.

↓

> If the waves run out of energy they <u>deposit</u> (drop) the material.

 b 1 mark for each correct line ('hydraulic action' to 'water is forced into cracks in the rock' already done).

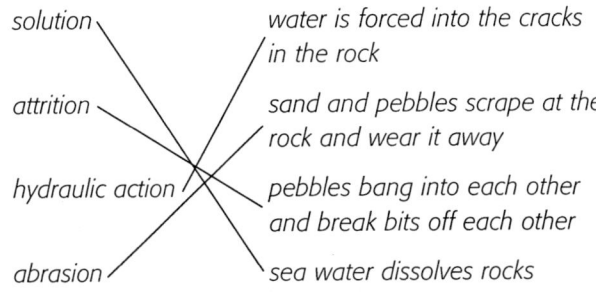

5 a 1 mark for adding arrow to diagram.

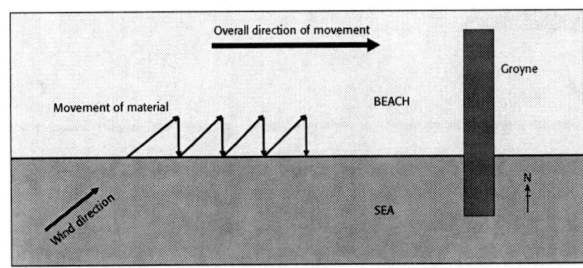

 b Sand is trapped on the western side of the groyne. The beach builds up higher (1 mark) and further out to sea (1 mark).
 c The beach will be removed (1 mark) so will be further inland/lower down (1 mark)

6 2 marks for drawing a diagram showing all 5 features (1 mark for an unclear diagram). 1 mark for each feature labelled.

7 a method is described – 1 mark per descriptive point.
 b 1 mark for each point, or 1 mark for a simple point and 1 or 2 for development – up to a maximum of 4 marks.
 c Up to 3 marks for stating people for and against plus up to 3 marks for explanation – up to a total of 6 marks.

Coasts

Name   **Class**   **Date**

Now I've reached the end of the Coasts chapter:

	Yes	Think so	No
◆ I know what causes waves.			
◆ I can describe at least eight coastal landforms, and how they were formed.			
◆ I know some of the ways we use land along the coast, and some of the conflicts that arise.			
◆ I can explain what causes cliffs to collapse.			
◆ I can give at least four ways of stopping or reducing coastal erosion.			
◆ I understand why we can't protect all the places that are at risk from erosion.			
◆ I know how we can fight erosion in a sustainable way.			

◆ I know what these terms mean:

erode ☐   transport ☐   deposit ☐   longshore drift ☐   beach ☐   bay ☐   headland ☐

cave ☐   arch ☐   stack ☐   stump ☐   wavecut platform ☐   spit ☐   salt marsh ☐

The part of this topic that I enjoyed most or found most interesting was:

Photocopiable worksheets

Learning activities

Assessment materials

[W] indicates material provided as editable Word files, as well as in PDF format, on the CD-ROM.

On the CD-ROM: pupil profile sheet; course theme, and lesson planning documents.

Name   Class

See how extreme weather can affect people's lives:

3 people die in heatwave

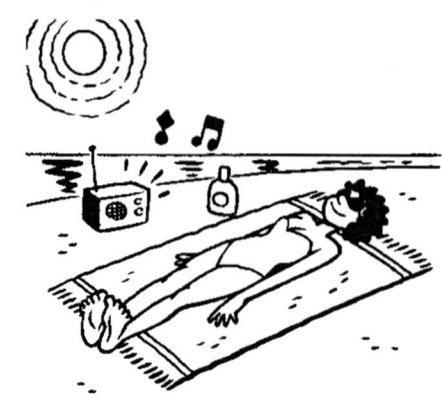

Villages cut off by snowdrifts

Weekend sports programme wrecked by floods

Houses without water after the worst drought in living memory

Copy this page layout – or be a star and design your own!

Imagine you are a reporter for a local newspaper.

Your job is to design and write a front page for one of the headlines above.

On a separate sheet of A4 paper:

1 Make up a good name for your newspaper.

2 Choose one of the headlines and write it out.

3 Now write the main article.

> **Think about** …
>
> • what the headline tells you;
>
> • what you know about weather and climate;
>
> • who will read your newspaper;
>
> • including suitable rainfall and temperature figures;
>
> • the effect of weather on local people;
>
> • how to make it exciting: eyewitness accounts, special stories.

4 Add extra details to your page, such as ads, pictures, a competition.

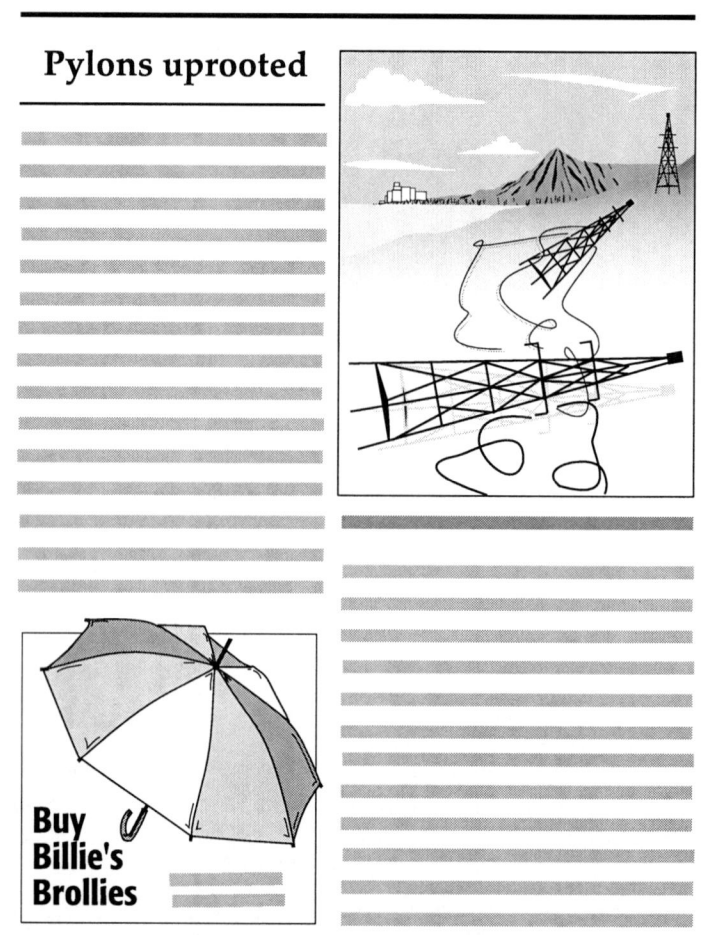

The Daily Record

Pylons uprooted

Buy Billie's Brollies

Name   Class

Contour lines join places at the same height above sea level.
Isobars join places at the same air pressure!

Below is a weather map for one December day. It shows a **depression**, a weather system
where a cold front is chasing a warm one. The isobars show how the pressure varies.

Read the notes around the weather map, then answer the questions.

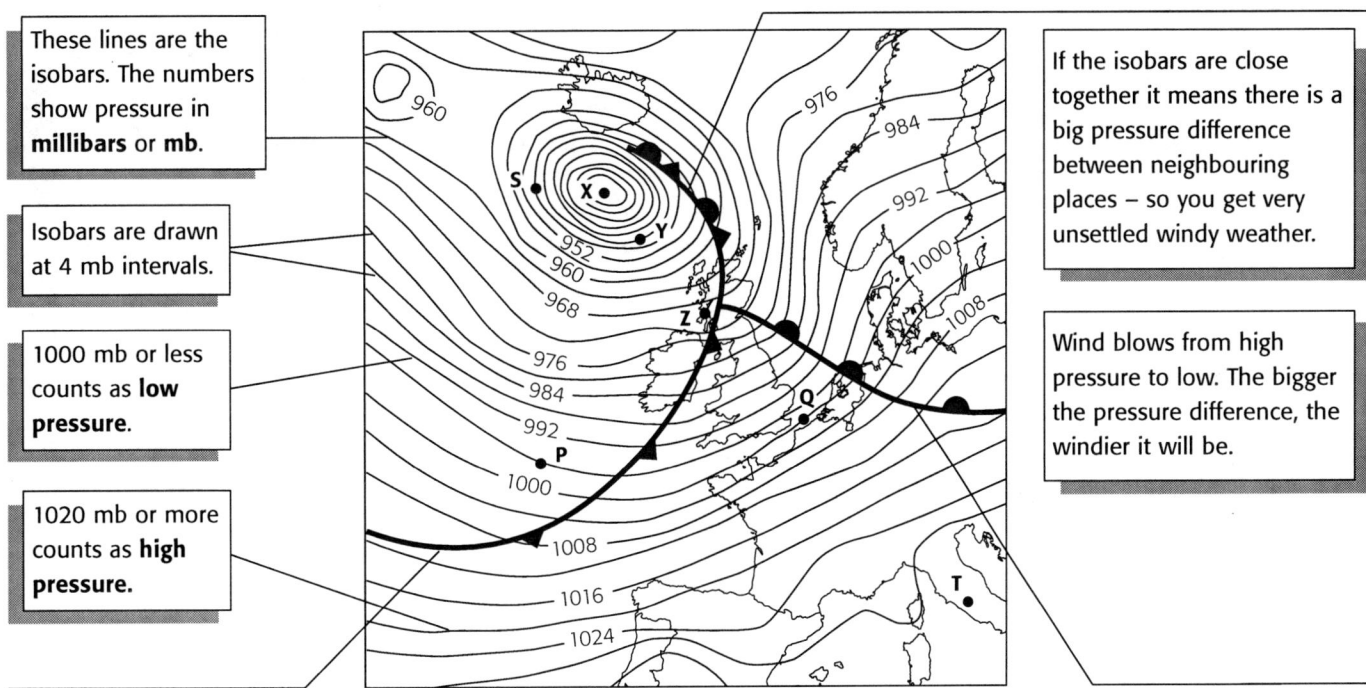

These lines are the isobars. The numbers show pressure in **millibars** or **mb**.

Isobars are drawn at 4 mb intervals.

1000 mb or less counts as **low pressure**.

1020 mb or more counts as **high pressure**.

If the isobars are close together it means there is a big pressure difference between neighbouring places – so you get very unsettled windy weather.

Wind blows from high pressure to low. The bigger the pressure difference, the windier it will be.

1 Fill in these labels on the correct blank lines on the map:

   warm front   **cold front**   **cold front has caught up with warm front**

2 Isobars are lines which _____

3 What is the pressure at P? _____ millibars

4 The pressure is lowest at the place labelled _____ on the map. It is about _____ millibars.

5 Which letter shows a place at high pressure? _____ Which country is it in? _____

6 Which place is likely to be warmer, P or Q? _____ Why? _____

   _____

7 Which place is likely to be windier, S or T? _____ Why? _____

   _____

8 In which direction is the wind likely to blow: from P to Z   or   from Z to P? _____

   Why? _____

9 Which place is more likely to have rain, T or Z? _____ Why? _____

   _____

10 Now, on the back of this sheet, see if you can write a paragraph comparing the weather at Z and T.

And now for the weather…?

*

Name _____ **Class** _____

Look at these drawings. Each is about either weather or climate.

A

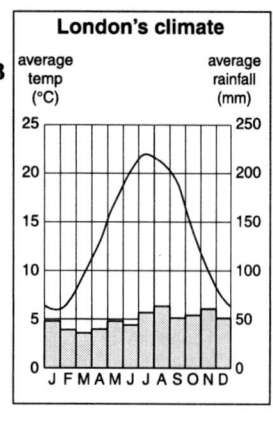

Tomorrow

B

London's climate

average temp (°C) / average rainfall (mm)

C

We always holiday in the Mediterranean. It's always hot and dry in summer. Even in winter it was 24 °C – much warmer than England

D Thermometer

30°C ⊢ (hot)

0°C ⊢ (freezing)

F Air pressure

E **Flood alert!**

Global warming blamed as Britain grows wetter and windier by the year

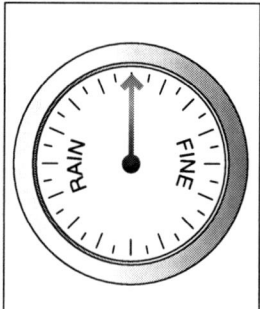

RAIN / FINE

1 Fill in the table below. Describe briefly what each diagram shows, in a box in the correct column. (**A** has been started for you.)

	Weather		Climate
A	This shows the weather forecast for …		

2 Now complete these sentences.

Weather is _____

_____

_____

Climate is _____

_____

_____

3 Draw two pictures to show the difference between weather and climate.

Name   Class

This writing frame will help you to make notes for some extended writing.
The topic is 'The climates of Europe'.

Each section represents a paragraph in your final report.

Use pages 38–39 in the pupils' book to help you.

1 For each paragraph:

   a make a list of points to mention, using the hints on the right;

   b write an opening sentence for the paragraph.

2 Now write your report in your exercise book.

Hints

What is Europe like?

Points:

Opening sentence:

▶ Describe the main physical features, e.g. mountains.

What climate zones are there in Europe?

Points:

Opening sentence:

▶ Describe each type of climate found in Europe.

▶ Write about the location of each type of climate.

▶ Mention a city found in each climate zone.

How does climate vary across Europe?

Points:

Opening sentence:

▶ How does climate change:
• from west to east?
• from north to south?

Why does climate vary across Europe?

Points:

Opening sentence:

▶ How is climate influenced by:
• latitude?
• distance from the coast?
• other factors?

Name   **Class**

You give travel advice for readers, in a national newspaper. Your job is to find the perfect holiday destination for each customer.

The Newman family from Manchester want a family holiday somewhere in Europe.

They want somewhere with a reasonable amount of sunshine.

Most of all they want somewhere where it is not likely to rain!

They don't want it to be too hot because they have three-year-old twins.

It would be nice if the holiday was on the coast but this is not essential.

They want a two-week holiday anytime in July.

Affordable locations include: Crete, Bucharest or Porto.

1 Study the climate data and decide on a suitable location for the Newmans.

2 On a separate sheet of paper, write and tell the Newmans where they should go and why. Include a climate graph (showing temperature and rainfall) to support your choice.

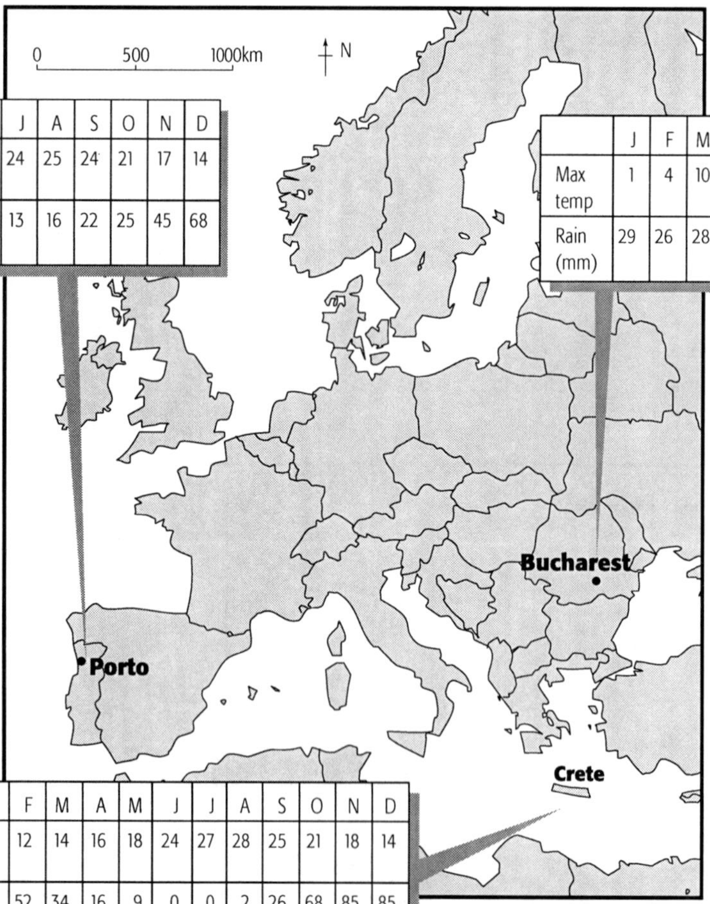

0   500   1000km   ↑ N

	J	F	M	A	M	J	J	A	S	O	N	D
Max temp	13	14	16	18	20	23	24	25	24	21	17	14
Rain (mm)	75	54	32	16	22	15	13	16	22	25	45	68

	J	F	M	A	M	J	J	A	S	O	N	D
Max temp	1	4	10	18	23	27	30	30	25	18	10	4
Rain (mm)	29	26	28	59	77	121	53	45	45	29	36	27

Porto offers a pleasant climate all year round. It gets hot in the summer, but never too hot because of the winds off the Atlantic Ocean. But it does rain in the summer: you can never be sure of having a rain-free holiday!

Bucharest is a growth area for tourism in the summer months. It gets really hot, over 30°C on average. There are no sea breezes to cool it down either but it does rain all year round. the weather is unpredictable: superb one week, raining all the next. Still, this is a hot place to go!

Bucharest ●

Porto

Crete

	J	F	M	A	M	J	J	A	S	O	N	D
Max temp	12	12	14	16	18	24	27	28	25	21	18	14
Rain (mm)	76	52	34	16	9	0	0	2	26	68	85	85

Crete is the largest island in the Mediterranean. In the summer it is almost like a desert: it almost never rains and can get very, very hot. Although the average temperatures in July and August are about 28°C, it can get as hot as 45°C. People have died on crete during heatwaves! Crete is the place to go if you want guaranteed sunshine.

Name   Class

Two types of satellite images can be used to forecast the weather,
visual images and **infra-red** (IR) images.
Both images show clouds in varying shades of grey and white.

This table shows you how to identify cloud types from each image.

Height	Thickness	Texture	Cloud type	Weather
Middle-level, so light grey on IR image	Thick, so bright on visual image	Lumpy, so will show shadows on visual image	Cumulus	Short, heavy showers of rain
Very high tops, so very bright on IR image	Very thick, so very bright on visual image	Lumpy, so will show shadows on visual image	Cumulo-nimbus	Heavy rain, sometimes storms, often fairly windy
Low, so grey on IR image (sometimes can't be seen at all)	Quite thick, so light grey on visual image	Smooth tops, so no shadows on visual image	Stratus	A bit of drizzle, overcast
Very high, so very bright on IR image	Very thin, so can't be seen easily on visual image	Smooth tops, so no shadows on visual image	Cirrus	Dry and often not very windy weather

Using the table above, have a go at analysing these images.

Visual image

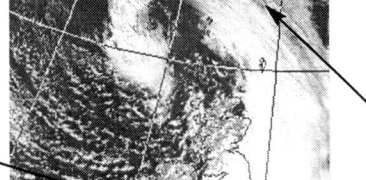

1 Fill in the gaps:

These clouds are bright. This means they could be _____ or_____ clouds.

2 Complete this sentence:

There are shadows in these cloudy areas, so the clouds could be_____ or _____

Infra-red image

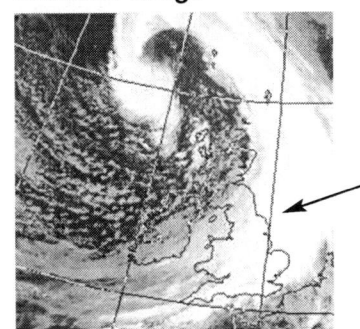

3 Complete this information:

These clouds are grey, so they could be_____ or _____ clouds.

4 Fill in the gaps:

These clouds are bright, so they could be_____ or _____ clouds.

5 Now use all this information to complete this paragraph:

Probable cloud types from these images are _____

This means the weather is likely to be _____

2A Hold the front page *

Rather than a handwritten front page, you could suggest that some pupils use a desktop publishing package. This worksheet then becomes ***.

2B Introducing isobars ***

1 'warm front' label on bottom right; 'cold front' label on bottom left; third label above the map

2 join places that are at equal air pressure

3 996

4 X, 924 mb

5 T, Italy

6 Q; it is in the warm air mass (behind the warm front), while P is in the cold air mass (behind the cold front)

7 S; isobars closer together around there (steeper pressure gradient)

8 from P to Z; winds blow from high pressure to low

9 Z; it is at low pressure (below 1000 mb), which means rising air and clouds, leading to rain. But T is at high pressure which means no clouds and therefore no rain.

10 Pupils may find this one difficult.

At **T** there is high pressure which means clear skies and no rain. There is little or no wind since there's only a gentle pressure gradient (the isobars are far apart). Since the sky is clear and the month is December, it will be cold. However T is

quite far south so it may not be icy. (But the temperature depends on local factors too, like the altitude at T).

At **Z**, on the other hand, the weather will be much more unsettled. Here the cold front is catching up with the warm front, and the pressure is very low, so there will be steeply banked cloud and lots of rain. The isobars are quite close together which is a sign of strong gusty wind. The cloud will help to keep heat in, but Z is a lot further north than T, and behind the cold front, so is probably quite a lot colder. (However the temperature at Z, as at T, will also depend on local factors.)

2C And now for the weather? *

1 Weather A, D, F. Climate B, C, E.

3 Weather is the state of the atmosphere in a place, at a given point in time. Climate is the average weather in a place.

2D Europe's climates **

Responses will vary.

2E Holiday helpline **

1, 2 None of the locations is perfect so responses willl vary. Crete offers almost guaranteed dry weather, but probably too hot; Bucharest is hot, but likely to be wet; Porto offers an intermediate, without extremes in temperature or rainfall. Some pupils might suggest a different location altogether. They should back up their choice with data.

The climate graphs should look like this:

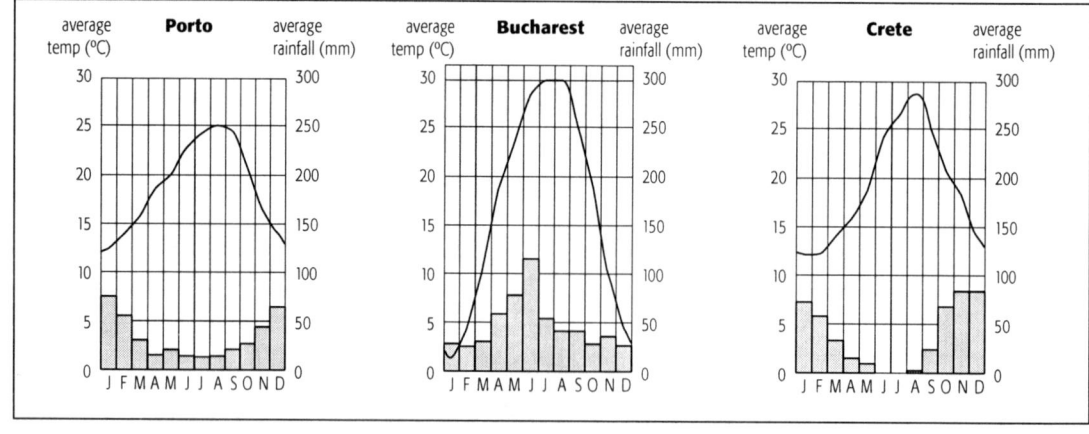

2F Analysing satellite images **

1 cumulus *or* cumulo-nimbus

2 cumulus *or* cumulo-nimbus

3 cumulus *or* stratus

4 cumulo-nimbus *or* cirrus

5 cumulus, cumulo-nimbus, and stratus; wet and windy.

How accurate is the weather forecast? **

Aims

∎ Pupils learn how to interpret weather forecasts
∎ Pupils revise the location of towns in the United Kingdom
∎ Pupils can devise simple measures of success: objective performance indicators
∎ Pupils can use numeracy skills to interpret data and draw conclusions

Introduction

These activities address Unit 10 of the QCA Scheme of Work (*How does the weather change?*). They can be done after unit 2.1 on pages 24-25 of **geog.2**.

The first activity tests pupils' ability to interpret weather forecasts. It introduces a method for comparing the accuracy of forecasts.

There are two follow-up activities. Activity 2 requires pupils to apply the method learnt in Activity 1. Activity 3 asks pupils to think about uses to which a weather forecast might be put.

Activity 1 (pages 67-69)

Pupils have to follow instructions to complete two tables based on a newspaper's weather forecast for the UK on 17 July. Then they assess how accurate the newspaper's weather forecast was.

Pupils will need a location map (page 71) and forecast enquiry tables (page 72).

The two completed tables are shown on page 66.

Activity 2 (page 69)

Pupils should work on their own or in pairs.

1   Each pupil/pair should look at the day's weather forecast in a different newspaper. They should record their findings in the blank forecast enquiry tables (page 73).

2   The next day pupils should find the weather summary table in the same newspaper. They should use the method learnt in Activity 1 to assess how accurate the newspaper's weather forecast was.

3   Pupils should compare their findings with those of other pupils to answer:
    a   which newspaper has the most accurate weather forecasts?
    b   which is the most accurate: forecasts of rainfall, or forecasts of temperature?

4   Pupils should write up their findings in their class books. They should also attempt to explain why newspapers sometimes get their forecasts wrong.

Activity 3 (page 70)

A further exercise using the same newspaper weather information as in Activity 1.

Pupils have to think about the uses to which a weather forecast might be put by a variety of people.

The following statements will help teachers to ensure that pupils have correctly interpreted the weather summary table from 17 July, so that they can judge for themselves whether they made reasonable decisions.

How accurate is the weather forecast? **

Actual conditions on 17 July:

- Rain fell between Oxford and Birmingham in the afternoon.
- It was sunny and dry in Belfast, with temperatures up to 19°C, but the sea was rough and is still forecast to be so.
- Wind veered between south and south west at Bristol Airport, gusting to 25mph. Best approached from the east, taking off to the west, into the wind.
- In Exmouth it was showery but warm at 18°C. Better for silage than hay, which needs to be cut dry.
- Temperature was 19°C as predicted in Norwich, while at Cromer itself there were 11.5 hours of sunshine!
- Manchester was very warm, with sunshine and showers. Morecombe had 7.4 hours of sunshine with a high of 20°C while Colwyn Bay though warm had only 1.9 hours, and it rained!

Completed tables for Activity 1

Table A - temperature

	Forecast temperature °C	Actual temperature °C	Temperature difference °C
Aberdeen	13	15	2
Glasgow	17	16	1
Belfast	14	19	5
Newcastle	16	16	0
Manchester	16	21	5
Norwich	19	19	0
Birmingham	15	18	3
London	17	21	4
Cardiff	16	15	1
Exmouth	15	18	3

Table B – rainfall

	Rain forecast? ✓ 0	Rain fell? ✓ 0	Rainfall difference? X
Aberdeen	0	✓	X
Glasgow	✓	0	X
Belfast	✓	0	X
Newcastle	0	0	—
Manchester	✓	✓	—
Norwich	0	0	—
Birmingham	✓	✓	—
London	0	✓	X
Cardiff	✓	✓	—
Exmouth	✓	✓	—

Name   **Class**

Most newspapers have weather forecasts. They predict what the weather will be like in the near future, with varying accuracy. But are they always right?

You're going to do a series of activities to find out.

Activity 1

The map below shows what weather was forecast for the UK on 17 July. Forecasts like this appear in most newspapers every day.

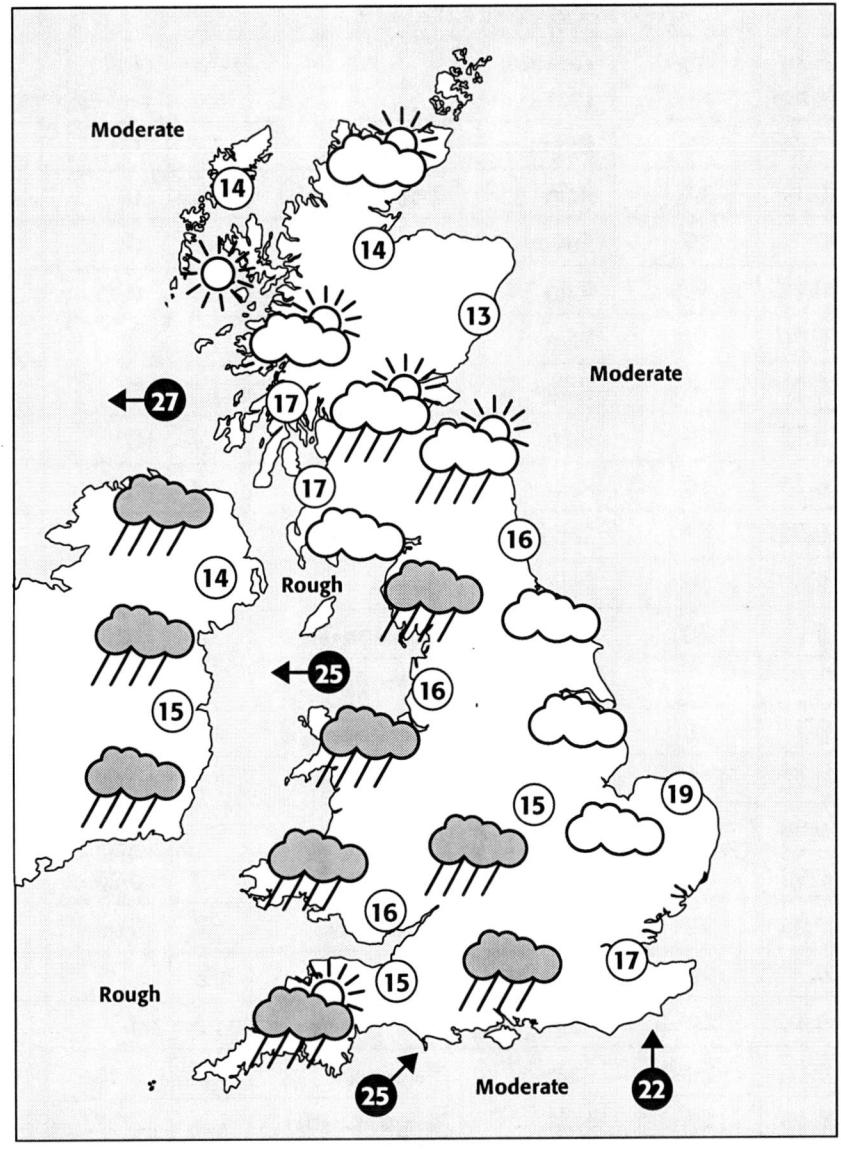

1   **a** Your teacher will give you one page containing two tables and another page containing a location map. In the second column of Table A, write the forecast temperature for each place (the location map will show you where they are). The first two have been done for you.

      b In the second column of Table B put a tick if rain was forecast, or a **O** if not. Again, the first two have been done for you.

2   Now look at the Weather summary table. Most newspapers have tables like this, they tell you what weather Britain actually had the day before.

This table tells you what weather Britain actually had on 17 July. It appeared in a newspaper on 18 July.

In the third column of Table A fill in the actual highest temperature for each place.

	Sun hrs	Rain inches	Max temp °C	Weather (day)		Sun hrs	Rain inches	Max temp °C	Weather (day)
Weather summary									
Aberdeen	9.2	0.01	15	Bright	**London**	3.6	0.15	21	Rain
Anglesey	0.9	0.11	17	Rain	**Lowestoft**	10.2	0	19	Bright
Belfast	5.1	0	19	Sunny	**Manchester**	6.5	0.04	21	Showers
Birmingham	2.6	0.15	18	Rain	**Margate**	7.5	0.11	22	Rain
Bognor Regis	3.3	0.20	17	Rain	**Morecambe**	7.4	0	20	Sunny
Bournemouth	2.1	0.96	16	Rain	**Newcastle**	1.1	0	16	Cloudy
Bristol	0	0.15	16	Rain	**Norwich**	7.8	0	19	Bright
Cardiff	1.2	0.13	15	Rain	**Oxford**	3.1	0.24	20	Rain pm
Clacton	7.4	0.02	17	Showers	**Penzance**	3.0	0.59	18	Bright
Colwyn Bay	1.9	0.01	19	Rain	**Poole**	3.0	0.93	16	Rain
Cromer	11.5	0	18	Sunny	**Ross-on-Wye**	3.1	0.57	17	Rain
Eastbourne	n/a				**Saunton**	0	0.14	16	Dull
Edinburgh	-	0	16	Bright	**Scarborough**	1.9	0	15	Cloudy
Exmouth	1.1	0.62	18	Showers	**Shrewsbury**	1.9	0.09	20	Rain
Falmouth	5.1	0.68	17	Rain	**Skegness**	0	0	17	Cloudy
Fishguard	0	0.02	16	Rain	**Southend**	5.7	0.20	19	Showers
Folkestone	8.6	0.05	22	Rain	**Southport**	7.4	0.06	21	Showers
Glasgow	-	0	16	Bright	**Southsea**	n/a			
Guernsey	2.8	0.56	19	Rain	**Stornoway**	11.0	0	18	Sunny
Hastings	6.5	0.06	19	Rain	**Swanage**	2.2	0.66	16	Rain
Herne Bay	7.5	0.13	23	Rain	**Teignmouth**	n/a			
Hunstanton	6.8	0	21	Sunny	**Tenby**	0.7	0.29	15	Showers
Isle of Man	6.5	0	19	Cloudy	**Tiree**	10.8	0	19	Bright
Isle of Wight	2.9	0.58	15	Rain	**Torquay**	4.3	0.01	18	Cloudy
Jersey	2.5	0.58	18	Rain	**Weymouth**	2.7	0.66	16	Showers
Leeds	4.0	0.98	19	Bright	Met Office report for 24 hours to 5pm yesterday				

Name   **Class**

3   Now you can fill in the **difference** between the **forecast** and the **actual** temperatures. You need to write this in the final column of your temperature table.

4   Now you need to work out the average score. To do this add up the differences and divide by the number of places. The lower this figure, the more accurate the forecast was.

5   If there is a **0** in the rain column of the Weather summary table, it has not rained, but if the figure is higher than **0** it has.

In the rainfall difference column of Table B, put an **X** each time there is a difference.

6   Add up the number of crosses. The lower the number, the better the forecast was.

Activity 2

Now you are going to carry out your own enquiry.

Your teacher will tell you whether you are going to do this on your own or in pairs.

1   First you need to choose a newspaper. Each person, or pair, should try to choose a different newspaper.

2   Find the page that has the weather forecast.

3   Your teacher will give you a sheet with blank forecast enquiry tables. Use the information on the newspaper's weather map to fill in the forecast temperature and rainfall columns in your two tables. (Hint: remember you can use your location map to help you.)

4   The next day you need to get hold of the same daily newspaper. Again, find the weather section. Now use the method that you learnt in Activity 1 to fill in the other columns in your tables.

5   When you've done this, compare your results with everyone else's.
   a Which newspaper has the most accurate weather forecasts?
   b Which is the most accurate: forecasts of rainfall, or forecasts of temperature?

6   Cut out your two tables and glue them into your class book. Underneath each one write a sentence about how accurate the weather forecast was. Write the heading 'Which newspaper has the most accurate forecasts?'. Underneath write a few sentences about what you found out when you compared your results with the rest of your class.

7   Finally, can you think of any reasons why the newspapers sometimes get their forecasts wrong? Write your reasons in your book under a suitable heading.

How accurate is the weather forecast?

**

Name   **Class**

Activity 3

Now you're going to think about uses to which the weather forecast might be put.

1   Look at the forecast map for 17 July again. You will also need the location map.

Try to answer the following questions:

   a Will slicks or wet weather tyres be needed for motor racing at Silverstone today?

   b Will a farmer in Devon cut the grass today for silage or hay, or will he wait until tomorrow?

   c Would an ice cream seller take his van to Cromer today?

   d If you lived in Manchester and fancied a day out today, which National Park would you go to, Snowdonia or the Lake District?

   e Would you take a leisure boat trip from Stranraer for a day trip to Belfast in Northern Ireland today?

   f Airline pilots land and take-off into the wind. Will air traffic control have them approaching Bristol Airport from the east or the west today?

2   Now look at the weather summary table.

   a What was the weather actually like in all these places?

   b Did you make sensible decisions?

3   **a** Was the weather forecast good enough?

   b Was the temperature or the rainfall predicted most accurately?

   c Was the accuracy better in some parts of the country than others?

Name   **Class**

Location map: the British Isles

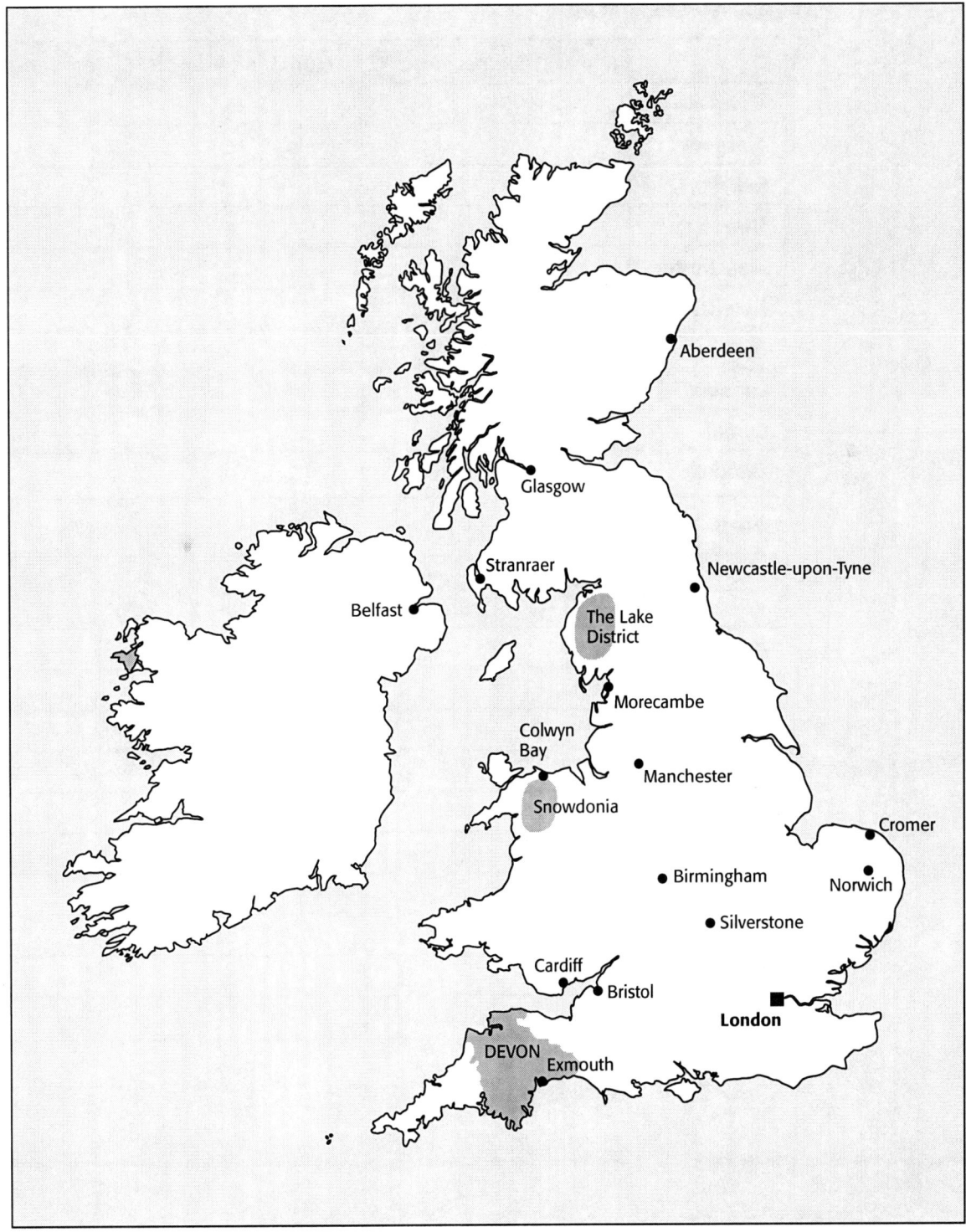

How accurate is the weather forecast? **

Name   Class

Forecast enquiry tables for Activity 1

Table A - temperature

	Forecast temperature °C	Actual temperature °C	Temperature difference °C
Aberdeen	13	15	2
Glasgow	17	16	1
Belfast			
Newcastle			
Manchester			
Norwich			
Birmingham			
London			
Cardiff			
Exmouth			

Table B – rainfall

	Rain forecast? ✓ 0	Rain fell? ✓ 0	Rainfall difference? X
Aberdeen	0	✓	X
Glasgow	✓	0	X
Belfast			
Newcastle			
Manchester			
Norwich			
Birmingham			
London			
Cardiff			
Exmouth			

Name   **Class**

Forecast enquiry tables for activity 2

Name: _____

Date: _____

Name of newspaper: _____

Table A – temperature

	Forecast temperature °C	Actual temperature °C	Temperature difference °C
Aberdeen			
Glasgow			
Belfast			
Newcastle			
Manchester			
Norwich			
Birmingham			
London			
Cardiff			
Exmouth			

	Rain forecast? ✓ 0	Rain fell? ✓ 0	Rainfall difference? X
Aberdeen			
Glasgow			
Belfast			
Newcastle			
Manchester			
Norwich			
Birmingham			
London			
Cardiff			
Exmouth			

Why does it rain? *

This is a fun consolidation exercise.

Aims

▮ Pupils know the terms frontal, relief, and convectional rainfall
▮ Pupils understand the processes of frontal, relief, and convectional rainfall
▮ Pupils practise teamwork skills

Introduction

This activity supports Unit 10 of the QCA Scheme of Work (*What are clouds and why does it rain?*). It is a card-sequencing activity that links with unit 2.2 on pages 26-27 of **geog.2**.

Activity

This activity should be done in pairs.

1 Give each pair an envelope containing the following:
   ▮ one set of cards about a cause of rainfall (pages 75-77)
   ▮ the instruction sheet to match the set of cards (pages 78-80)
   ▮ a blank overhead
   ▮ an overhead pen.

2 Instruct pupils to put the cards in the correct sequence. (This could be run as a competition with a prize for the first correct pair for each set of cards.)

3 Instruct pupils to follow the instructions in their envelope.

Name   Class

| FRONTAL RAINFALL | sometimes a warm air mass meets a cold one |

| the warm air mass slides up over the cold one, since it is lighter | as the warm air rises, it cools |

| as it cools, the water vapour in it condenses to make tiny water droplets | these droplets form a gently sloping bank of clouds |

| droplets in the clouds join to form larger drops, which fall as rain | |

Name   **Class**

CONVECTIONAL RAINFALL	the sun's heat warms the ground
CONVECTIONAL RAINFALL	because the air is warm it rises upwards
as the air rises it cools	as it cools, the water vapour in it condenses to form tiny water droplets
the droplets form clouds	inside the clouds droplets join to make larger drops, which fall as rain

Why does it rain?

RELIEF RAINFALL	warm moist air is blown in from the Atlantic Ocean

the wind meets a line of high hills or mountains	the air is forced to rise

as the air rises it cools	as the air cools, the water vapour in it condenses to form tiny water droplets

the droplets form clouds	inside the clouds droplets join to make larger drops, which fall as rain

the rain falls on the high land facing into the wind (the windward side)	the other side of the high land (the leeward side) stays dry and sheltered

Why does it rain? *

Name   **Class**

Instruction sheet for

frontal rainfall

All rain is caused by air rising. But it rises for different reasons – so we give rain different names. **Frontal rainfall** is one of these names.

1   Read your cards. They describe what happens when we get frontal rainfall. You need to put the cards in the correct order.

2   On your blank overhead, draw a diagram describing how frontal rainfall happens. You can use the cards to help you label your diagram.

3   Underneath your diagram write the following paragraph (some of the words are missing so you will need to fill in the gaps):

> **Frontal rainfall is caused by travelling _____ . In the UK these often move in from the Atlantic Ocean. This means we get lots of frontal rainfall in the _____ and in the _____ . We get frontal rainfall throughout the year, but especially in _____ .**

Now you are going to tell the rest of your class what happens when we get frontal rainfall. Use your overhead to help you.

Why does it rain?

*

Name   **Class**

Instruction sheet for

convectional rainfall

All rain is caused by air rising. But it rises for different reasons – so we give rain different names. **Convectional rainfall** is one of these names.

1 Read your cards. They describe what happens when we get convectional rainfall. You need to put the cards in the correct order.

2 On your blank overhead draw a diagram describing how convectional rainfall happens. You can use the cards to help you label your diagram.

3 The paragraph below tells you **where** and **when** we are likely to get convectional rainfall in the UK. You need to cross out the wrong words leaving the right words.

Convectional rainfall is more likely to form in the **summer/winter** than in **summer/winter**. It is more likely to fall **inland/on the coast** than **inland/on the coast**. It is more likely to fall in **Africa/Iceland** than in **Africa/Iceland**.

4 Write the correct paragraph under your diagram.

Now you are going to tell the rest of your class what happens when we get convectional rainfall. Use your overhead to help you.

Name   **Class**

Instruction sheet for

relief rainfall

All rain is caused by air rising. But it rises for different reasons – so we give rain different names. **Relief rainfall** is one of these names.

1   Read your cards. They describe what happens when we get relief rainfall. You need to put the cards in the correct order.

2   On your blank overhead draw a diagram describing how relief rainfall happens. You can use your cards to help you label your diagram.

3   The paragraph below tells you **where** we are likely to get relief rainfall. you need to cross out the wrong words leaving the right words.

   Relief rainfall is quite common in Britain. If falls mostly in the **west/east** where most of the **high/low** ground is located. Relief rain falls on the **windward/leeward** side of high ground. The **leeward/windward** side stays dry.

4   Write the correct paragraph under your diagram.

Now you are going to tell the rest of your class what happens when we get relief rainfall. Use your overhead to help you.

Weather and climate

The assessment opportunities for Weather and climate are as follows:

▮ The **level-marked assessment** 'All about weather' on pages 82-87.

In this assessment, pupils need to:
a identify how key weather elements are measured;
b give a description of how relief and convectional rainfall happen;
c use weather maps to prepare a weather forecast for the UK.

A **feedback form** for the level-marked assessment is provided on page 88.

▮ The **scored test** on pages 89-93.

▮ Opportunities for interim assessments provided by **geog.2**:

How accurate is the weather forecast? (an investigation) on pages 65-73 of this file.

Why does it rain? (a card-based activity, with the opportunity for pupils to work in pairs) on pages 74-80 of this file.

Activities 12, 13, 16, 24, 26, and 31 in the *Further suggestions for class and homework* section on pages 60-61 of the *geog.2 teacher's handbook*.

Worksheet B: Help from satellites for *And now the weather …* (a webfile) in *geog.2, Weather and climate* on *geog.world*.

▮ The **self-assessment form** for the whole Weather and climate chapter on page 94.

Weather and climate

Name	Class	Date

All about weather

The level at which I am currently working is ☐

so my target level for this assessment is ☐

because

Assessment task

This assessment task is about measuring, recording and forecasting the weather. You will:

- identify how key weather elements are measured;
- give a description of how relief and convectional rainfall happen;
- use weather maps to prepare a weather forecast for the UK.

You have been given a range of resources to help you: a table with weather terms, definitions and methods of measurement, a set of statements relating to how relief and convectional rainfall happen, and a series of weather maps.

Answer these questions on a separate piece of paper.

1 Look at figure 1. It gives some key weather terms and some of the methods used to measure weather. Make a copy of the table and fill in all the gaps using the words beneath the table (hint: some information is missing so you'll have to add it yourself!).

2 Now look at figure 2. These statements describe how relief and convectional rainfall happen, but they're all jumbled up! Sort the statements into two groups, one for each kind of rainfall, then write them out in the correct order.

3 Imagine you present the weather forecast on a national TV news programme. You have to put together a forecast for tomorrow's weather based on either figure 3 or 4 (you can choose). You only have a five-minute slot and there's a lot to fit in; you need to talk about:
   • the weather conditions in all the different parts of the UK (e.g. the South West);
   • how the weather conditions might affect human activities;
   • what weather systems are present.

Hint: figure 5 will help you understand the weather maps.

Before you start work, make sure you understand the task and what you have to do. And look at the **success criteria** on the next page, so that you know how to achieve your target level – or better!

Level 3
- You are able to match some weather terms with their descriptions and methods of measurement.
- You give some simple weather descriptions using a weather map and key.

Level 4
- You are able to match most weather terms with their descriptions and methods of measurement. Your attempts to fill in the missing information are mostly correct.
- You have an idea of which processes lead to convectional rainfall, and which to relief rainfall, and can place some parts of the process in the correct sequence.
- You describe the weather conditions in a number of different places, using some appropriate terminology.
- You make some simple statements about how weather can affect human activities.

Level 5
- You are able to match all given weather terms with their descriptions and methods of measurement. Your attempts to fill in the missing information are correct.
- You place the processes leading to convectional rainfall, and those leading relief rainfall, in the correct order.
- You make some accurate statements based on a weather map and key, with comments on a variety of weather elements.
- You identify correctly the weather system shown on a satellite image.
- You state in more detail how the different weather conditions can affect various activities.

Level 6
- You describe fully the weather conditions for a variety of places across the British Isles, using a weather map and key.
- You state how the weather conditions can directly influence the behaviour and activities of people.
- You identify correctly the weather system shown on a satellite image and make some attempt to relate it to the weather conditions shown on the map.

Level 7
- You use a wider range of skills to describe and explain the variations in the weather conditions across the British Isles, as shown by a weather map.
- You understand how the weather can affect human activity.
- You explain the conditions in relation to the features of the weather system shown on a satellite image.
- You show a full understanding of a wide range of specific terminology and write your ideas in a clear way, and to an appropriate length.

Level 8
- In addition to the descriptors for level 7, you describe the weather conditions shown on the weather map in complete detail, and explain comprehensively the conditions in relation to the weather system present.
- You are able to explain complex information shown on the weather map.
- You understand how the weather can affect the activities of different groups of people.
- You give some detail about how the passage of the weather system is likely to affect weather conditions in the near future.
- A high level of literacy is demonstrated throughout.

Exceptional performance

In addition to Level 8…
- You evaluate critically the material provided.
- You show wider understanding of the topic, evaluate your own work and suggest further lines for enquiry.

Figure 1 Measuring the weather

Weather term	Means ...	Measured using ...
air pressure		
		thermometer
	how fast the wind blows	
wind direction		anemometer
		visibility meter
precipitation		

the greatest distance you can see, in km or m   the weight of air pressing down on the Earth's surface
visibility   wind speed   how hot or cold something is, measured in degrees Centigrade   rain gauge
temperature   wind direction   weather vane

Figure 2 Two kinds of rainfall

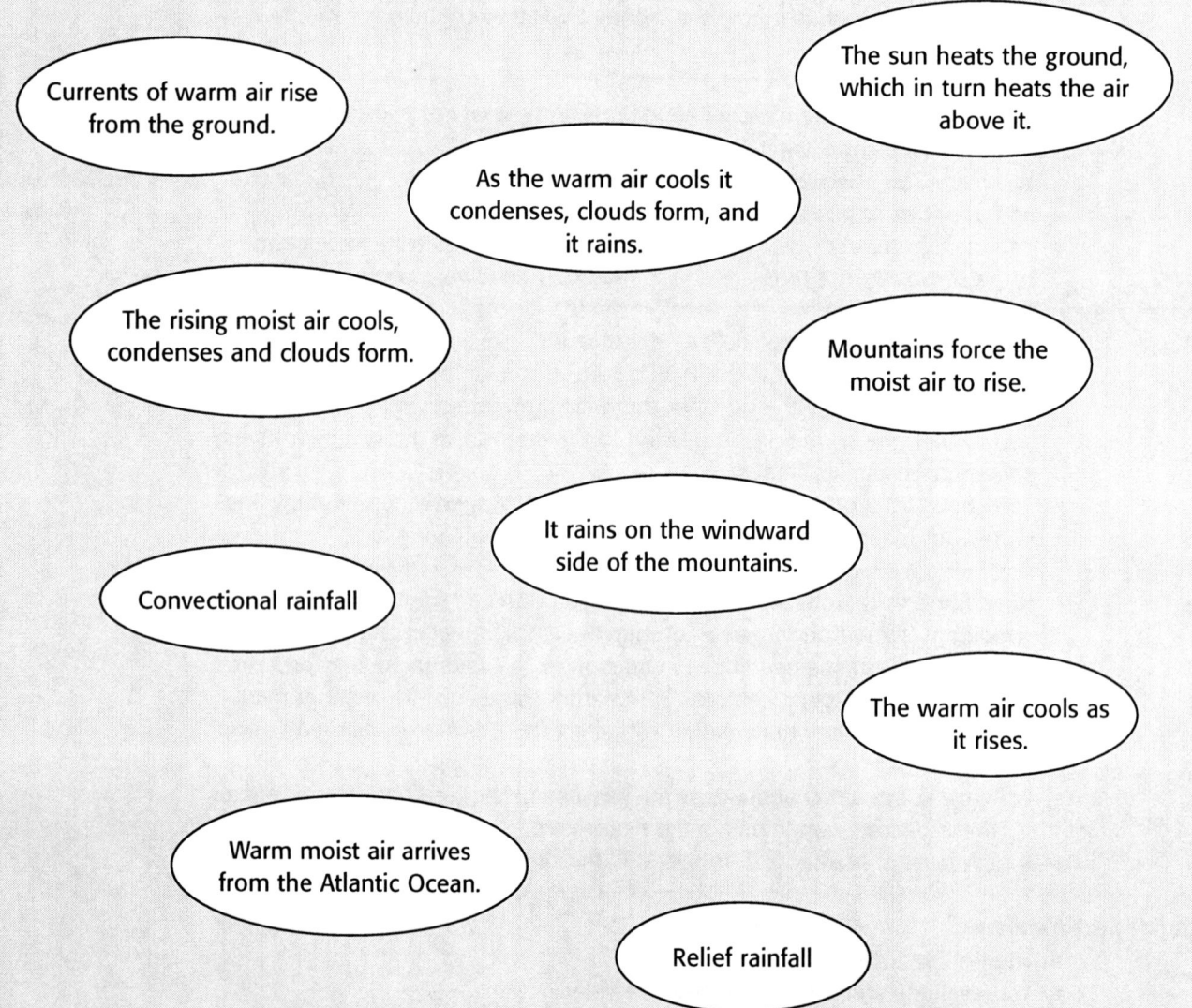

geog.2: 2 Weather and climate

Figure 3 Weather maps for the UK

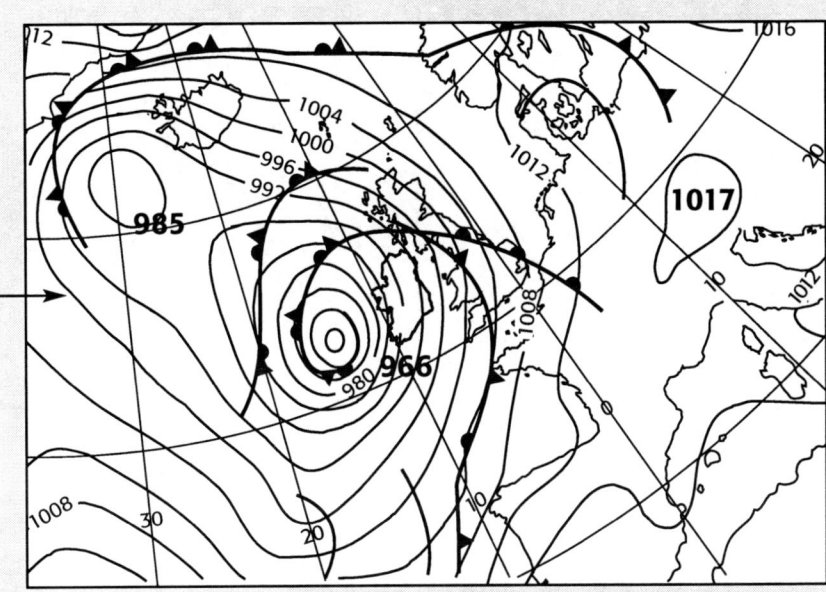

The lines on this map are called *isobars*. They tell you how high the pressure is (compare the numbers to those on the similar map in Figure 4; in which map are they mostly higher?).

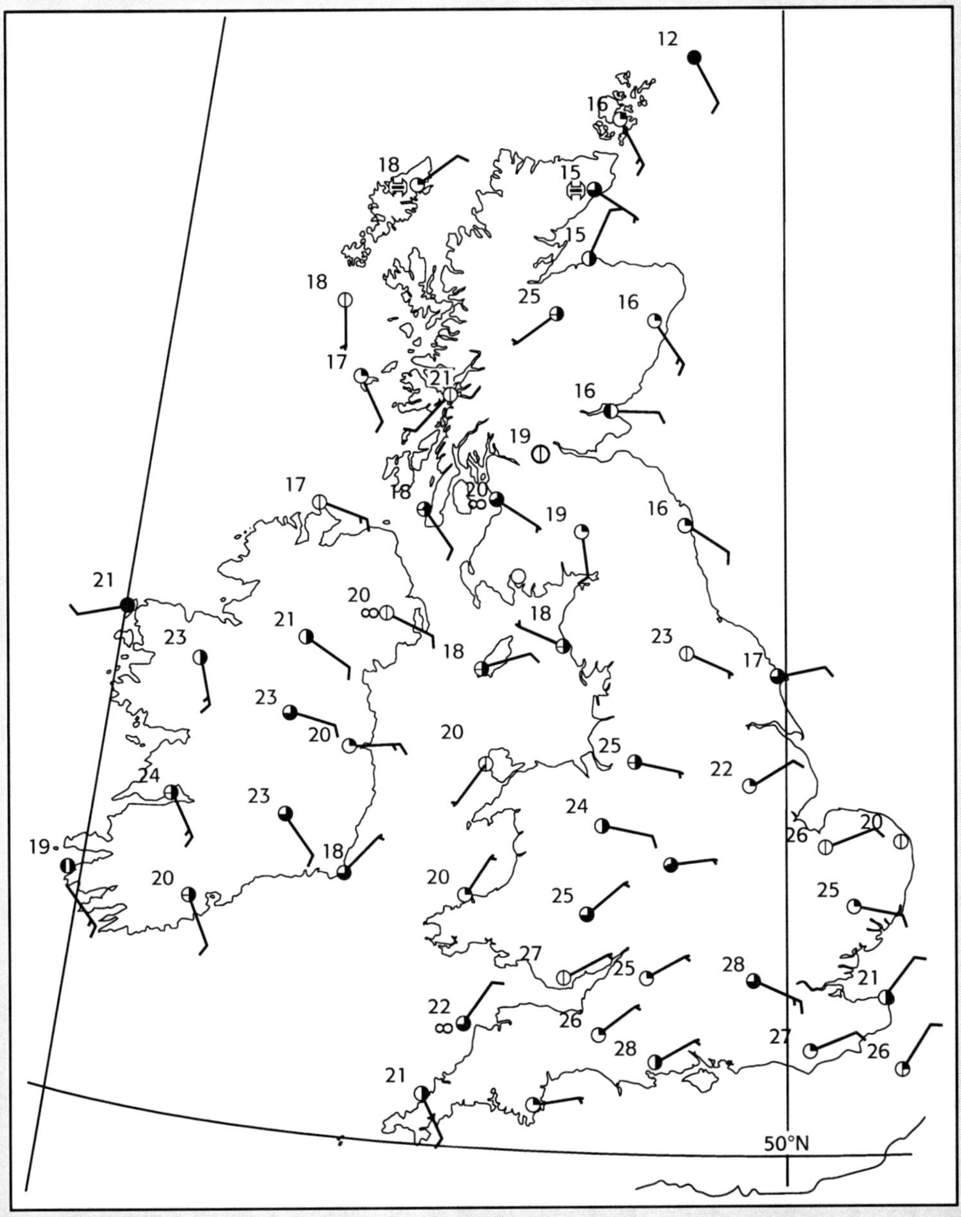

Figure 3 Weather maps for the UK

Figure 4 Weather maps for the UK

Compare the numbers on this map with those on the similar map in Figure 3. in which map are the numbers mostly higher? (This should give you a clue about the weather system shown here!)

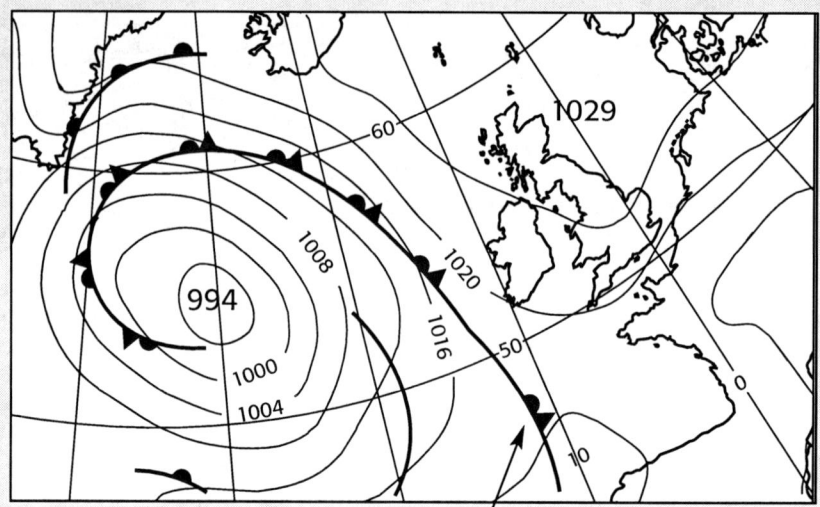

Having these two symbols together is known as an *occluded front*. It's what happens when one front catches up with the other!

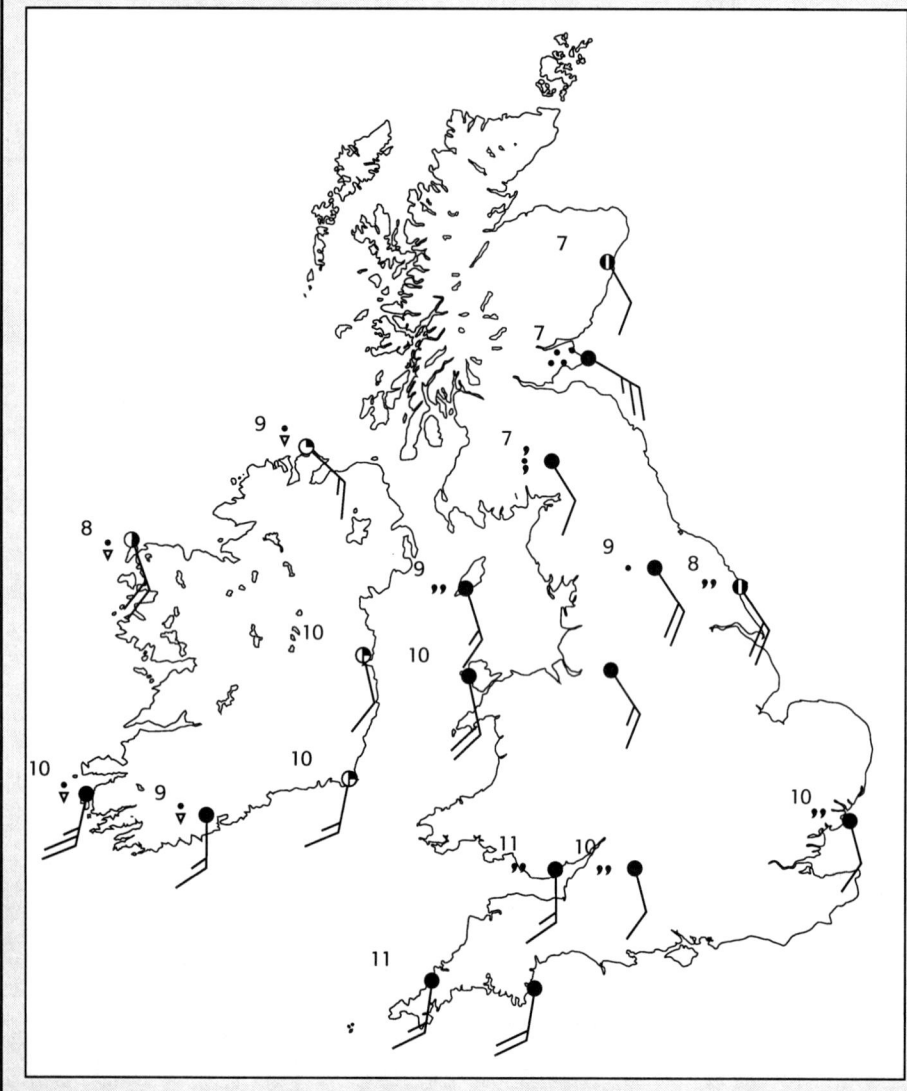

Figure 4 Weather maps for the UK

Figure 5 Symbols used on weather maps

Are the weather symbols used in figures 3 and 4 familiar to you? Probably not! Meteorologists use slightly different weather symbols to the ones we see on the TV and in the newspapers. This key will help you to make sense of the weather maps.

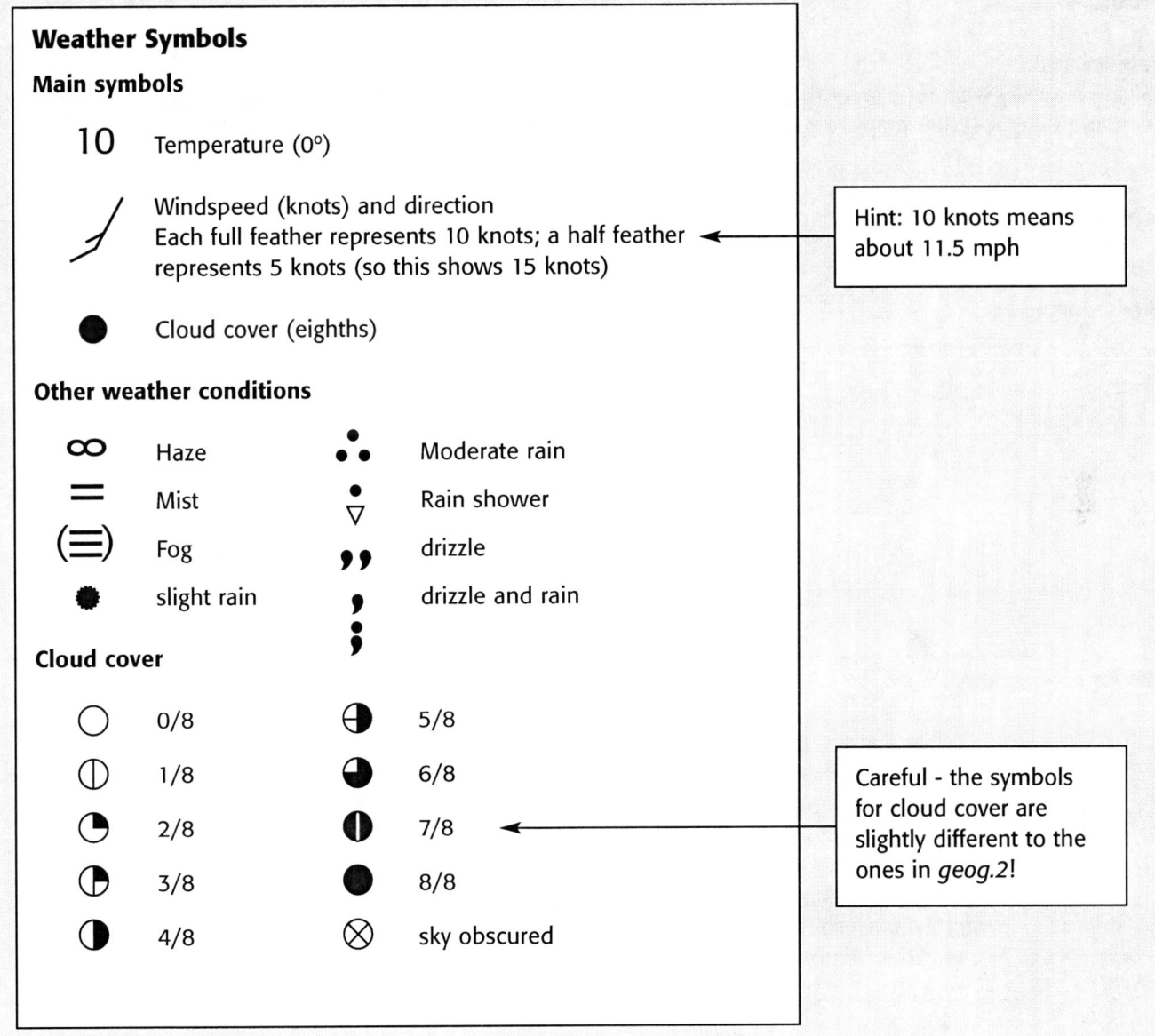

Weather Symbols

Main symbols

10   Temperature (0°)

Windspeed (knots) and direction
Each full feather represents 10 knots; a half feather represents 5 knots (so this shows 15 knots)

Hint: 10 knots means about 11.5 mph

●   Cloud cover (eighths)

Other weather conditions

∞   Haze   Moderate rain

=   Mist   Rain shower

(≡)   Fog   drizzle

✱   slight rain   drizzle and rain

Cloud cover

○   0/8   5/8

◐   1/8   6/8

◕   2/8   7/8

◑   3/8   8/8

◐   4/8   ⊗   sky obscured

Careful - the symbols for cloud cover are slightly different to the ones in *geog.2*!

Weather and climate

Name   **Class**   **Date**

All about weather

Assessment task
Identifying how key weather elements are measured; giving a description of how relief and conventional rainfall happen; and using weather maps to prepare a weather forecast for the UK.

Level awarded:

Teacher's comments:

Targets for improvement:

- Describe ideas in greater detail. ❏
- Suggest more reasons/processes to explain geographical ideas. ❏
- Try to use more geographical words and terms in your writing. ❏
- Try to support your writing with further, researched ideas. ❏
- Improve accuracy and/or presentation skills. ❏
- Use a greater range of presentation styles/techniques in your work. ❏
- Improve personal organisation and homework to raise your achievement level. ❏
- Ask for help about ideas you don't understand. ❏

Student's comments:

Weather and climate Test

Read these instructions carefully before you start:
✓ Write your name, class, and the date in the spaces above.
✓ Your teacher will tell you how long you have to complete this test.
✓ Start time _____ End time _____
✓ Read the questions through before you start.
✓ Check your answers at the end.

1 Which one of these sentences tells us what **weather** is? Put a tick in the box by the right answer.

Weather is …

❑ how often it rains

❑ the state of the atmosphere around us

❑ what time of the year it is   *[1 mark]*

2 Below is a paragraph about measuring the weather, but there are gaps in it! You need to choose from the words below to complete the paragraph. Be careful, some of the words aren't useful!

weather vane	thermometer	degrees	precipitation
millibars	barometer	centimetres	ruler	meteorologists

People who study the weather are called _____. They measure

temperature using a _____, and the answer is in degrees centigrade.

Air pressure is measured using a barometer, and the answer is in _____.

_____ is measured in millimetres using a rain gauge.   *[4 marks]*

3 Here are some words and their definitions, but they are all mixed up. Draw lines to join up the correct words and definitions.

air pressure   *how far we can see, measured in metres or kilometres*

wind direction   *how 'heavy' the air is*

cloud cover   *where the wind is blowing from*

visibility   *how much of the sky is covered in cloud, measured in oktas*

                                                        [4 marks]

4   **a** Write ONE sentence about **what** the weather is like when the air pressure is HIGH. *[2 marks]*

_____

_____

b Write ONE sentence about **why** the weather is like this in HIGH pressure.   *[2 marks]*

_____

_____

5 There are three types of rain; convection, relief, and frontal rain.   *[6 marks]*

   a In the box, draw a diagram to show ONE type of rainfall.

   b Add labels to your diagram to show what is happening.

   c Give your diagram a title.

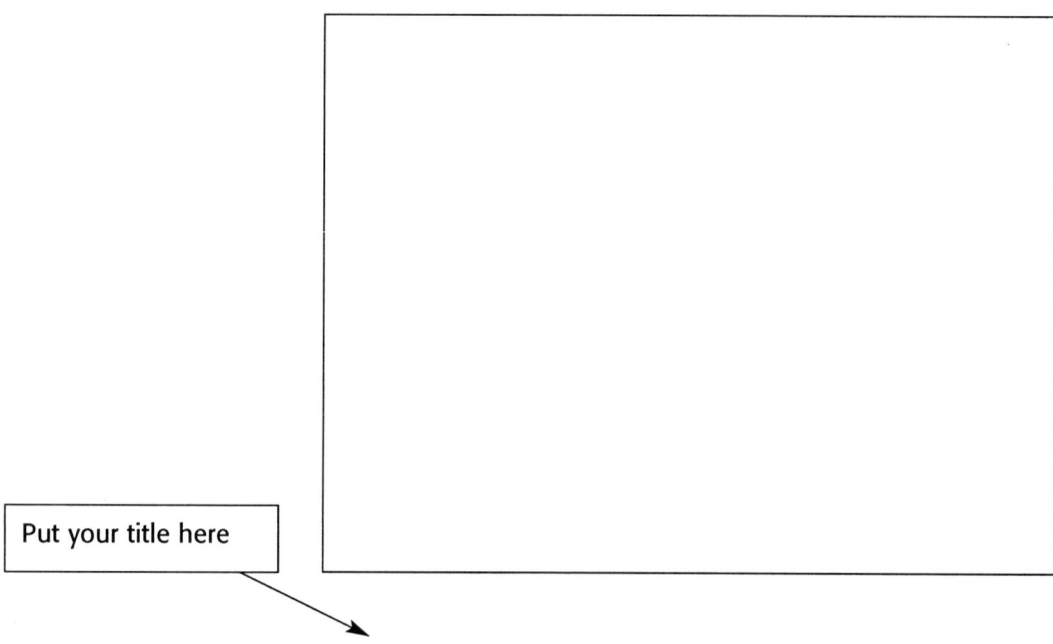

Put your title here

_____

6 An air mass is a huge block of air. It can be warm or cold, damp or dry depending on where it comes from. When an air mass arrives, it affects our weather.

Look at this map of air masses coming to Britain.

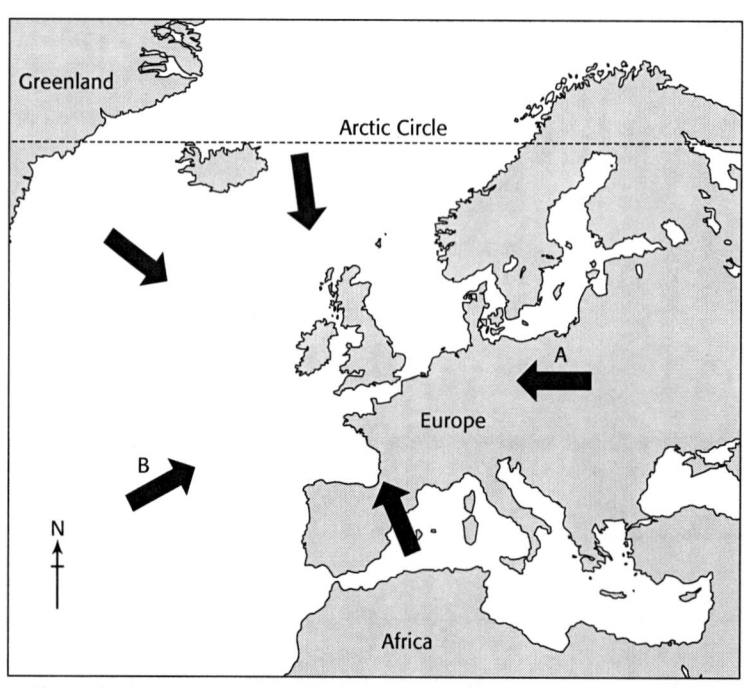

a What sort of weather would you expect from air mass A? *[2 marks]*

_____

_____

b What sort of weather would you expect from air mass B? *[2 marks]*

_____

_____

7 **Climate** is the average of weather over a long period. It can be shown on a climate graph.
You are going to complete this climate graph for Athens.

Month	J	F	M	A	M	J	J	A	S	O	N	D
Temperature (°C)	10	10	12	17	20	25	29	30	24	20	14	9
Rainfall (mm)	6	4	5	3	3	2	1	1	1	4	5	6

c Use this data to finish drawing the line graph for temperature. Draw the line in red. *[3 marks]*

e Write a title on this line. *[1 mark]*

d Now use this data to draw the bar graph for rainfall. Shade the bars in blue. *[5 marks]*

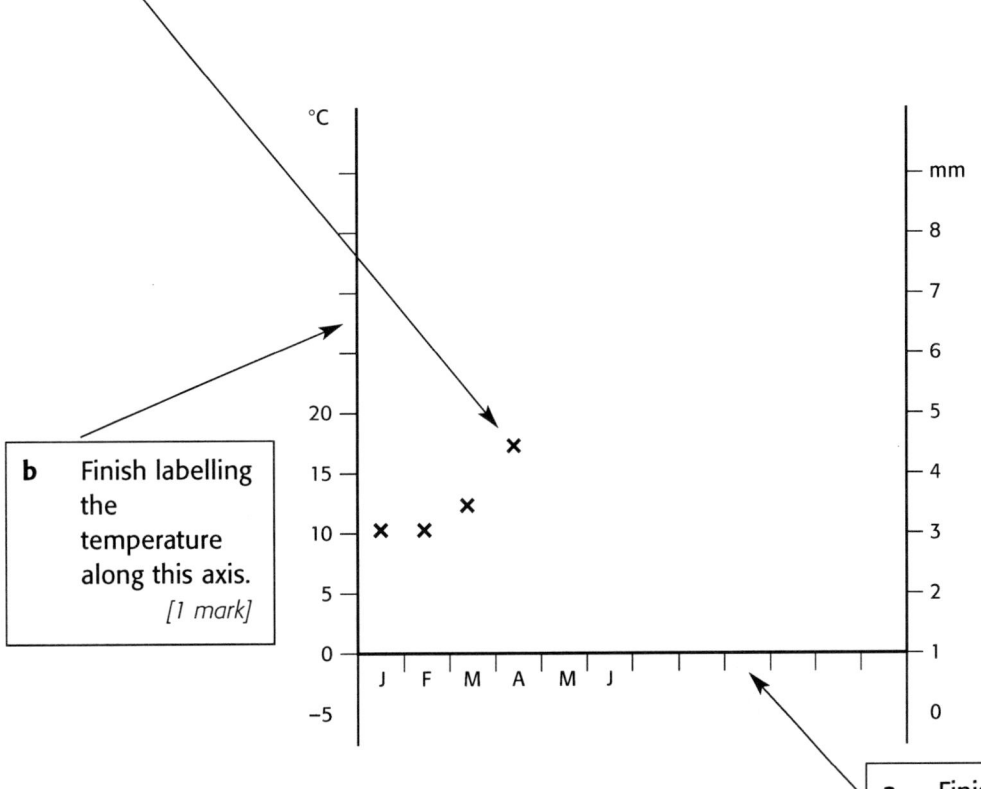

b Finish labelling the temperature along this axis. *[1 mark]*

a Finish labelling the months along this axis. *[1 mark]*

8 The graph on the right shows the climate in London.

a Use the graphs for London and Athens to fill in the table.

[6 marks]

	Highest temperature	Lowest temperature	Most rain	Least rain
London	22 °C			
Athens			6 mm	

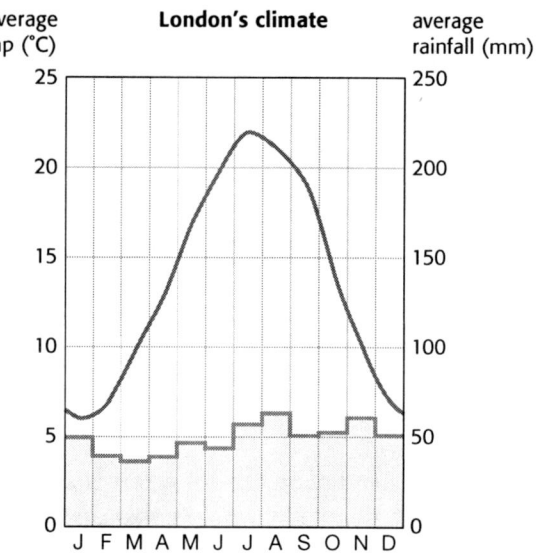

average temp (°C) **London's climate** average rainfall (mm)

b The main wind direction in Britain is from the south west. How does this explain the higher rainfall in London?

[2 marks]

_____

_____

c What are the main differences in temperature between the two places?　*[2 marks]*

_____

_____

d Give reasons to explain these differences.　*[6 marks]*

_____

_____

_____

_____

_____

_____

_____

_____

_____

_____

Total marks: 50　Total score:　/50

1 Weather is the state of the atmosphere around us. (1 mark)

2 1 mark for each correct word placement.
People who study the weather are called <u>meteorologists</u>. They measure temperature using a <u>thermometer</u>, and the answer is in degrees centigrade. Air pressure is measured using a barometer, and the answer is in <u>millibars</u>. <u>Precipitation</u> is measured in millimetres using a rain gauge.

3 1 mark for each correct line

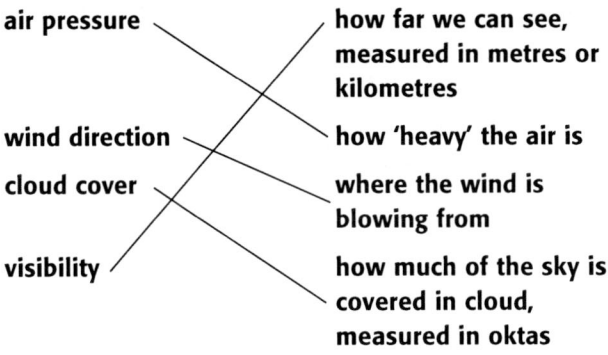

air pressure — how far we can see, measured in metres or kilometres

wind direction — how 'heavy' the air is

cloud cover — where the wind is blowing from

visibility — how much of the sky is covered in cloud, measured in oktas

4 a Cloudless, no rain or wind, could be hot in summer, very cold in winter ($\frac{1}{2}$ mark for any correct point).

b Cool air is sinking ($\frac{1}{2}$ mark), so it gets warmer ($\frac{1}{2}$ mark), so water evaporates ($\frac{1}{2}$ mark), so no cloud or rain ($\frac{1}{2}$ mark).
May also explain that there is no wind because there is no gap formed by rising air ($\frac{1}{2}$ mark), so no air has to rush in to fill the gap ($\frac{1}{2}$ mark).

Maximum of 2 marks for 4 b).

5 a 1 mark for diagram.
b 4 marks for labels - must be processes (e.g. air is rising), not features (e.g. hills).
c 1 mark for a sensible title.

6 a dry (1 mark), cold in winter OR warm in summer (1 mark).
b wet (1 mark), warm (1 mark).

7 2 marks for each correct labelling of axes. 1 mark for accurate crosses, 1 mark for joining crosses with a smooth line (no ruler) and 1 mark for using red. 3 marks for drawing bars correctly (2 if almost all correct, 1 if some correct), 1 mark for using a ruler to draw bars, 1 mark for colouring blue. 1 mark for adding a sensible title.

8 a 1 mark for each correct number in the table (London's 'highest temperature' and Athens' 'most rain' already done).

	Highest temp.	Lowest temp.	Most rain	Least rain
London	22 °C	6 °C	60 mm	40 mm
Athens	30 °C	9 °C	6 mm	1 mm

b Rain comes over ocean (Atlantic - pupils might not mention name) (1 mark), so carries lots of moisture (1 mark).

c Athens is hotter (1 mark), 1 mark for either:
- hottest temperature is 8 degrees more in Athens
    or:
- London's coldest temperature is 3 degrees less than in Athens.

d 1 mark for each simple idea (e.g. latitude) up to 3 marks, with a second mark in each case for expanding – up to a maximum of 6 marks.

Weather and climate

Name   **Class**   **Date**

Now I've reached the end of the Weather and climate chapter:

	Yes	Think so	No
◆ I know some of the ways of measuring weather, and the units that are used.			
◆ I know what the three different kinds of rainfall are, and how each one forms.			
◆ I can describe the type of weather linked with:			
low pressure			
high pressure in summer			
high pressure in winter			
◆ I can explain why the weather in the UK can change so quickly.			
◆ I can identify the following on a weather map:			
warm front			
cold front			
depression			
◆ I know what satellite images can tell us about the weather.			
◆ I know what the difference is between weather and climate.			
◆ I know what a climate graph is, and how to draw one.			
◆ I know some of the factors that influence climate, including the main one.			
◆ I can describe the general pattern of Europe's climate zones.			
◆ I know some of the ways in which climate affects our lives.			

◆ I know what these weather terms mean:

temperature ❑   *precipitation* ❑   *air pressure* ❑   *wind speed* ❑   *wind direction* ❑

cloud cover ❑   *visibility* ❑   *warm front* ❑   *cold front* ❑   *depression* ❑

The part of this topic that I enjoyed most or found most interesting was:

Ecosystems

Photocopiable worksheets

Learning activities

Assessment materials

[W] indicates material provided as editable Word files, as well as in PDF format, on the CD-ROM.

On the CD-ROM: pupil profile sheet; course theme, and lesson planning documents.

Name   Class

In the pampas (grasslands) of South America the climate is just right for grass. Never hot enough to dry all the grass up, or cold enough to stop it growing, and there's rain all year round.

This diagram shows part of a food web in the pampas, which depends on grass for its survival.

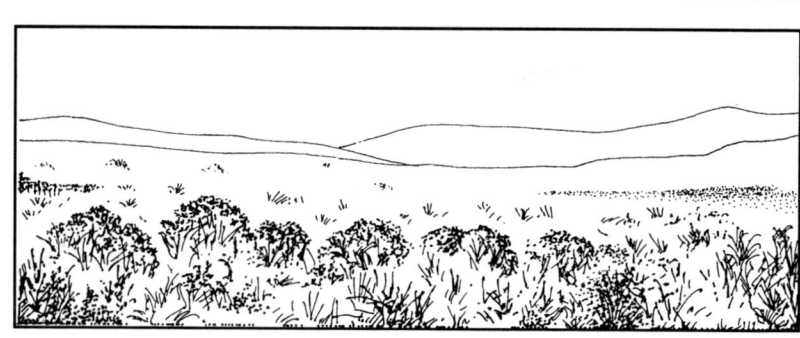

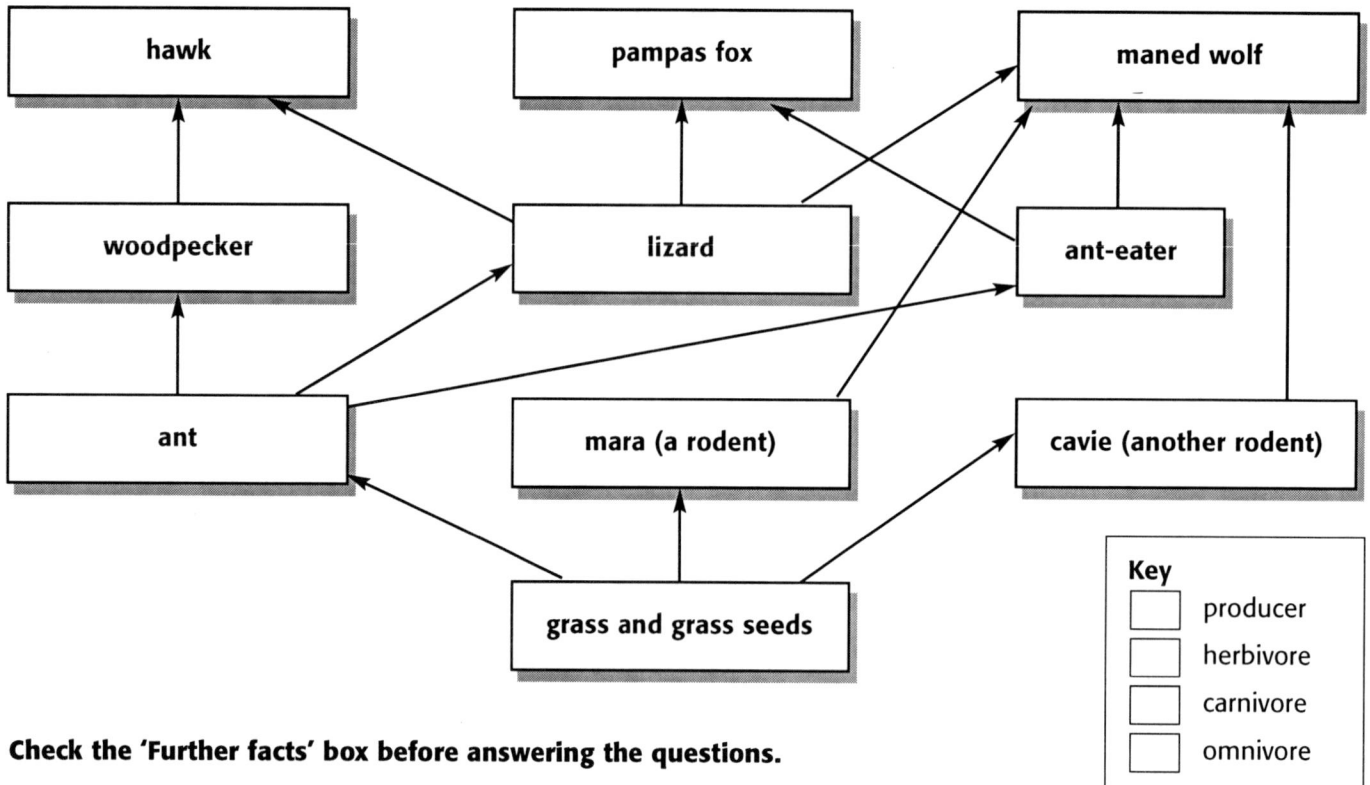

Key

☐ producer
☐ herbivore
☐ carnivore
☐ omnivore

Check the 'Further facts' box before answering the questions.

1 Plants make their own food using sunlight. They are called **producers**. Colour in green the box showing the producer.

2 Using the 'Further facts', add two more arrows from the producer box.

3 Animals that eat only plants are called **herbivores**. Colour the boxes of the herbivores in yellow.

4 Animals that eat both plants and animals are called **omnivores**. Colour the omnivore boxes in blue.

5 Animals that eat *only* other animals are called **carnivores**. Colour these boxes in red.

6 Colour in the key.

7 Copy out and complete this **food chain**. (Use your food web to help you.)

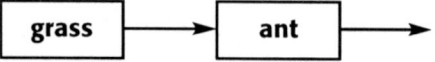

8 On the back of this sheet write out another food chain that exists in the pampas.

Further facts

• Woodpeckers eat grass seeds as well as insects.

• Maned wolves like fruit as well as flesh!

• The pampas fox eats grass seeds and berries too.

• Ants also eat flies and other insects.

• Maras and cavies are strictly vegetarian!

• Hawks, ant-eaters and lizards don't eat plants.

Name   Class

**When humans make use of ecosystems
the results can be good – or bad.**

1 Look at results A to I below. Use them
to complete the table, by writing in the
letters. (One has been done for you.)

You can use a letter more than once,
and write more than one in a space.

Activity	Positive (good) result	Negative (bad) result
Farming		
Mining coal		
Taking water from a river	C	
Clearing land for building		
Fishing		

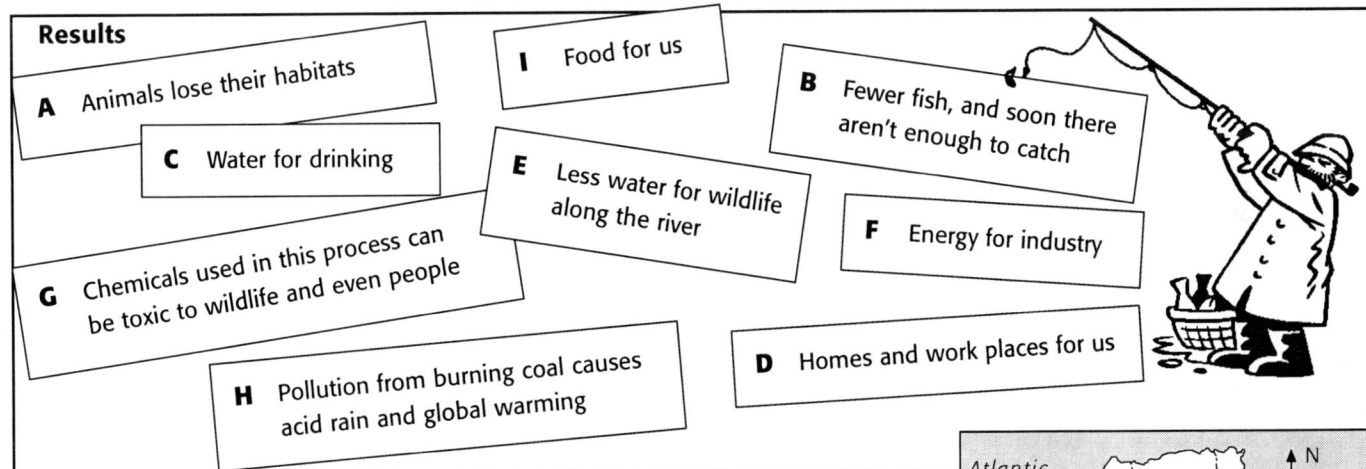

Results

A Animals lose their habitats

I Food for us

B Fewer fish, and soon there aren't enough to catch

C Water for drinking

E Less water for wildlife along the river

F Energy for industry

G Chemicals used in this process can be toxic to wildlife and even people

H Pollution from burning coal causes acid rain and global warming

D Homes and work places for us

**We humans can also suffer when we damage ecosystems. These boxes
explain what's happening in the Sahel – an area of unreliable rainfall just
south of the Sahara Desert. But they are not in the right order!**

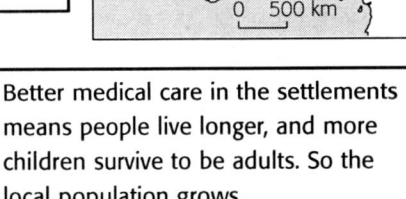

○ That means there are more and more farmers keeping animals on less and less land. So every blade of grass gets eaten.

○ Less topsoil means less grass grows. So the animals have less to eat. So life for the farmers gets harder and harder.

○ In the past, people of the Sahel followed the rains, so that their animals had fresh grass to eat. They lived in tents. This is called nomadic farming.

○ Better medical care in the settlements means people live longer, and more children survive to be adults. So the local population grows.

○ But today, many prefer to live in permanent homes. So more and more land is being taken over for settlements.

○ That leaves the ground bare. So some of the soil gets blown away by the wind.

2 Join the boxes in the correct order and number them 1 to 7.

3 Think of ways to make farming in the Sahel more sustainable. Write your ideas on the back of your sheet.

○ When it does rain, the dusty topsoil gets washed away because there's no grass or trees to protect it. This problem is worst on slopes.

Name   **Class**

Ecosystems are made up of biotic (living) and abiotic (non-living) parts.
The living parts are plants, animals, and bacteria.
The non-living parts are the climate, rocks, soil and water.

1 This text is about the ecosystem of the Andes. Underline the sentences:
   a about the abiotic part *only*, in one colour
   b about the interaction between the two parts, in another colour
   c about the biotic part *only*, in a third colour

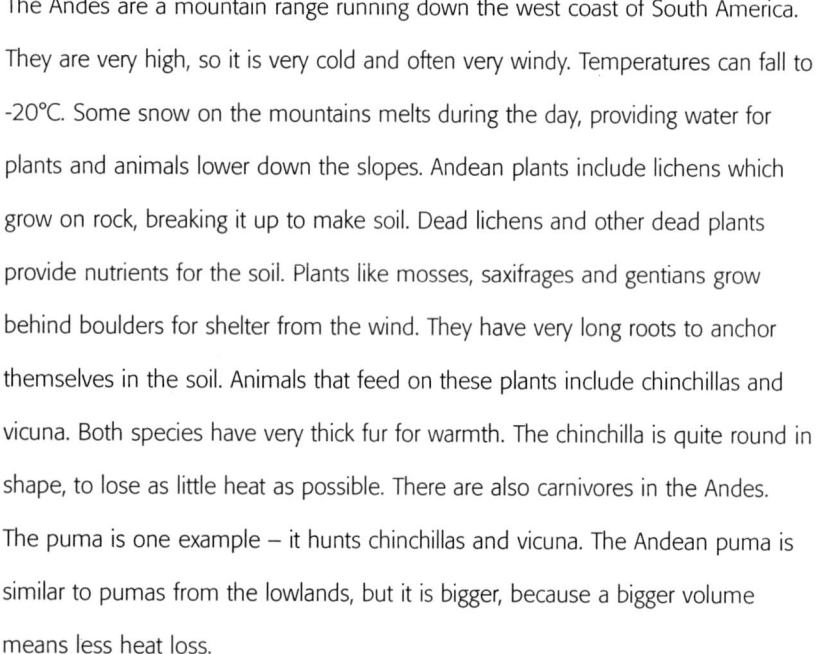

The Andes are a mountain range running down the west coast of South America.
They are very high, so it is very cold and often very windy. Temperatures can fall to
-20°C. Some snow on the mountains melts during the day, providing water for
plants and animals lower down the slopes. Andean plants include lichens which
grow on rock, breaking it up to make soil. Dead lichens and other dead plants
provide nutrients for the soil. Plants like mosses, saxifrages and gentians grow
behind boulders for shelter from the wind. They have very long roots to anchor
themselves in the soil. Animals that feed on these plants include chinchillas and
vicuna. Both species have very thick fur for warmth. The chinchilla is quite round in
shape, to lose as little heat as possible. There are also carnivores in the Andes.
The puma is one example – it hunts chinchillas and vicuna. The Andean puma is
similar to pumas from the lowlands, but it is bigger, because a bigger volume
means less heat loss.

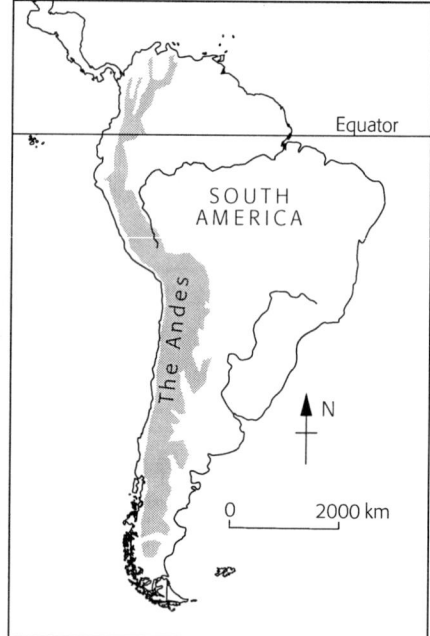

Now do 2–5 below in your exercise book.

2 Write the title 'The Ecosystem of the Andes' at the top of a page, cut out the text
box and map, and stick them on the page. Add a key for your underlining.

3 Now answer these questions.
   a In the Andean ecosystem, how do the soil and plants depend on each other?
   b Why do plants need rocks and boulders?
   c Write down one Andean food chain.

4 To survive in a harsh environment, plants and animals need to change or **adapt**.
Make a table like this one and complete it using information from the text box.

Plant adaptation	Why it is needed	Animal adaptation	Why it is needed

5 Ecosystems have many **inter-relationships**. A change in one part causes changes
in other parts. What else do you think would happen if ...
   a all the chinchillas were hunted for their fur?
   b global warming made the area a few degrees warmer and less windy?
   c more farmers came to live in the mountains?

Name   Class

Plants grow in places where the climate suits them.
Many develop special features to help them cope with the conditions they live in.
They *adapt* to their environment.

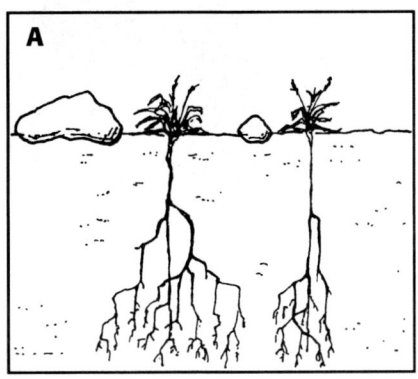
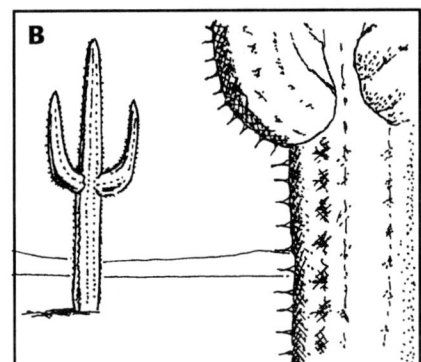

1   Cut out the three pictures of plants.

2   Cut out these descriptions, and match them to the correct picture.

Leaves have become thin spikes so that they won't lose much water. Photosynthesis takes place in the swollen green stem, which can store water.   **D**

It needs a lot of sun. It doesn't grow well in shade. But it can survive a dry season because its roots grow deep to fnd water.   **E**

Many plants have tall trunks to reach sunlight. Their leaves have waxy coats, and points called drip tips, to let rain flow off easily.   **F**

3   Cut out the three climate graphs and match them to the pictures and descriptions.
(Remember, the line shows the temperature, and the bars show the rainfall.)

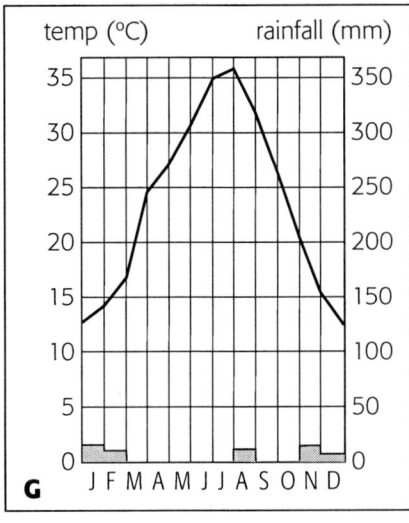
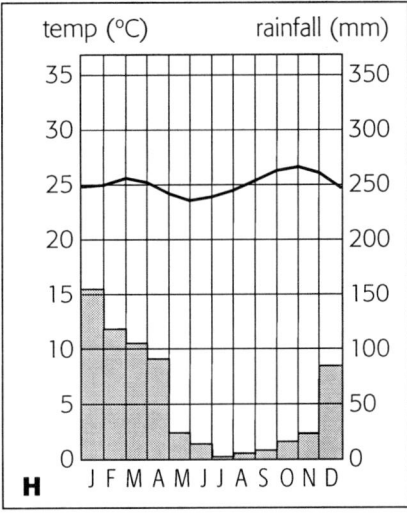
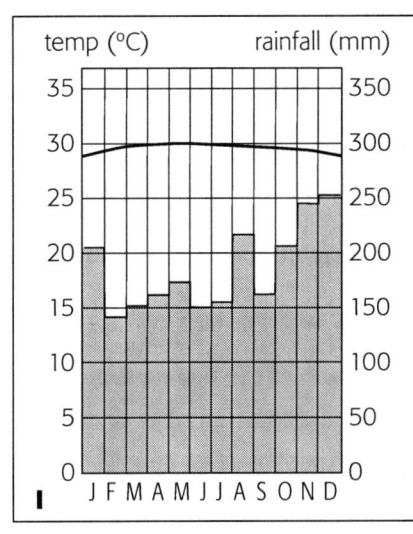

Now do these in your exercise book.

4   Stick in the plant pictures, descriptions and graphs in their groups.

5 **a**   Which plants grow in the wettest area? What helps them cope with the rain?

   b   Which area is the driest? What adaptations help plants to survive here?

6   Now see if you can name the three biomes. Write the names below the groups.

Name   Class

When an animal species survives in only a few places, and there aren't many individuals left, it is in danger of extinction. The giant panda is an example.

This map will show the number of **endangered species** in some parts of Asia.

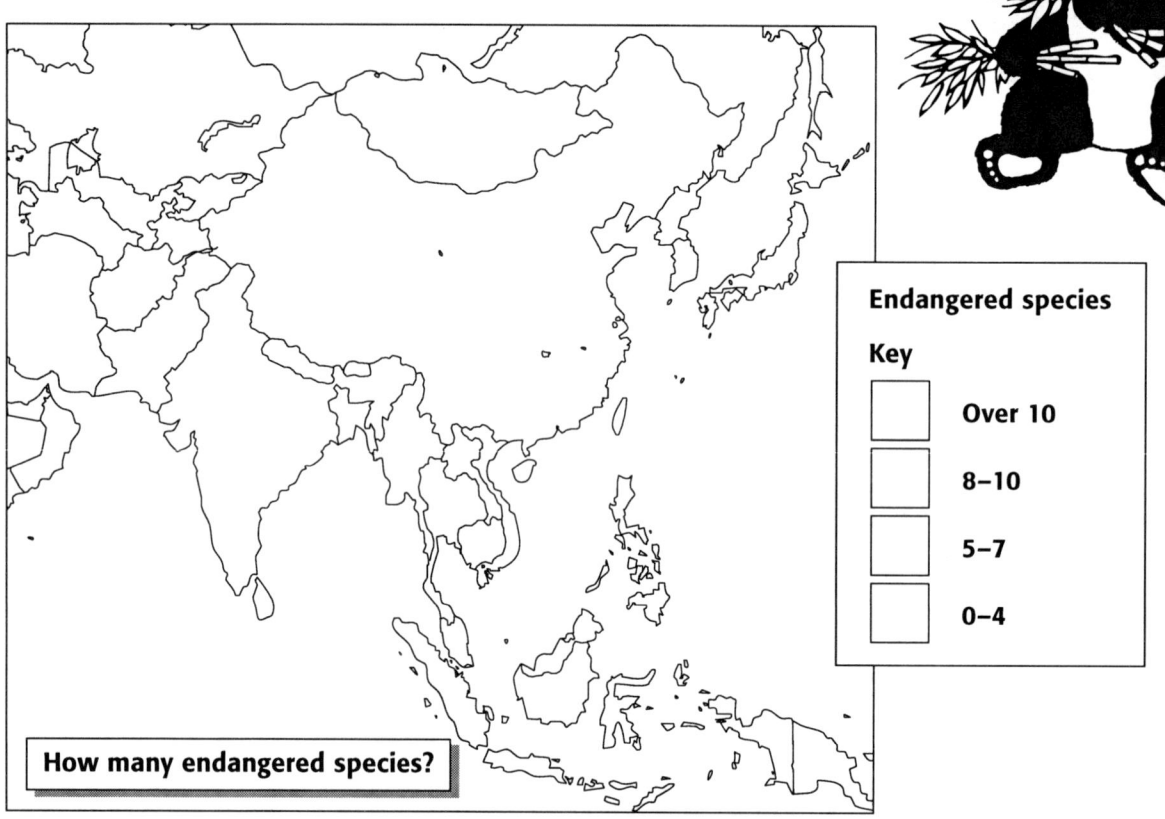

Endangered species

Key

☐   Over 10

☐   8–10

☐   5–7

☐   0–4

How many endangered species?

1 Look at the map key. To which group does China belong? Shade that box in the key. Then shade in China to match, on the map. (Use an atlas to help you.)

2 Do the same for the other four countries in the table. Use a different colour or shading for each box in the key.

Now use your exercise book for 3–5 below.

3 Cut out the map and stick it in your exercise book.

4 Which of the five countries has:

   a the least number of species at risk?

   b most species at risk?

5 Study the Philippines factfile.

   a Why are so many animals at risk, in the Philippines? Write a rough list of possible reasons. (Your teacher may ask you to work in pairs.)

   b Share your ideas with the whole class, and discuss them.

   c Now write out your final answer for **a**. You could give the reasons as bullet points, or as continuous prose. Give your answer a title.

Country	Number of endangered species	For example
China	9	giant panda
Japan	6	brown bear
Philippines	16	dugong
Taiwan	4	tiger
Bangladesh	2	Asian elephant

Philippines factfile
- Cities growing by 4.9% per year
- Population in 1995: 69 million
- Population in 2004: 86 million
- Deforestation: 3.2 thousand km² per year. Most of the rainforest has gone already.
- 20% of the country's income is spent paying back loans from other countries.

Name **Class**

1 Find all the words in the list in the word search. You can circle or colour them.

p	t	g	v	f	o	r	e	s	t	x	y	p	s	h
r	s	s	d	j	a	n	n	a	v	a	s	u	o	e
o	t	s	e	z	s	s	v	t	l	p	s	h	t	r
d	n	c	o	r	e	l	i	g	m	t	j	u	e	b
u	a	f	z	i	o	u	r	t	a	y	u	q	s	i
c	l	w	c	y	l	f	o	i	w	n	s	e	u	v
e	p	e	r	o	v	i	n	r	a	c	u	m	o	o
r	p	d	g	n	t	a	m	i	z	c	o	b	r	r
s	y	z	l	r	b	v	e	x	a	w	u	e	e	e
s	h	w	e	l	h	s	n	t	l	r	d	w	f	r
e	s	s	e	r	e	h	t	a	e	w	i	d	i	x
r	e	s	o	p	m	o	c	e	d	s	c	o	n	e
d	e	c	o	s	y	s	t	e	m	s	e	o	o	z
w	o	o	d	l	a	n	d	k	r	v	d	f	c	e
o	g	z	e	x	t	i	n	c	t	d	l	i	w	o

carnivore
coniferous
deciduous
decomposer
desert
ecosystem
environment
extinct
foodweb
forest
herbivore
plants
producer
rainforest
savanna
soil
species
sustainable
weather
woodland

2 Now use the words to complete the sentences below. You may use each word only once.

HINT: Cross out each word from the list as you use it.

A A _____ is a diagram that shows how animals and plants are linked by eating.

B When a species dies out it is _____ .

C A _____ is an animal that eats other animals.

D Trees which lose their leaves in winter are _____ .

E In England there is a famous National Park called the New _____ , where wild ponies are part of the ecosystem.

F The scientific name for a type of plant or animal is _____ .

G Most plants grow in _____ .

H _____ includes sunshine, rain and wind.

I In a _____ there are lots of trees growing.

J A plant makes its own food, so it is called a _____ .

K An _____ can be any size. It could be as small as a pond or as huge as a rainforest.

L Fir trees are _____ .

M A really dry place is called a _____ .

N Something which breaks down dead material is called a _____ .

O In the Amazon basin there is _____ .

P Everything around us is our _____ .

Q Things which grow in the soil and make their own food are called _____ .

R A _____ is an animal that eats only plants.

S If people use an ecosystem without damaging it then what they are doing is _____ .

3A Food webs **

1 grass   **2** arrows to woodpecker and pampas fox

3 only mara and cavie

4 ant, woodpecker, pampas fox, maned wolf

5 lizard, ant-eater, hawk

7 There are several choices: grass, ant, woodpecker, hawk;
grass, ant, lizard, hawk / pampas fox / maned wolf;
grass, ant, ant-eater, pampas fox / maned wolf.

8 Any of those from 7 that the pupil has not used already;
or grass, mara, maned wolf; or grass, cavie, maned wolf.

3B People in ecosystems **

1 The positive results are in bold, the negative in italics:
Farming: **I**; *A, G.* Mining coal: **F**; *A, H.* Taking water from a
river: **C**; *E, A.* Clearing land for building: **D**; *A.* Fishing: **I**; *B.*

2 1 In the past ....   2 But today, many prefer ....
3 Better medical care .....   4 That means there are more and
more farmers ....   5 That leaves the ground bare ....
6 When it does rain .....   7 Less topsoil means ....

3 Ideas: terrace slopes in some way both to trap moisture when
rains do come, and reduce soil erosion; grow thorny hedges or
put up fences to prevent wind erosion; grow trees that can cope
with drought, as both windbreaks and a source of fuel; let grazing
areas lie fallow from time to time if at all possible; use efficient
fuel stoves to reduce demand on firewood and conserve trees;
see if there are breeds of grass that grow faster and cope better
with drought; switch partly from keeping animals to growing
crops, to reduce the impact of grazing; choose crops that can
withstand drought best; find a way to store water when rains do
come; dig deep wells for irrigation in dry weather; diversify in
other ways – for example through traditional crafts that could be
sold to tourists, or sustainable tourism in the desert, or even light
industry (using solar power?); seek foreign aid; work together to
get the best results; control family size?

3C The ecosystem of the Andes ***

1 The information about the abiotic parts is underlined below.
The information about interaction between the biotic and
abiotic parts is in italics. The rest is about the biotic part only.

<u>The Andes are a mountain range running down the west coast of
South America. They are very high, so it is very cold and often very
windy. Temperatures can fall to –20°C.</u> *Some snow on the
mountains melts during the day, providing water for plants and
animals lower down the slopes. Andean plants include lichens which
grow on rock, breaking it up to make soil. Dead lichens and other
dead plants provide nutrients for the soil.* Plants like mosses,
saxifrages and gentians grow behind boulders for shelter from the
wind. They have very long roots to anchor themselves in the soil.
Animals that feed on these plants include chinchillas and vicuna. Both
species have very thick fur for warmth. The chinchilla is quite round in
shape, to lose as little heat as possible. There are also carnivores in
the Andes. The puma is one example – it hunts chinchillas and
vicuna. The Andean puma is similar to pumas from the lowlands, but
it is bigger, because a bigger volume means less heat loss.

3 **a** Lichens help to break up rock to make soil (biological
weathering). Dead lichens and other dead plants add nutrients
to soil. Soil provides the nutrients for plant growth, and anchors
the plant's roots. **b** Rocks weather into soil, and they provide
shelter. **c** Several possible answers:
mosses / saxifrages / gentians ➜ chinchilla / vicuna ➜ Andean
puma.

4 **Plants**: long roots to anchor them, grow behind boulders for
shelter, lichens have adapted to survive on rock. **Animals**:
adapted to feed on mosses, saxifrages and gentians (or each
other), thick fur for warmth, rounded shape to minimise heat
loss, larger volume to minimise heat loss.

5 **a** Pumas will grow short of food so risk extinction – or eat all
the vicuna so both become extinct; the plant population will
grow as fewer are eaten; the soil will gain more nutrients
from decayed plants, so more sophisticated plants may
develop.

   b More water everywhere since more snow melts; bogs could
develop; vegetation will grow faster and thicker; more soil
produced as both chemical and biological weathering
speed up (chemical weathering increases with
temperature); in general plants and animals will be able to
colonise further up the slope than before; more complex
vegetation will develop in the warmth (perhaps moving in
from further down the slope); the animal population will
grow, since there is more food; new species could move in,
possibly including more large carnivores to feed on the
smaller animals; animals will adapt their fur coats and body
shape to suit the warmer climate (and / or move further up
the slope).

   c Clearing land for farming would drive the wildlife from it, so
all the species would reduce in number.

3D How do plants adapt to their environments? *

2 & 3 The groups are: A, E, H; B, D, G; C, F, I.

5 **a** tall trees, drip tips   **b** G; spikes, swollen stem

6 A, E, H: savanna. B, D, G: hot desert C, F, I: rainforest.

3E Species at risk of extinction **

4 **a** Bangladesh **b** Philippines.

5 High rate of population growth means land deforested for
homes, timber, fuel, farming etc. (Logging is in fact the main
culprit.) Deforestation means habitats destroyed.
The high level of debt probably means: many poor people are
dependent on wood for fuel; slash and burn agriculture since
farmers can't afford machinery or chemical fertilisers; no money
for conservation or education about it; and a need to earn
foreign currency from logging.

3F Ecosystems word search *

A foodweb, **B** extinct, **C** carnivore, **D** deciduous, **E** forest,
F species, **G** soil, **H** weather, **I** woodland, **J** producer,
K ecosystem, **L** coniferous, **M** desert, **N** decomposer,
O rainforest, **P** environment **Q** plants, **R** herbivore,
S sustainable

What eats what? The ecosystem puzzle   */**/***

Aims

■ Pupils understand the concept of the food web
■ Pupils understand the structure of the polar ecosystem
■ Pupils can interpret a web matrix
■ Pupils can use logical processes to work out which animals are represented on the food web

Introduction

This activity addresses Unit 11 of the QCA Scheme of Work (*Investigation of ecosystems*). It is a logic puzzle that can be done after unit 3.1 on pages 44-45 of **geog.2**.

The activity can be managed at three levels of difficulty:
■ with label boxes
■ with a logic matrix
■ with a set of named boxes showing the links.

Activity

Pupils have to complete a polar food web diagram by working out which animal eats what. The completed food web is provided for your information on page 104.

Level 1 (hardest)
Issue pupils with the partially-completed food web on page 105. Instruct them to work out, by themselves, the correct word for each empty box, using the options at the bottom of the sheet.

Level 2
Issue pupils with the partially-completed food web on page 105 and the logic matrix on page 106. Instruct them to use the matrix to work out what goes in each box.

Level 3
Give each pupil the partially-completed food web on page 107 and the cut out boxes on page 108. Instruct pupils to cut out the 10 boxes and put them in the right positions on the diagram.

Follow-up work
Tell pupils to write encyclopaedia entries for three of the animals from the polar food web. Some guidance for this is provided on page 109.

The encyclopaedia entries could be written using a word processing or desktop publishing package.

What eats what? The ecosystem puzzle   */**/***

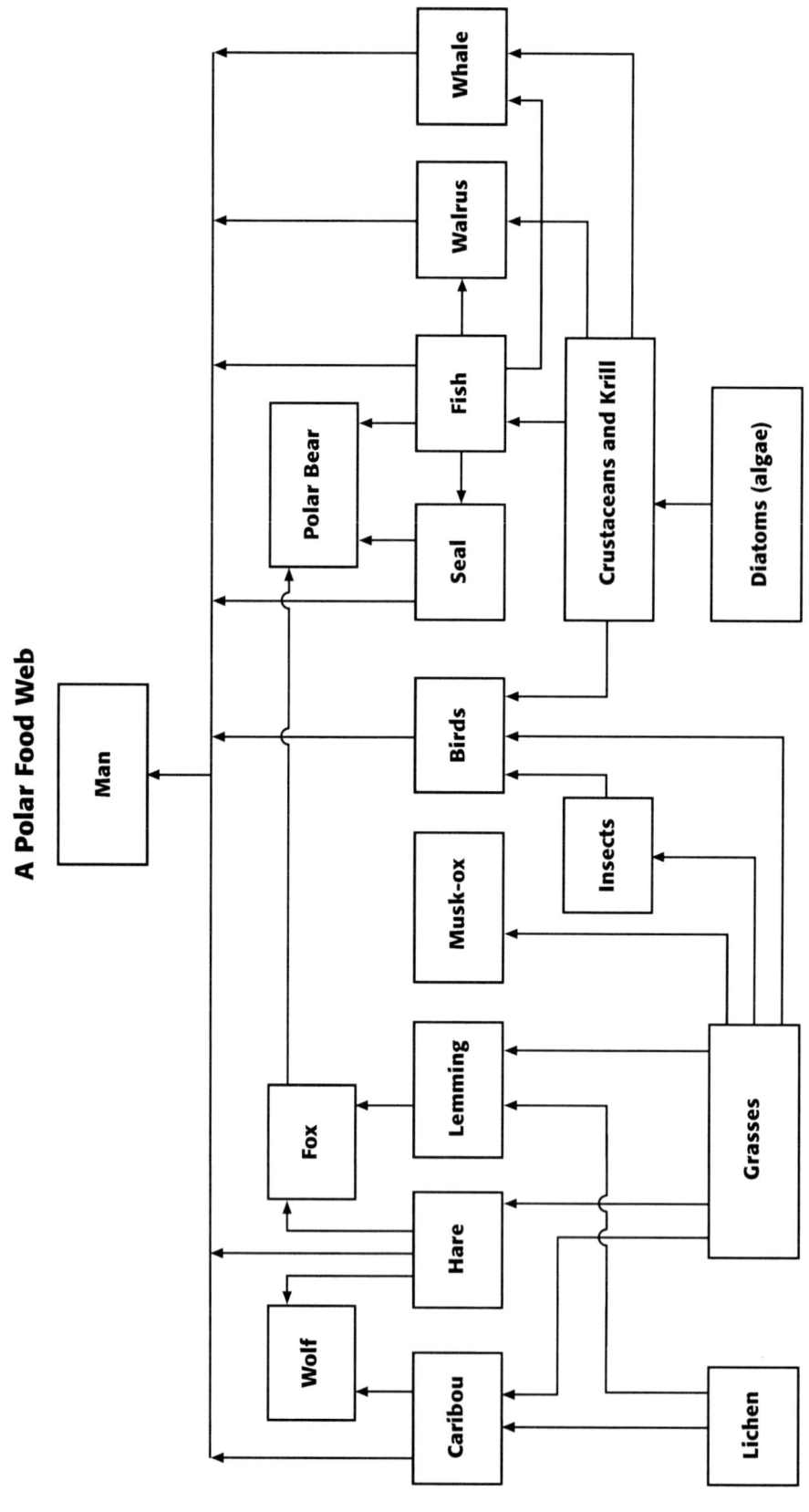

A Polar Food Web

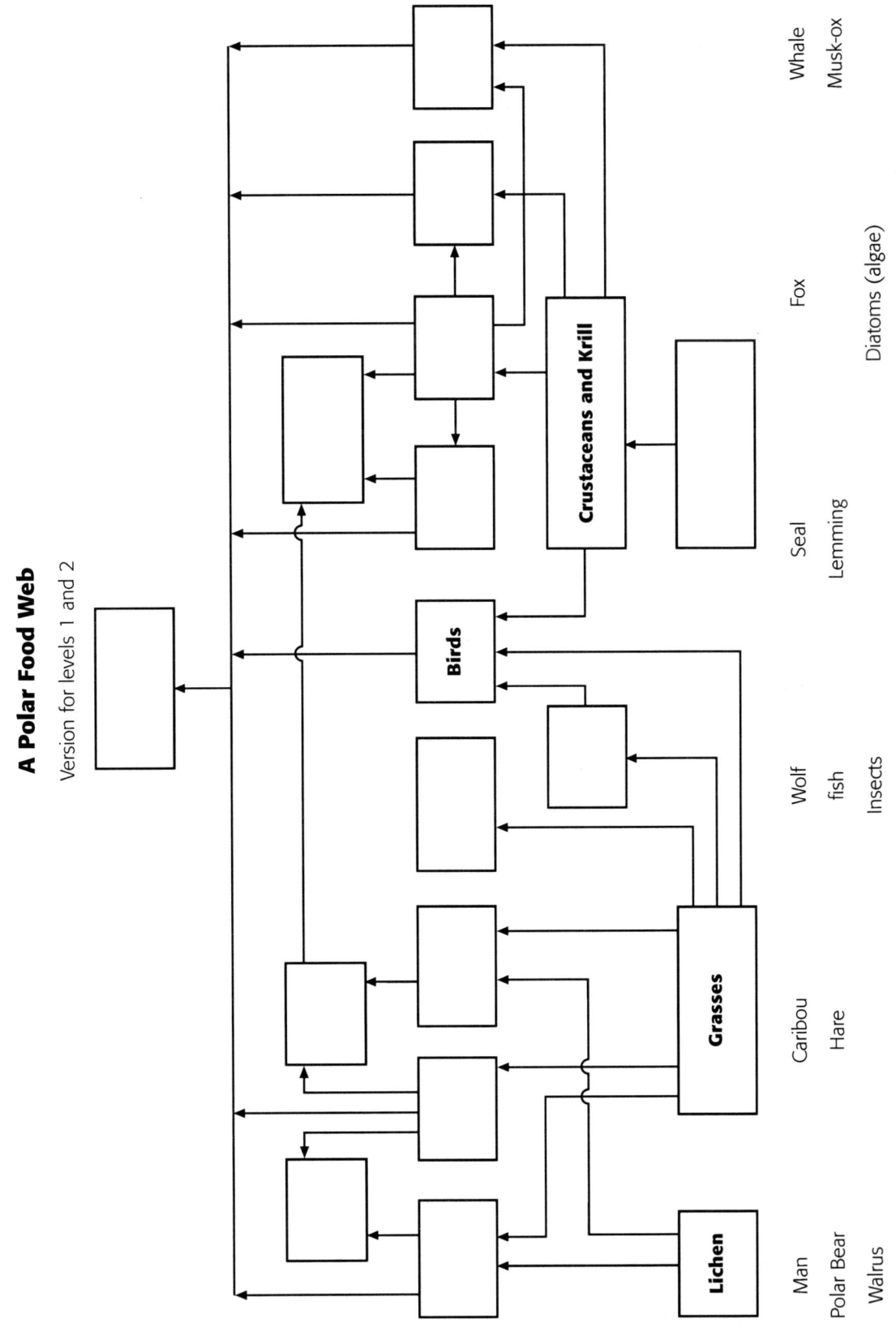

A Polar Food Web

Version for levels 1 and 2

Whale
Musk-ox

Diatoms (algae)

Fox

Crustaceans and Krill

Seal
Lemming

Birds

Wolf
fish
Insects

Grasses

Caribou
Hare

Lichen

Man
Polar Bear
Walrus

Name   **Class**

Polar food web – logic matrix

A tick in the table below means that the creature at the top of the column eats the thing in the row. So a row of ticks means that the thing in the row is eaten by a lot of the creatures in the columns. A column of ticks means that the creature at the top of the column eats most of the others.

Use this table to help you fill in the empty boxes on the polar food web. For example, the food web shows something eating lichen and grasses, which is itself eaten by two other things. The table below shows that the lemming eats lichen and grasses, but is only eaten by the fox. So it looks as though the answer is the caribou.

Eaters

Eaten	Man	Wolf	Fox	Polar Bear	Caribou	Hare	Lemming	Musk-ox	Birds	Seals	Fish	Walrus	Whales	Insects	Crustaceans Krill
Man															
Wolf															
Fox				✓											
Polar Bear															
Caribou	✓	✓													
Hare	✓	✓	✓												
Lemming			✓												
Musk-ox															
Birds	✓														
Seals	✓			✓											
Fish	✓			✓						✓		✓	✓		
Walrus	✓														
Whales	✓														
Insects									✓						
Crustaceans Krill									✓		✓	✓	✓		
Lichen					✓		✓								
Grasses					✓	✓	✓	✓	✓					✓	
Diatoms (algae)															✓

Name

Class

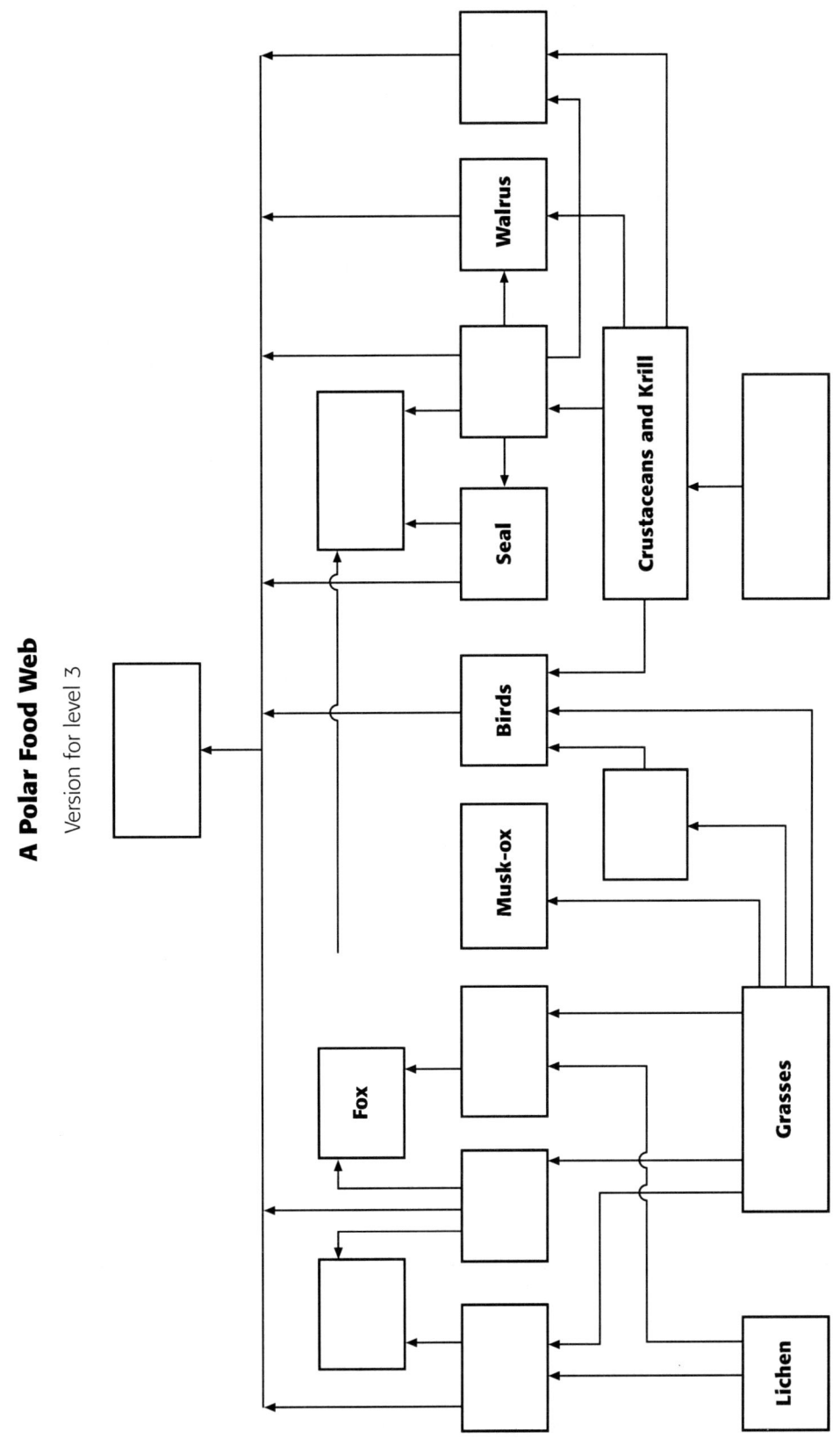

A Polar Food Web

Version for level 3

Walrus

Crustaceans and Krill

Seal

Birds

Musk-ox

Fox

Grasses

Lichen

Name   **Class**

Cut-out cards for level 3

Cut out the 10 creatures and stick them on the food web diagram in the right places.

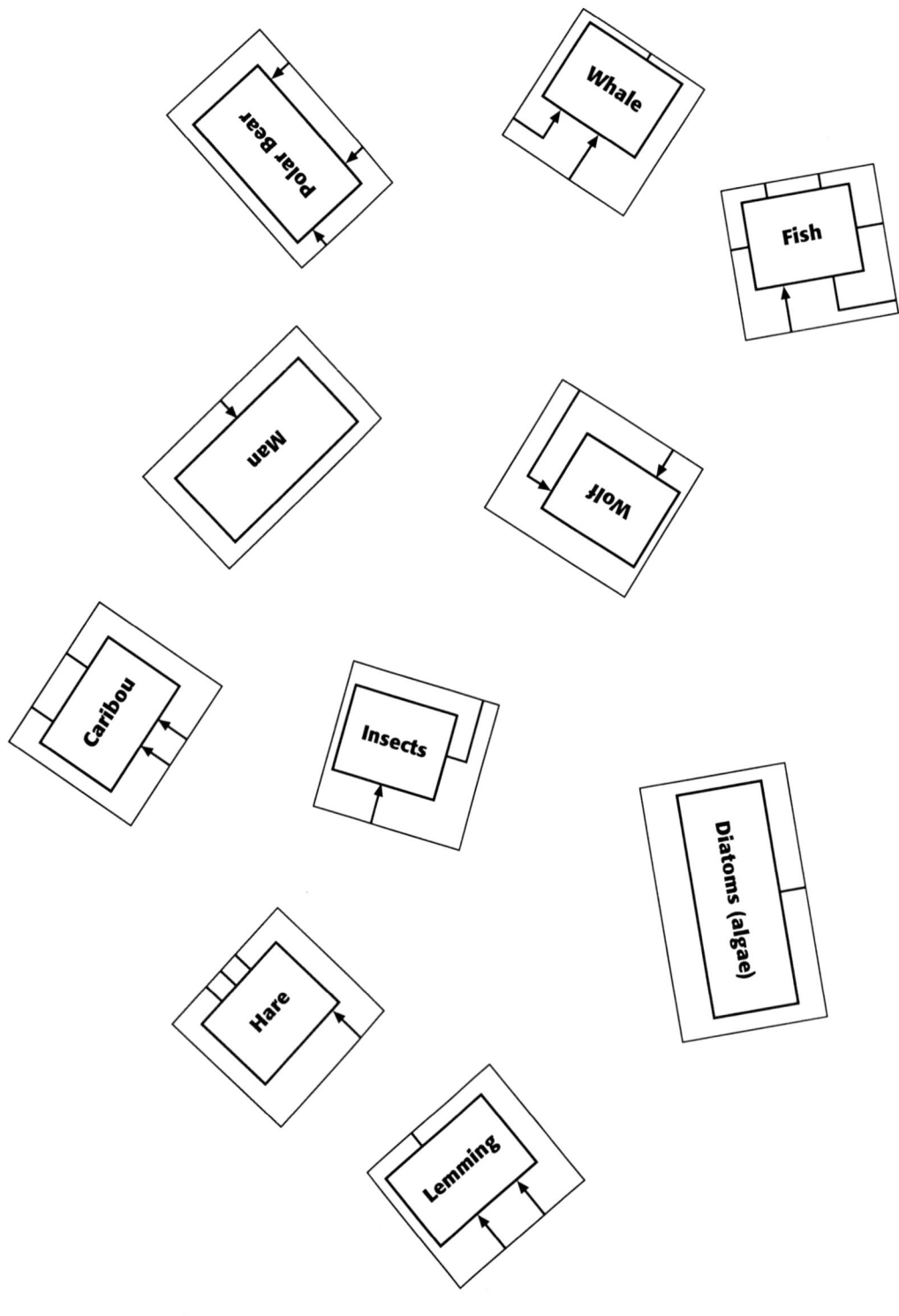

Name   Class

Follow-up work

Now you're going to find out more about some of the animals that live in polar environments.

Choose THREE animals from the polar food web. You're now going to write descriptions of these three animals for an encyclopaedia.

You already know what these animals like to eat. To find out more you will need to do some research. A really good place to look for information is the Internet. Try typing the name of the animal into a search engine such as www.google.com.

Good things to find out about are:
∎   where the animal lives
∎   how it has adapted to its surroundings
∎   what it looks like
∎   what it likes doing
You should also try to include a picture of the animal. You could try drawing one yourself or printing one from the Internet.

Here is a description of a polar bear:

Polar bear

The polar bear is a large mammal. It is a ferocious animal that lives in polar regions of the northern hemisphere.

Polar bears are well adapted to their arctic surroundings. They have thick winter coats and layers of fat beneath their skin to protect them from the cold.

The favourite meal of a polar bear is seal, but they also like to eat fish and foxes. They have a very good sense of smell, which helps them track down their next meal.

Polar bears are great swimmers. They use their large front paws as powerful oars. Under water they keep their eyes open but close their nostrils. A polar bear may remain underwater for over a minute.

Polar bears tend to live for about 25 years.

Tropical rainforest – 20 questions

Aims

▪ Pupils know the animals, plants, soils, and conditions that prevail in the rainforest

▪ Pupils exercise and develop thinking skills, notably a decision-tree strategy using yes or no answers

▪ Pupils develop social skills, such as friendly competition and the ability to win or lose graciously

Introduction

This activity addresses Units 11 and 14 of the QCA Scheme of Work (*Investigating Brazil; Can the earth cope? Ecosystems, population and resources*).

This activity introduces a valuable revision technique to use before an assessment. It can be adapted to almost any other subject. Instead of 'animal, vegetable, mineral, or abstract', try 'people, place, or thing'.

Activity (page 111)

1 Read through pages 50-51 of **geog.2** with the class.

2 Divide the class into pairs.

3 Instruct one pair to choose an object or idea from pages 50-51 of **geog.2**. They should identify which of the following categories it belongs to:
animal (e.g. tree frogs, sloths, apes)
vegetable (e.g. lianas, ferns, green algae)
mineral (e.g. soil, water, nutrients from soil)
abstract (e.g. tall, straight, hot).
(The majority of pupils will select an animal or vegetable.)

4 Another pair should then attempt to identify the object or idea using as few questions as possible. They can ask a maximum of 20 questions.

5 Tell pupils to write down the questions briefly. This not only records how many questions have been asked, but will prevent the same question being asked twice.

This activity can also be done without reference to the **geog.2** students' book. Simply instruct pupils to think of something that is found in the tropical rainforest using their background knowledge.

Tropical rainforest – 20 questions

Name   **Class**

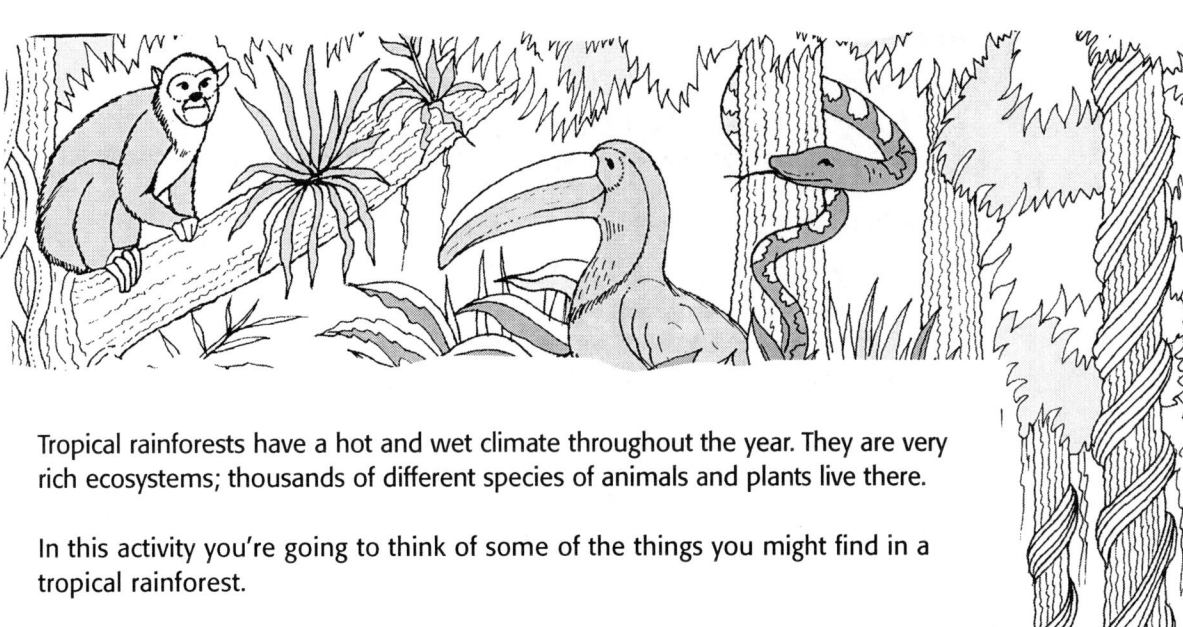

Tropical rainforests have a hot and wet climate throughout the year. They are very rich ecosystems; thousands of different species of animals and plants live there.

In this activity you're going to think of some of the things you might find in a tropical rainforest.

The class will be divided into pairs, with each pair competing against another pair.

Activity

This game is based on the idea that everything in the world can be described as either:
▌ **animal** – an animal, or made from animals
▌ **vegetable** – a plant, or made from plants
▌ **mineral** – something made from metal, stone, or soil.

Things can also be 'abstract' – which means a 'thought' or an 'idea'.
There are examples of all of these on pages 50 and 51 of **geog.2**.

Instructions

1 With your partner, choose something from pages 50-51 of the textbook.

2 Work out whether it is animal, vegetable, mineral, or abstract.

3 Say to the other pair "I am .... " (tell them whether you are animal, vegetable, mineral, or abstract).

4 The other pair then has just 20 questions to guess what you are.

5 The questions must expect the answer 'yes' or 'no' only,
   e.g.   don't ask, "How tall are you?"
          do ask, "Are you a tall animal?"

          don't ask, "Do you have teeth or a beak?"
          do ask, "Do you have teeth?"

6 It is wise to make a quick note of the questions as they are asked, so that the same question is not asked twice.

7 If you can't agree about something ask your teacher, their decision is final!

8 After 20 questions, or if the answer is guessed correctly, you should swap roles with the other pair.

Design your own animal

*

Aims

▮ Pupils know the characteristics of one ecosystem
▮ Pupils know what adaptations animals might have
▮ Pupils understand how these adaptations help animals to survive in an ecosystem

Introduction

This activity consolidates ideas about the characteristics of four different ecosystems and about the adaptations that animals make to their environment. It builds on work done in chapter 3 'Ecosystems' in **geog.2**, and addresses Unit 14 of the QCA Scheme of Work (*Can the earth cope? Ecosystems, population and resources*).

Lesson preparation

▮ Decide whether pupils will work in pairs or individually.
▮ Photocopy enough sets of feature cards (page 114). Cut them up and put them in envelopes.
▮ Then photocopy the ecosystem descriptions (page 115). Cut them up into individual descriptions. Stick one description on the front of each envelope.
▮ Photocopy enough of the pupil instruction sheets (page 113).
▮ You will need plain paper, backing paper, rulers, scissors and glue.

Activity

1 Each pair or individual should be given an envelope containing a set of feature cards. These cards describe a variety of adaptations that animals might have.

2 Pupils should read the ecosystem description on the outside of their envelope, and then look at the cards inside.

3 They have to decide which cards are relevant to their particular ecosystem, and put the irrelevant cards to one side.

4 Pupils should then use the relevant cards to design an animal for their ecosystem.

5 Pupils should be told to present their design as a display, with annotations to explain their choices of adaptations.

Lesson ideas

To start the lesson, you could hold a question-and-answer session on animals and their adaptations. Then give out the envelopes and the pupil instruction sheets. Pupils can then follow the instructions on their sheets, asking for display materials as they need them.

Design your own animal

Name   **Class**

In this activity you are going to use what you know about an ecosystem to design an animal that could live there.

Activity

1   Your teacher has given you an envelope. On the outside there is a description of an ecosystem. Read it and underline the important facts.

2   Now open your envelope and have a look at the cards inside. They describe ways in which animals can adapt to survive in different places.
    Decide which things would be useful for an animal living in your ecosystem. Put the other cards back in the envelope.

3   Now look at the cards that you've kept. Use them (and any ideas of your own) to design your animal. Work on scrap paper first.

4   When you are happy with your design, draw the animal on plain paper. Remember to colour it in the correct colours.

5   Now label each part of the animal and say why you chose to design it that way.

6   Think of a name for your animal and write it as a title. Add your name to your work.

7   Stick your design onto backing paper.

Design your own animal

Name   Class

Big feet Would stop you sinking into sand or snow	**Layer of fat** Would be very useful if it's cold	**Being tall** Would help you to see, or to reach food that's high up
Dark skin Would stop you getting sunburnt	**Camouflage colour** Would be useful for hiding from your enemies	**Excellent sight** Would help you see your prey, or your enemies!
Big ears Would help you hear your prey, or your enemies!	**Long tail** Would be useful for climbing trees	**Waterproof fur or feathers** Would stop you getting wet
Claws Would be useful for lots of things: climbing, killing prey, gripping food	**Fingers** Would be helpful for gripping your food and climbing trees	**Few skin pores** These let moisture out, so if you only have a few, you'll save water
Sharp teeth Would be useful for ripping meat	**Water storage** Would be useful if you don't live near water	**Thick fur** Would help to keep you warm
Nocturnal This means that you only come out at night - good if you don't like daytime	**Pale colouring** This reflects sunlight, so would stop you getting too hot	**Wings** Would help you escape your enemies, or get into the trees easily
Tough skin Would protect you from thorns	**Strong leg muscles** Would be good for travelling long distances	**Long arms** Would help you get about in tree tops
Being short Would be good if your food is low down near the ground	**Bare skin** Would help you sweat, so would stop you getting too hot	**Defences** Would help protect you from your enemies

Design your own animal

Name   Class

Hot desert ecosystem

★ Temperatures of over 30°C during the day in summer.

★ Cold at night.

★ Almost no rainfall, except in occasional storms.

★ Hardly any plants.

★ Some areas of deep sand, some areas of pebbles and bare rock.

Tropical rainforest

★ Temperatures of over 25°C during the day all year round.

★ Warm and humid even at night.

★ Heavy rainfall almost every day.

★ Lots of trees, but not much vegetation on the ground.

★ Trees produce flowers, fruits, and seeds at different times, so there is food all year round.

Savanna

★ Temperatures of around 25°C during the day all year round.

★ Quite a lot of rain in the winter.

★ Almost no rain in the summer, the dry season.

★ Lots of tall grass with some thorny trees.

★ Food and water are very difficult to find in the dry season.

Tundra (places like the Canadian Arctic)

★ Temperatures of below freezing in winter.

★ Ground is frozen hard in winter and soggy in summer.

★ Heavy snow in winter.

★ Plants only grow in summer and they are short because it is windy.

★ Very bright sunshine reflecting from the snow in winter.

Ecosystems

The assessment opportunities for Ecosystems are as follows:

■ The **level-marked assessment** 'Conflict over deforestation in the tropical rainforests' on pages 117-118.

   In this assessment, pupils need to:
   a undertake some research about the issues surrounding deforestation in the rainforest
   b show an understanding about the theme of sustainability
   c carefully plan and produce a piece of extended writing.

   A **feedback form** for the level-marked assessment is provided on page 119.

■ The **scored test** on pages 120-125.

■ Opportunities for interim assessments provided by **geog.2**:

   What eats what? The ecosystem puzzle (a logic puzzle, with writing follow up) on pages 103-109 of this file.

   Design your own animal (a fun activity; pupils can work individually or in pairs) on pages 112-115 of this file.

   Activities 6, 8, 13, 15, 18, 20, 21, 23, and 27 in the *Further suggestions for class and homework* section on pages 82-83 of the *geog.2 teacher's handbook*.

   Worksheet B: Expedition for Desert survival (a webfile) in geog.2, *Ecosystems on geog.world*.

■ The **self-assessment form** for the whole Ecosystems chapter on page 126.

Ecosystems

Name   **Class**   **Date**

Conflict over deforestation in the tropical rainforests

The level at which I am currently working is

so my target level for this assessment is

because

Assessment task

This assessment is about deforestation in the world's tropical rainforests. You will:

a do some background research into the issues surrounding deforestation in the rainforest;

b show that you understand what sustainability means;

c plan and write a piece of extended writing. The title for your work is:

Conflict over deforestation in the tropical rainforests

For millions of years the tropical rainforests lay undisturbed, then some humans realised that they could exploit them and the destruction began. Not all human activity in the rainforests has to be destructive, however; there are ways of using them sustainably. You need to think about the various ways the rainforests are used, and whether there are better ways of managing them.

1 Research information which will help you to write your essay. (Hint: reread class and homework notes on this topic, and try the Internet for extra information.

2 Start to plan your extended writing; in it you should try to:
  • define what you mean by sustainability;
  • identify any positive and sustainable practices being carried out in the rainforest;
  • describe any negative and unsustainable activities that exploit the rainforest;
  • discuss the impact of any negative and unsustainable activities on the rainforest and, at a global scale, on the planet;
  • discuss what different groups of people think about the exploitation of the rainforest;
  • show how the rainforest is affected by the break up of the interrelationships that exist between different parts of the forest;
  • suggest how the rainforest could be managed to allow for more sustainable human economic activity, using economic restrictions and encouraging ecotourism, for example;
  • say how different groups may react to any of the management options you suggest.

Before you start work, make sure you understand the task and what you have to do. And look at the **success criteria** on the next page, so that you know how to achieve your target level – or better!

---

geog.2: 3 Ecosystems

Level 3
- You show a basic understanding of how deforestation can affect the rainforest environment and have mentioned a range of products that are taken from the forest and used to generate wealth.
- Your use of some geographical words is accurate.

Level 4
- You show that you understand how people can have both a positive and negative impact on the rainforest ecosystem, using some quite detailed examples about what products from the rainforest are exploited.
- You make good use of some geographical terms to show your understanding.

Level 5
- You structure your extended writing well and demonstrate quite a good understanding of what is meant by sustainable practice.
- You use a range of quite detailed examples to describe the positive and negative impacts that human economic activity is having on the ecosystem.
- You describe, in some simple statements, what different groups of people might think about using the rainforest and, also, about how it could be managed in the future.

Level 6
- You demonstrate a more detailed understanding of the conflicting demands that are placed upon the rainforest ecosystem and have been able to explain why conflict exists.
- You structure your work very carefully to show the range of ways in which the forest is exploited, and the ways in which it could be more sustainably managed.
- You appreciate that different management approaches can lead to different solutions.

Level 7
- You describe and explain the interactions between people and the rainforest and you demonstrate how this can change the characteristics of places in positive and negative ways. You explain the conflicts over deforestation at local, regional and global scales.
- You demonstrate a detailed understanding of what is meant by sustainable development and you know how it affects the management of environments.
- You appreciate the differing values and attitudes placed on the environment.
- Your extended writing is well structured, making good use of examples and specific terminology, with evidence of significant additional research.
- You demonstrate excellent presentation skills.

Level 8
- In addition to the descriptors for level 7, you recognise more thoroughly the causes and consequences of deforestation in the rainforest.
- You appreciate more fully the local, regional and global context which makes this issue of vital importance.
- You give evidence of having carried out excellent additional research.
- You use a wide range of examples to illustrate how the rainforest could be managed more sustainably and make reference to the issues in other global forests where this approach is also required.
- Your writing has a clear and logical sequence with excellent use of specific terminology and presentation skills.

Exceptional performance

In addition to Level 8...
- You evaluate critically your sources of evidence and present coherent and well-substantiated conclusions.
- You assess the relative merits of tackling environmental issues and justify your viewpoints about different approaches.
- You evaluate your work by suggesting improvements in approach and extensions to your study.

© OUP: this may be reproduced for class use solely within the purchaser's school or college

Ecosystems

Name   **Class**   **Date**

Conflict over deforestation in the tropical rainforests

Assessment task
A piece of extended writing about the issues surrounding deforestation in tropical rainforests.

Level awarded:

Teacher's comments:

Targets for improvement:

- Describe ideas in greater detail. ❑
- Suggest more reasons/processes to explain geographical ideas. ❑
- Try to use more geographical words and terms in your writing. ❑
- Try to support your writing with further, researched ideas. ❑
- Improve accuracy and/or presentation skills. ❑
- Use a greater range of presentation styles/techniques in your work. ❑
- Improve personal organisation and homework to raise your achievement level. ❑
- Ask for help about ideas you don't understand. ❑

Student's comments:

Ecosystems Test

Name	Class	Date

1 Ecosystems are made up of living and non-living things. This list includes things you'd find in an ecosystem. Tick all the ones that are **living**. *[3 marks]*

❑ Plants ❑ Soil ❑ Animals ❑ Climate ❑ Bacteria

2 An important part of an ecosystem is the **food chain**. This shows what eats what.

a Below is a food chain for a wood, but it is not complete. Choose from the words in the box to finish off the food chain. *[2 marks]*

oak leaf	ladybird	wolf	mouse

	→	caterpillar	→		→	fox

b i Which living thing in the food chain is a **producer**? _____ *[1 mark]*

ii Which living thing in the food chain is a **herbivore**? _____ *[1 mark]*

c **Decomposers**, like worms and bacteria, rot material in an ecosystem. Why is this really important for the ecosystem? *[2 marks]*

_____

_____

3 There are eight main types of ecosystem (biomes) in the world. Four of them are listed in the box.

hot desert	savanna	tropical rainforest	deciduous forest

Fill in the name of the biome for each of these climate descriptions. *[4 marks]*

Hot. Quite a lot of rain but has a dry season when there is almost no rain. Biome: _____	Very hot for most of the year, then cooler. Almost no rain all year. Biome: _____
Hot and very wet all year. Biome: _____	Never gets very hot. Rains quite a bit all through the year. Biome: _____

4 This question is about the tropical rainforest.

a Here is a diagram of the structure of the rainforest. You need to label each layer. *[4 marks]*

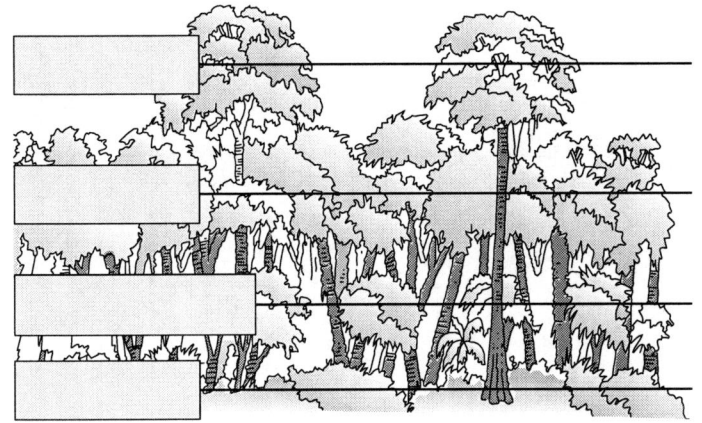

Options:
Under canopy
Emergents
canopy
Forest floor

b Why are so many rainforest trees so tall? Think about competition. *[1 mark]*

_____

_____

c What are drip tips for? Think about rainfall and how it affects leaves. *[1 mark]*

_____

_____

d Why do most animals live in the canopy layer? Think about food. *[2 marks]*

_____

_____

5 Many rainforests are being destroyed. This table shows the percentage of forest lost over each year in some countries.

Country	Brazil	Tanzania	Malawi	Ecuador	Singapore	Philippines	Haiti	Jamaica
% of forest lost each year	0.6	1.2	1.4	1.8	2.3	3.4	5.1	7.8

Follow each of the instructions in the boxes to complete the map overleaf.

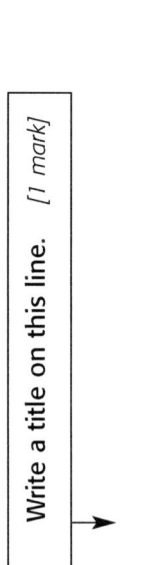

a Three of the bars have been done for you. They are all 0.5 cm wide. Draw a rectangle 0.5 cm wide and 1.8 cm tall near Ecuador. Join the bar to Ecuador with a line. *[1 mark]*

b Now draw a rectangle near Singapore. Remember to make it the same width as the rest. Look at the table to work out how tall it should be. *[1 mark]*

c Now complete bars for the other countries in the table. *[3 marks]*

d Write a title on this line. *[1 mark]*

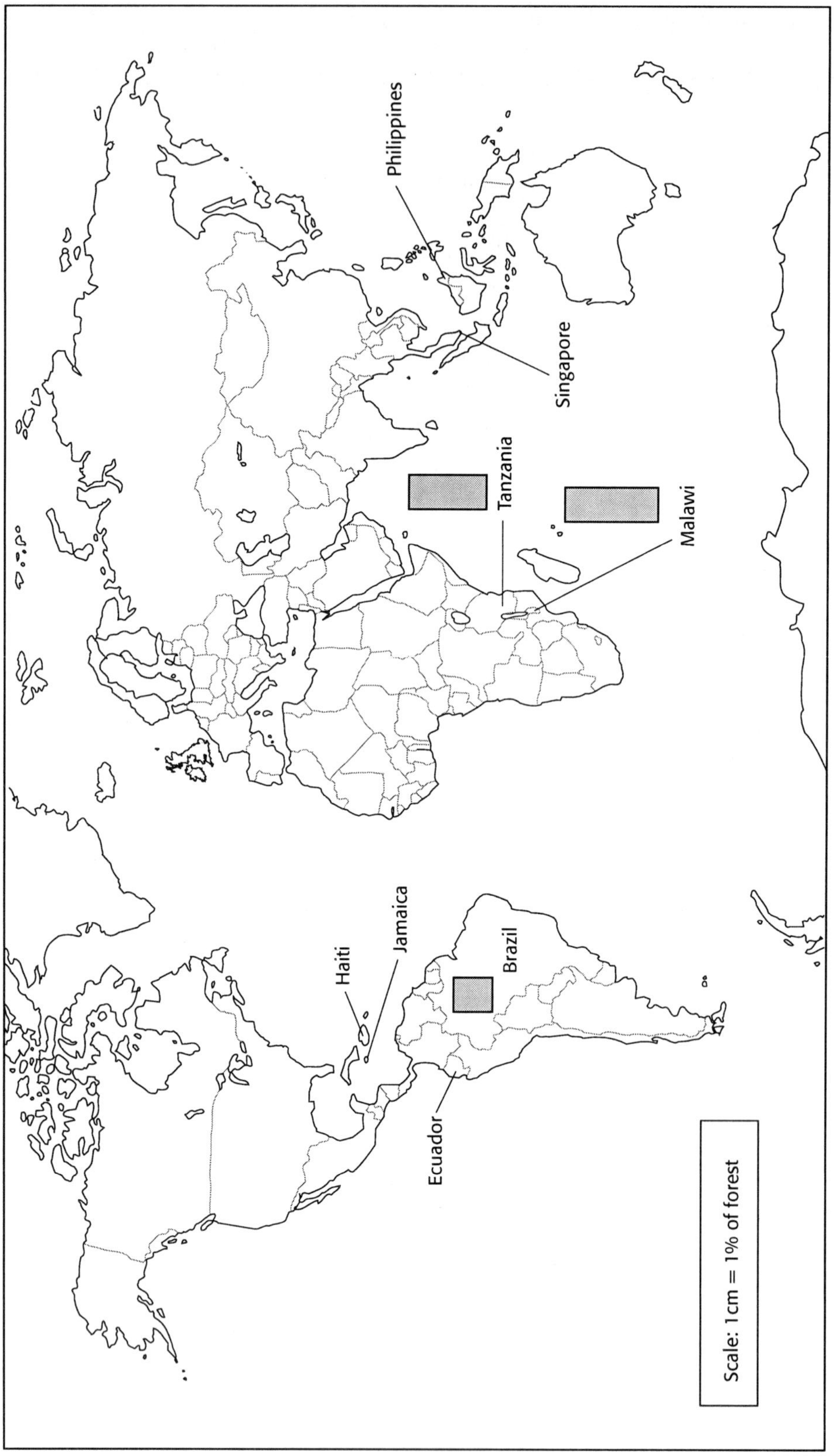

Philippines

Singapore

Tanzania

Malawi

Jamaica

Haiti

Brazil

Ecuador

Scale: 1cm = 1% of forest

e Which country has the least deforestation each year? *[1 mark]*

f Which country has the most deforestation each year? *[1 mark]*

g There are lots of reasons for deforestation. Suggest 3 reasons for the forests being destroyed in this country. *[3 marks]*

_____

_____

_____

h Deforestation can cause many bad things. Explain TWO bad things that will happen if deforestation happens in a place. *[4 marks]*

_____

_____

_____

_____

6 **Savanna** is grassland that has lots of rain in parts of the year and very little at other times. The plants and animals that live there have adapted to the conditions. Choose TWO of these plants or animals and explain why they are like they are.

Why do giraffes have long necks?

_____

_____ *[2 marks]*

Why do acacia trees have little leaves?

_____

_____ *[2 marks]*

Why do baobab trees have thick trunks?

_____

_____ *[2 marks]*

Why do bushes have thorns?

_____

_____ *[2 marks]*

7 Farmers in the savanna are **pastoralists**. This means that they graze cattle and follow the rains to find grass. They also grow some crops and cut trees for firewood.

In recent years the pastoralists haven't been able to move around so much because there are more people and there is less land available.

a How does the fact that the farmers stay longer in one place damage the soil? *[4 marks]*

_____

_____

_____

_____

b In Machakos, farmers have changed the way they work to make the soil better. They have planted hedges around their fields, terraced the slopes, used manure and compost, and planted trees and crops that they will be able to sell.

Explain how these things have helped to improve the farmland in Machakos.   *[6 marks]*

_____

_____

_____

_____

_____

_____

_____

_____

_____

_____

_____

_____

_____

_____

Total marks: 50	**Total score:**	**/50**

1 1 mark for each correct tick.
- ✓ Plants
- ✓ Animals
- ✓ Bacteria

2 a 1 mark for each correct name in the box (caterpillar and fox already done).

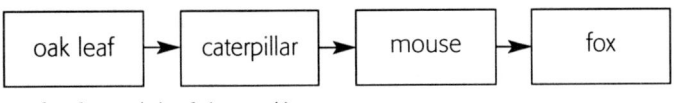

| oak leaf | → | caterpillar | → | mouse | → | fox |

b i oak leaf (1 mark)
  ii caterpillar (1 mark)

c Decomposers change dead matter into nutrients (1 mark) and then the plant can use the nutrients (1 mark).

3 1 mark for each correct label

| Hot. Quite a lot of rain but has a dry season when there is almost no rain.

 Biome: savanna | Very hot for most of the year, then cooler. Almost no rain all year.

 Biome: hot desert |

| Hot and very wet all year.

 Biome: tropical rainforest | Never gets very hot. Rains quite a bit all through the year.

 Biome: deciduous forest |

4 1 mark for each correct label.

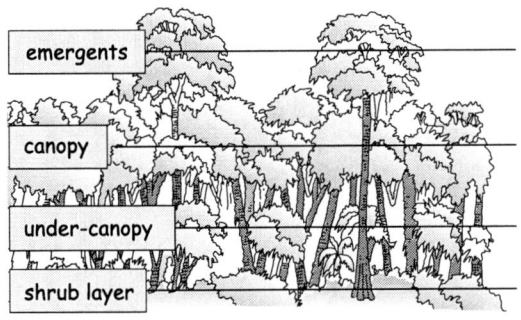

- emergents
- canopy
- under-canopy
- shrub layer

b trying to reach sunlight/competition for light (1 mark).
c allow excess water to fall off leaf (1 mark).
d more food (1 mark) more shelter (1 mark).

5 a-d 1 mark for each correct bar (location and scale), 1 mark for a sensible title (total of 6 marks for this question).
e Brazil (1 mark).
f Jamaica (1 mark).
g 1 mark for each of any three sensible reasons (e.g. timber trade, clearing land for farming, road building, mining, land for cattle farming).

h 1 mark for a bad effect, second mark for explaining it (e.g. soil gets washed away (1 mark) because the trees no longer shelter it (1 mark)). Maximum of 4 marks for this question.

6 Only TWO boxes should be filled in.

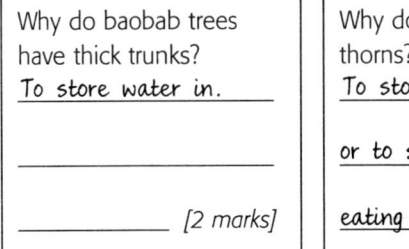

| Why do giraffes have long necks?
 so they can reach to

 get leaves off trees

 _____ [2 marks] | Why do acacia trees have little leaves?
 So that less water is

 lost through the leaves.

 _____ [2 marks] |

| Why do baobab trees have thick trunks?
 To store water in.

 _____

 _____ [2 marks] | Why do bushes have thorns?
 To stop water being lost

 or to stop animals from

 eating them. [2 marks] |

7 a More animals eating the grass so the soil is left bare (1 mark). Growing crops takes nutrients from the soil (1 mark). Trees cut down for firewood so they can't protect the soil (1 mark). All this means the soil gets eroded (1 mark).
May also explain soil gets a baked crust on top or is washed away in rains - credit both these points with 1 mark each.
Maximum of 4 marks for this section.

b 1 mark each for up to three simple explanations, with a second mark in each case for elucidation – up to a maximum of 6 marks.
Examples include:
Hedges around fields slow wind speed (1 mark), so reduce the energy of the wind and therefore limit wind erosion (1 mark).
Terracing reduces the slope of the fields (1 mark), so there is less surface run-off and less soil removed in run-off (1 mark).
Manure and compost increase the soil fertility (1 mark) – they also make it lump together better (colloids), and the lumps (colloids) are harder to erode (1 mark).
Planting trees and crops for sale mean increased income (1 mark) for spending on other soil protection measures (1 mark).

Ecosystems

Name	Class	Date

Now I've reached the end of the Ecosystems chapter:

	Yes	Think so	No
◆ I can explain why plants are a key part of any ecosystem.			
◆ I understand how destroying one part of an ecosystem can have an affect on the whole thing.			
◆ I know where tropical rainforests are in the world, and can describe their climate.			
◆ I know the ways in which vegetation adapts to the climate, in the rainforests.			
◆ I can describe how and why humans are destroying the rainforests.			
◆ I can give an example of sustainable living in the rainforest.			
◆ I know where the savanna ecosystem can be found in the world. I can describe the climate in the savanna.			
◆ I know the ways in which vegetation adapts to the climate, in the savanna.			
◆ I can describe how and why humans are destroying the savanna.			
◆ I can give an example of sustainable living in the savanna.			

◆ I know what these weather terms mean:

ecosystem ☐   producer ☐   consumer ☐   decomposer ☐   food chain ☐

food web ☐   biome ☐   sustainable ☐

The part of this topic that I enjoyed most or found most interesting was:

Photocopiable worksheets

Learning activities

Assessment materials

[W] indicates material provided as editable Word files, as well as in PDF format, on the CD-ROM.

On the CD-ROM: pupil profile sheet; course theme, and lesson planning documents.

Name **Class**

Experts can only 'estimate' future world population growth.
That means they can only make a good guess.
The table below shows two estimates for population change
up to 2050.

1 Use the data to complete the graph.
Draw one line for each set of figures.
Label them 'high estimate' and 'low estimate'.

2000	6.0 billion	6.0 billion
2005	6.5 billion	6.4 billion
2010	6.8 billion	6.6 billion
2015	7.2 billion	6.9 billion
2020	7.5 billion	7.0 billion
2030	8.2 billion	6.8 billion
2040	8.8 billion	6.3 billion
2050	9.3 billion	6.0 billion

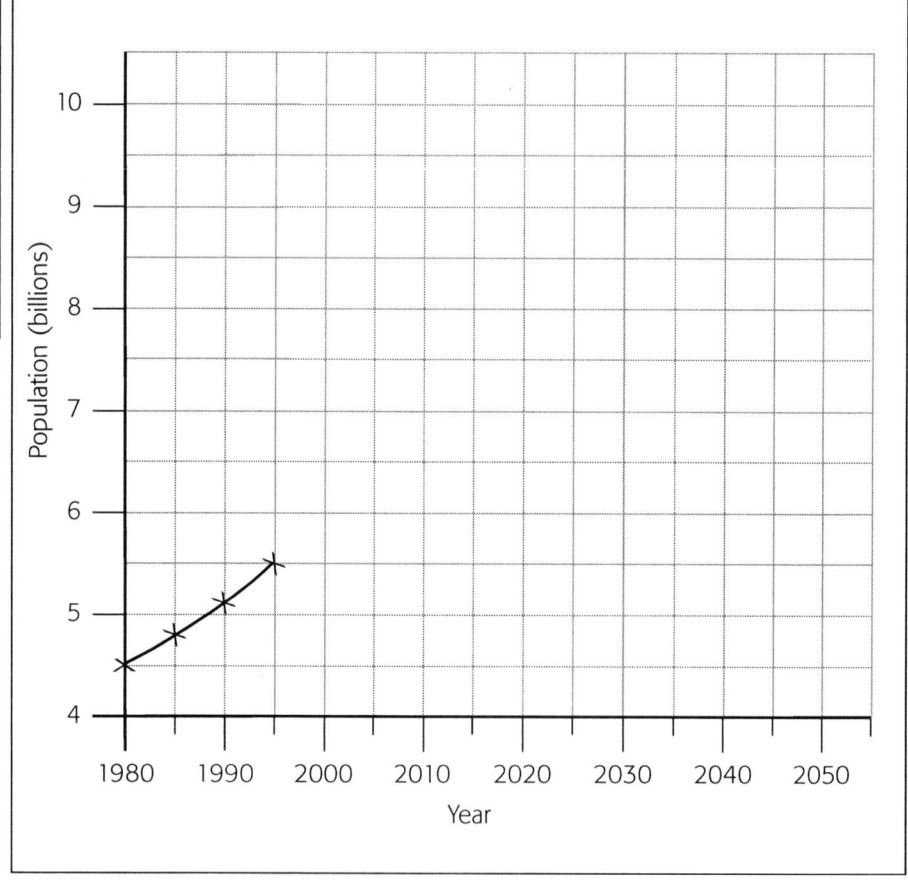

Now answer these questions in your exercise book.

2 It is difficult to know exactly how many people are alive today. Why is that?

3 To produce an estimate, experts have to make certain assumptions.
Think of reasons for the big difference between these two estimates.

4 What problems might there be if population grows like the highest line
on your graph?

5 Could there be problems if the population of the world starts to fall?
Give reasons.

Do you remember …?

The **birth rate (BR)** is the number of births for every thousand of the population, per year.

The **death rate (DR)** is the number of deaths for every thousand of the population, per year.

Population growth or **natural increase** can be found by subtracting the DR from the BR. It is given as a percentage.

The graph on the right shows the birth and death rates for Mexico in the 20th century.

1 What do you think happened from 1910 to 1920?

_____

_____

Birth and death rates for Mexico

2 Use the data in the table (below right) to complete the outline graph for Sweden.

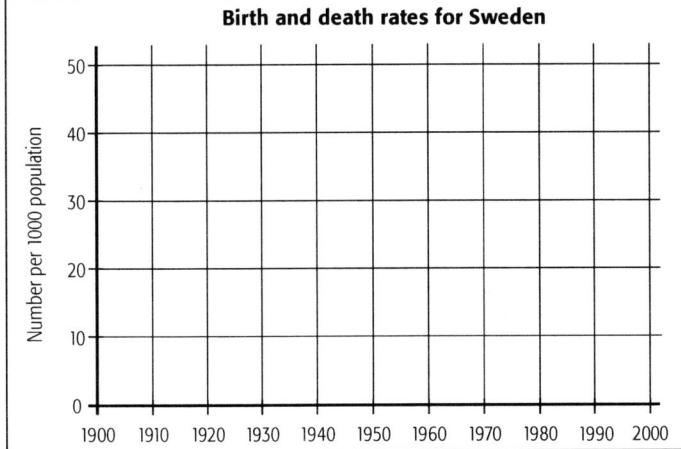

Birth and death rates for Sweden

Data for Sweden		
Year	BR	DR
1900	27	15
1910	19	16
1920	16	14
1930	13	12
1940	18	11
1950	16	10
1960	14	11
1970	13	11
1980	12	11
1990	12	10
2000	11	10

3 On the Sweden graph, label (in neat writing):
   a high BR   **c** falling DR   **e** rapid population growth
   b low BR   **d** falling BR   **f** population falling

Now answer these questions in your exercise book.

4 Describe the overall **trend** in the birth and death rates:
   a for Sweden   **b** for Mexico

5 Suggest some reasons for these trends.

6 Which country had the larger increase in population in the 20th century? Give reasons for your answer.

Name   **Class**

The table gives data for the 25 countries of the European Union or EU.
(Not all European countries are in the EU.)

1 Work out the population density for each country by dividing the population of the country by its area:

$$\text{population density} = \frac{\text{population}}{\text{area}}$$

Give your answer to the nearest whole number.

2 Using an atlas, label the 25 EU countries on an outline map of Europe. See how neatly you can write. You may need to write some labels out to the side.

Your next task is to create a chloropleth map showing population density.

3 Decide on four categories of equal size, eg 0–100, 101–200, and write these beside the key below. (The last one could be 301 and over.)

4 Shade in the key. Use four shades of one colour, starting with a very light one, and getting darker as you go down the key.

5 Cut out the key and paste it on to your outline map of Europe (without covering up any of the 25 EU countries!).

6 Shade the EU countries on the map according to your key.

In your exercise book:

7 Describe the pattern of population density shown on your map.

8 Try to explain the pattern.

Country	Area (sq km)	Population	Population density (people per sq km)
Austria	84 000	8 000 000	
Belgium	33 000	10 000 000	
Cyprus	9 000	800 000	
Czech Republic	79 000	10 000 000	
Denmark	43 000	5 000 000	
Estonia	45 000	1 400 000	
Finland	338 000	5 000 000	
France	552 000	60 000 000	
Germany	349 000	82 000 000	
Greece	129 000	11 000 000	
Hungary	93 000	10 000 000	
Ireland	69 000	4 000 000	
Italy	294 000	58 000 000	
Latvia	65 000	2 400 000	
Lithuania	65 000	3 500 000	
Luxembourg	2 600	400 000	
Malta	316	400 000	
Netherlands	37 000	16 000 000	
Poland	313 000	39 000 000	
Portugal	92 000	11 000 000	
Slovakia	49 000	5 400 000	
Slovenia	20 000	2 000 000	
Spain	499 000	40 000 000	
Sweden	412 000	9 000 000	
UK	244 000	60 000 000	

Key   population density (people per sq km)

☐

☐

☐

☐

Name   Class

___

Resources are the things people need to live, and do their work.

1 Name a job for which this is an essential resource.

a rain   _____   b timber _____

c thread   _____   d wind   _____

e a camera _____   f petrol _____

2 Below are some words used to describe resources, and their definitions.

  a Complete each definition, using a word from this 'Missing' bag.

  b Join each word box to its definition box with a wavy arrow.

  c Colour each pair of boxes to match.
     (A different colour for each pair.)

Missing resources — more, rice, atmosphere, live, factories, physical, dance, can't

| non-renewable | basic | We can't _____ without them. |

| primary | | |

| renewable | Can be recycled or we can easily make or grow _____ . | Once we use them all up we _____ get more. |

| manufactured | Made by people, often in _____ . | Found naturally in the earth, sea or _____ , or we can grow them. |

3 Next, in each empty box above, draw and label one resource that you use at home.
   (For example you could include one fuel.)

4 Now draw a line from each resource in **3** to any word box that describes it.
   (You might need to join it to more than one box!)

___

Name   Class

800 million people go to bed hungry every night.

1 You are a young farmer in a poor country where the climate is hot and dry, and the rain unreliable. You like to work hard. You have many ideas for improving your farm. But you still go to bed hungry every night. How does it happen?

To see how, complete this vicious circle by writing **A – I** in the correct boxes in the circle. (One has been done for you.)

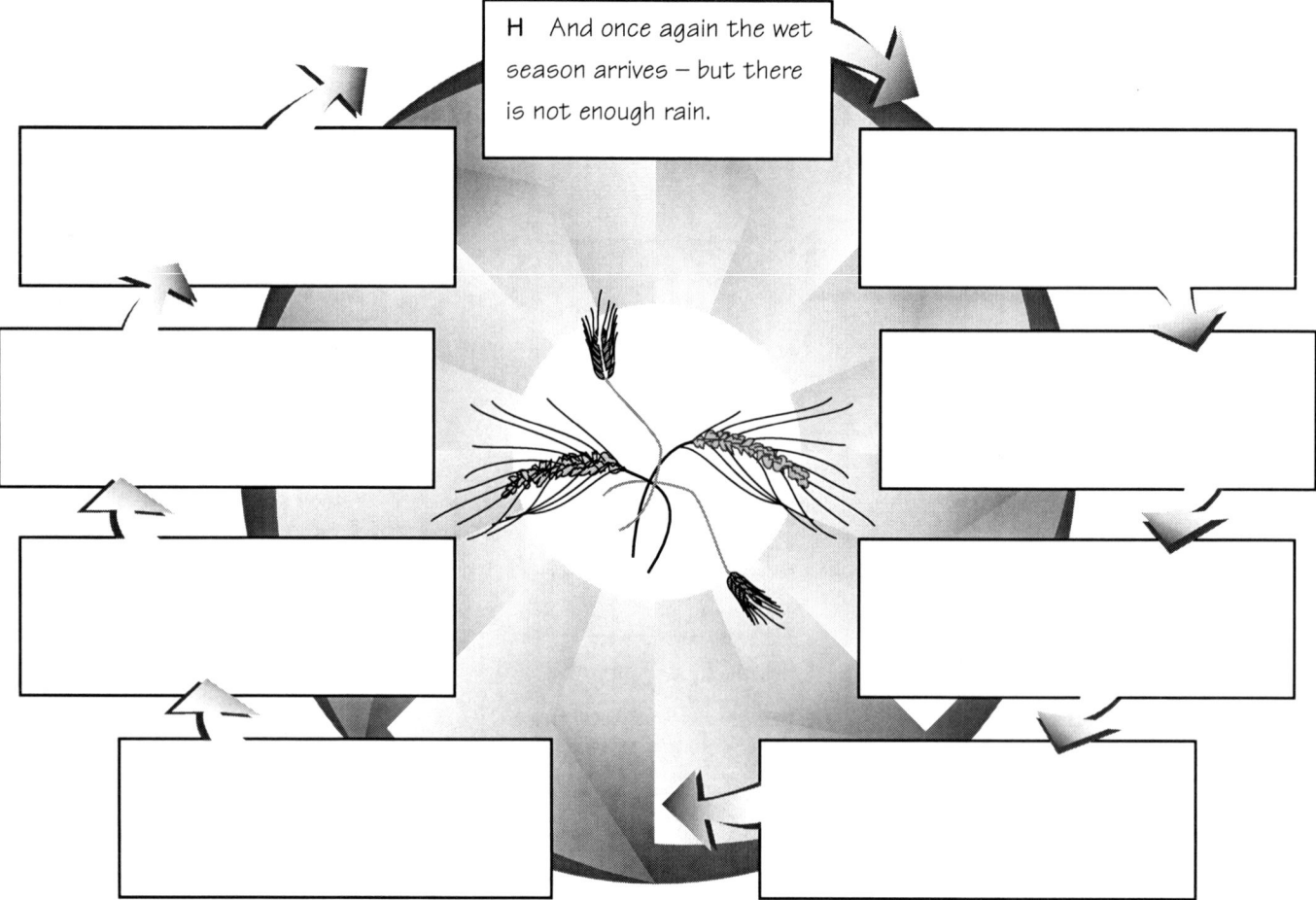

H   And once again the wet season arrives – but there is not enough rain.

A … and there is not even enough to feed your family …

B … which means you can't sell any crops, as you'd planned.

C Soon you do not have enough energy to work hard …

D Instead you store them away, eating very sparingly every day.

E … and since you didn't sell crops, you have no money for tools or fertiliser either.

F So you just poke holes in the hard ground with a stick, and plant seeds for next year.

G So your crops grow weak and stunted …

H And once again the wet season arrives – but there is not enough rain.

I So every day you and your family feel a little hungrier.

2 Suddenly the climate improves. The rains fall regularly in each wet season. Now draw a 'virtuous circle' on the back of this page to show how your life changes.

4A How many people? **

1

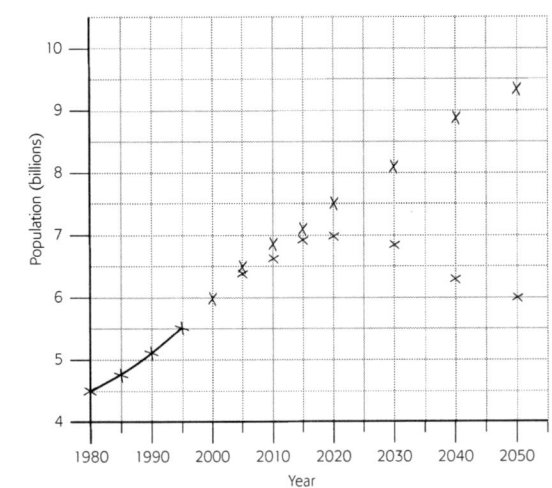

2 It is impossible to count everyone in every country. You need to send out forms, which some people won't want to fill in – for example if they are there illegally, or hiding from someone. In areas where a lot of people can't read, you need to send out interviewers with forms. It may be impossible to reach people in isolated places. By the time you have finished counting, some more people will have been born and some will have died, so the census will be out of date immediately.

3 To estimate, you must make lots of assumptions. For example, about how birth and death rates will change in different countries as they develop. Different experts will make different assumptions.

4 Shortages of basic resources (food, water, fuel, land), overcrowding, especially in cities, more people living in poverty, increased pollution, increased deforestation, pressure on services (health care, education), tension between countries and people due to unequal distribution of resources (for example water wars).

5 An ageing population, an increasing number of elderly people being supported by a declining number of people of working age; not enough people to do essential jobs; more houses, roads, power stations etc. than we need!

4B Comparing birth and death rates **

1 The population fell because the death rate was higher than the birth rate. There could have been famine or war or a fatal epidemic. (In fact 1910 was the year of the Mexican revolution which plunged the country into disorder for several years.)

2 & 3

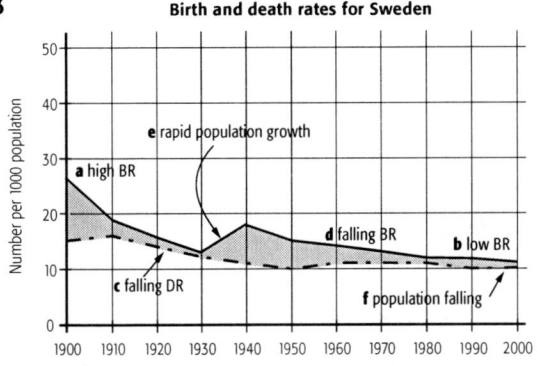

Birth and death rates for Sweden

4 a Sweden: *Overall*, both declined at roughly equal rates from 1900; but there were blips, for example around 1940 when the birth rate rose. Both are now at a similar low rate.
b Mexico: Again an *overall* decline in both since 1900 (with a blip for death rates in the first decade). However the birth rate stayed fairly steady, at a high rate, until around 1970 and then it fell fast. The death rate declined fairly steadily by comparison. Both appear to be levelling off now but the gap between birth and death rates is larger for Mexico than for Sweden.

5 A high death rate is due to disease, poor nutrition and so on. As countries develop and health care and nutrition improve, the death rate falls. A high birth rate is often related to poverty, with children seen as security for the future – so large families are common in many poor countries; it is also a sign that birth control methods are not available. As a country develops, and wealth grows, and particularly as women get educated and get better jobs, the birth rate generally falls. So the fall for both measures, for both countries, is a sign of their continuing development. The larger gap between birth and death rates suggests that Mexico is less developed.

6 Mexico, because the gap between birth and death rates is greater there; so it has the greater natural increase.

4C Population density **

1 The population density figures to the nearest whole number are as follows: Austria 95, Belgium 303, Cyprus 89, Czech Republic 127, Denmark 116, Estonia 31, Finland 15, France 109, Germany 235, Greece 85, Hungary 108, Ireland 58, Italy 197, Latvia 37, Lithuania 54, Luxembourg 154, Malta 1266, Netherlands 432, Poland 125, Portugal 120, Slovakia 110, Slovenia 100, Spain 80, Sweden 22, UK 246.

7 The highest density of population is in Malta / the UK / Belgium / Germany / Netherlands (But remind pupils that it is an *average* figure. There are areas of high density in all the countries.)

8 Malta, Belgium and the Netherlands are small, with quite large populations, which means a high population density. Some countries, such as Italy, have large unpopulated mountain areas, reducing their overall figure. There's also a link with industry: more industry, such as Germany, usually means a higher population density.

4D A question of resources *

1 Typical answers: **a** farmer, gardener **b** carpenter, builder **c** tailor **d** windsurfing instructor, manager of windfarm **e** photographer **f** taxi driver, racing driver, bus driver

4E Hunger: a vicious circle ***

1 H, G, A, B, D, I, C, E, F

2 Pupils' diagrams could show stages like these: wet season arrives, and rain falls as usual ➔ crops grow well
➔ you have more than you need to feed the family
➔ you can sell excess crops ➔ you can spend some of the money you earn on fertilisers, machinery, better seed, perhaps even more land ➔ so your farmland improves
➔ you plant crops for next year.

A mystery   **

In this activity, pupils use thinking skills and the information provided to solve a mystery: *What caused the argument that shattered the peace and quiet in a park in Pune, India, on a balmy Thursday evening?*

Aims

This activity gives pupils the opportunity to:

- sort relevant facts from irrelevant ones
- link relevant facts in a logical way
- learn a little about the issues surrounding GM crops andpoverty in India
- form a hypothesis
- present and discuss their solution

Lesson preparation

- Decide how many groups of pupils you will have. Small, mixed-ability groups of just three pupils are recommended, so that all pupils become involved.
- Prepare a set of 31 statement cards and a 'setting the scene summary' for each group (pages 135-137). Put these in an envelope. Write the *Mystery* question (above) on the envelope.
- Decide which follow-up activity you are going to use, and photocopy the relevant page (page 138 or 139).

Activity

1 Divide the class into groups. Make sure each group has enough space to spread out their 31 statements.

2 Tell the class what you want them to do. You could explain that:
   - they are about to become detectives.
   - they need to read about the scene of the mystery first, then they should read all the statements in the envelope and ask about any they do not understand.
   - they must think about each statement and decide whether it helps to solve the mystery. If it is not relevant, they should discard it.
   - they should use the remaining statements to construct the points that each man might have made.
   - they should check the discarded statements from time to time, to make sure they are not relevant.
   - they must come up with a *full* explanation for what the argument was about and what each man said, and include all the relevant facts.

Follow-up activity:

To follow up this mystery there are two possible activities:

1 A set of questions (page 138) could be read out to the whole class, or given to each group prior to whole-class feedback. If you prefer not to use the questions, you could ask a couple of groups to present their explanation verbally and then ask other groups to comment. You could also ask pupils about the way they worked. For example, how they moved the paper strips about, and why; how their explanation changed as they went through the activity, and why; and how they worked together. This will start them thinking about working methods.

2 Pupils could be asked to make their own written record of the solution to the mystery, in the form of a writing frame (page 139).

For a full discussion of the *Mystery* strategy, and other examples, see the excellent *Thinking through Geography* by David Leat et al., which was our inspiration for this activity.

A mystery

Name   **Class**

A mystery

The scene:
Pune, India.

It was a quiet, warm evening. On some open space by the road near the Agricultural College, people were relaxing after a hard day's work, squatting on the ground talking and playing cards.

Two men walked out of the hotel talking together and stopped at the park. They sat down on the grass and continued their discussion. Suddenly there was loud shouting. The two men started pushing each other and yelling.

The mystery:
What caused the argument that shattered the peace and quiet in a park in Pune, India, on a balmy Thursday evening?

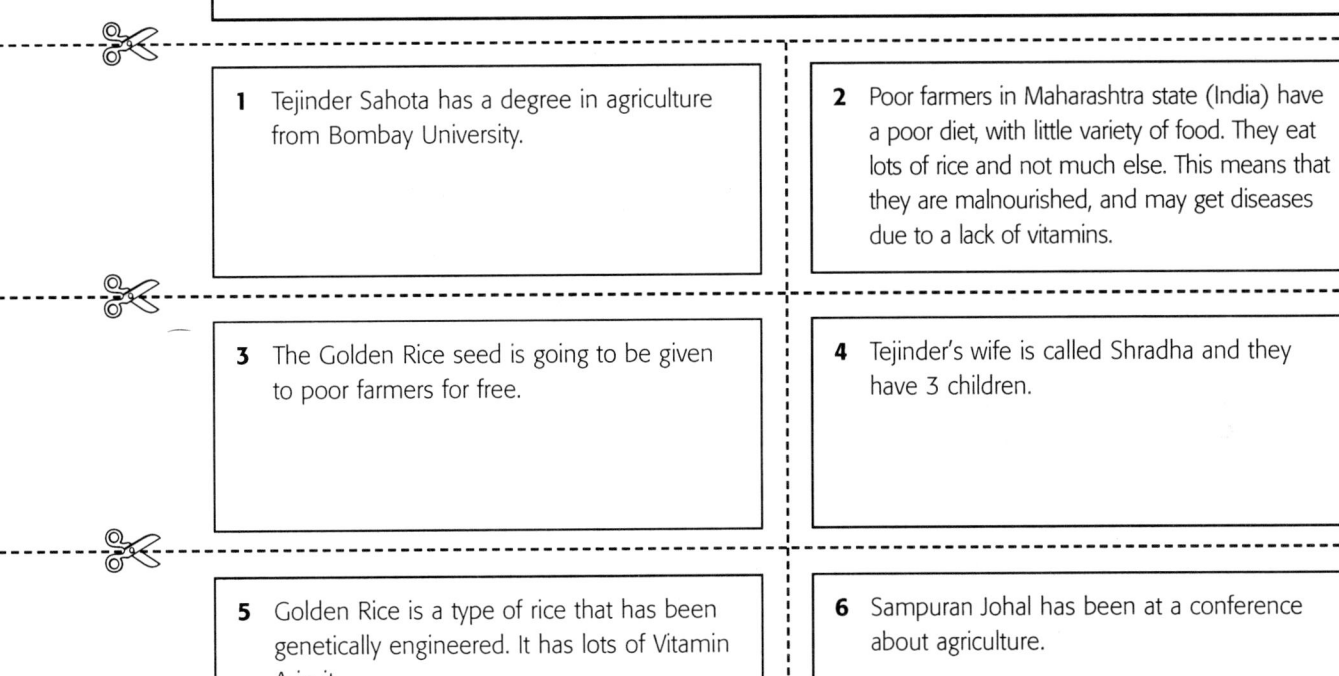

1 Tejinder Sahota has a degree in agriculture from Bombay University.

2 Poor farmers in Maharashtra state (India) have a poor diet, with little variety of food. They eat lots of rice and not much else. This means that they are malnourished, and may get diseases due to a lack of vitamins.

3 The Golden Rice seed is going to be given to poor farmers for free.

4 Tejinder's wife is called Shradha and they have 3 children.

5 Golden Rice is a type of rice that has been genetically engineered. It has lots of Vitamin A in it.

6 Sampuran Johal has been at a conference about agriculture.

7 Lack of Vitamin A in people's diets makes children go blind and also causes 1 million deaths every year.

---

geog.2: 4 People and resources

Name   **Class**

---

8 Red palm oil is rich in Vitamin A and is cheap to extract. It doesn't need to be genetically modified (GM) or tested, so it can be used straight away.

9 Golden Rice would be part of a poor person's diet, not the only food they eat, so they wouldn't need to eat 12 times what they do now. It's not the only thing that needs to be done to help poor farmers.

10 Pune is spelled Poona in English.

11 To get enough Vitamin A from Golden Rice, people will need to eat 12 times more rice each day than they do now. They can't afford to buy this much extra rice.

12 Tejinder is wearing jeans and a T-shirt.

13 The GM food company thinks that Golden Rice could save 4000 lives a day over the whole of Asia.

14 Tejinder Sahota is worried about the malnutrition of the poor farmers. He thinks the solution is to divide the land more fairly so that all families have enough space to grow what they need to eat.

15 A conference about agriculture has just ended at the Agricultural College in Pune.

16 There were 400 people at the conference.

17 Rice is a grain. It grows on stalks.

18 Sampuran is an advisor to a GM food company that has developed a type of rice called Golden Rice.

19 Maharashtra state is on the west coast of India.

Name   **Class**

---

20 GM food is quite new. It is possible that the new genes put into the food might change over time. This means that the rice might not always have the same amounts of Vitamin A.

21 Tejinder Sahota wants the poor farmers to get more money for their crops. Then they can buy better food without having to rely on what they can grow.

22 Sampuran and Tejinder met at the chess club at Madras University.

23 The Vitamin A in Golden Rice is in the form of a chemical called beta-carotene. This is the same chemical that makes carrots orange. It is this chemical that makes the rice yellowish and that's why it's called Golden Rice.

24 People in Asia have grown rice for thousands of years.

25 Sampuran Johal has a degree in biological sciences from Madras University.

26 Tejinder has been at a conference about agriculture at the Agricultural College in Pune.

27 It cost $2.6 million and took 10 years to develop Golden Rice.

28 78% of malnourished children live in countries where there is spare food.

29 Tejinder works for a charity that is trying to improve life for poor farmers in Maharashtra state in India.

30 There is a new coffee shop in Pune, which opened in 2001. Cappuccino is the most popular drink served there.

31 Tejinder and Sampuran are both really worried about poor farmers and feel very strongly about what should be done to help them.

A mystery

Name   **Class**

Solving the Mystery

What caused the argument that shattered the peace and quiet in a park in Pune, India, on a balmy Thursday evening?

Follow-up questions

1   Who were the men who were arguing?

_____

2   How do they know each other?

_____

3   Why were the two men in Pune?

_____

4   What jobs do the two men have?

_____

5   What worries them both about the lives of poor farmers in Maharashtra state?

_____

_____

6   What does Sampuran want to do to improve things for the farmers?

_____

_____

7   What does Tejinder think about this?

_____

_____

8   Who do you think is right?

_____

_____

_____

_____

_____

Name   Class

Writing frame

It was a quiet, warm evening. On some open space near the Agricultural College people were relaxing after a hard day's work, squatting on the ground talking and playing cards.

Two men walked out of the hotel talking together and stopped at the park. They sat down on the grass and continued their discussion. Suddenly there was loud shouting. The two men start pushing each other and yelling.

Our reporter has investigated the incident.

One of the men arguing was _____ . He has a degree in

_____ from the University of _____ He works as

_____ .

The other man arguing was _____ , he _____

_____

_____ .

The two men had just left a conference about _____ . It was held at

_____ . The men knew each other already because

_____ .

They stopped to talk before going home. They were worried about poor

farmers because _____

_____ .

_____ thinks that Golden Rice is the best solution. He thinks it

would be a good thing because _____ .

_____ .

_____ thinks that Golden Rice is a bad idea because

_____

_____ .

He thinks it would be better to _____

_____

_____ .

People and resources

The assessment opportunities for People and resources are as follows:

■ The **level-marked assessment** 'World population growth' on pages 141-144.

 In this assessment, pupils need to:
 • write a description of a graph showing world population growth;
 • understand the causes of global population change;
 • consider current and future problems that could result from overcrowding on our planet.

 A **feedback form** for the level-marked assessment is provided on page 145.

■ The **scored test** on pages 146-150.

■ Opportunities for interim assessments provided by **geog.2**:

 A mystery (a thinking / sorting activity, with the opportunity or pupils to work in small groups) on pages 134-139 of this file.

 Activities 11, 17, 18, 20, 21, 24, and 25 in the *Further suggestions for class and homework* section on pages 92-93 of the *geog.2 teacher's handbook*.

 Worksheet A: Making the most of your rice for *Rice – the amazing grain* (a webfile) in *geog.2, People and resources* on *geog.world*.

 Worksheet B: World rice production for *Rice – the amazing grain* (a webfile) in *geog.2, People and resources* on *geog.world*.

■ The **self-assessment form** for the whole People and resources chapter on page 151.

People and resources

Name	Class	Date

World population growth

The level at which I am currently working is

~~so~~ my ~~target~~ level for this assessment is

because   EBI:

Assessment task

In this assessment you will answer questions about world population growth. You will:
- analyse a graph showing population growth over time;
- think about some of the causes of world population growth;
- think about possible problems caused by living on a crowded planet.

1 Study Figure 1 then answer these questions.
   a Describe how the world's population has changed since 1700.
   b Do you think *The population explosion!* is a suitable title for the graph? Why?
   c Give a definition for each of these terms, (Remember: write in full sentences.)
   - birth rate
   - natural increase
   - infant mortality
   - death rate
   - life expectancy

2 Now look at Figure 2. It gives population data for the UK and Mali, for 2003.
   a How did the population change in each country in 2003?
   b In which country did the population increase more rapidly?
   c What could Mali do to try and reduce its infant mortality rate?
   d Why should people in the UK plan their pensions very carefully?

3 Choose two countries where population density is high. Give reasons why each country might be so crowded (try to think of physical factors as well as social ones). *Social = Human*

4 Choose two countries where population density is low. Give reasons why each country might be so sparsely populated (again, try to think of physical factors as well as social ones). *Social = Human*

5 You work for the World Health Organisation (WHO). You've become worried about how the world will cope with the rapid rise in population. You're particularly concerned with how *(LIC)* countries in the developing world will cope.
   Write a letter to the leader of the WHO expressing your concerns.

Before you start work, make sure you understand the task and what you have to do. And look at the **success criteria** on the next two pages, so that you know how to achieve your target level – or better.

Level 3
- You understand the meaning of some of the population terms.
- You can read some information from the graph and show some understanding of the phrase 'population explosion'.
- You recognise some problems that might result from the planet becoming overcrowded.

Level 4
- You show an understanding of most of the population terms and recognise where in the world population is dense, and where it is sparse.
- You give an accurate analysis of a graph showing world population growth.
- You recognise a range of problems that might result from the planet becoming overcrowded.
- You use a good standard of literacy in your work and make use of some appropriate terminology.

Level 5
- In addition to level 4, you give simple reasons to explain why some parts of the world are densely populated, and some sparsely, using some named examples.
- You describe fully the growth in the world's population over the last three centuries, and recognise some of the implications of this.
- Your letter identifies a wide range of problems associated with population growth, and gives some explanation about why these problems will get worse.
- You use a good range of appropriate terminology.

Level 6
- You have a full command of the population terminology used in this assessment.
- You apply your knowledge of these terms to describe and explain accurately how the world's population has risen and the consequences that this could have for nations at different stages of development.
- You recognise the problems that the world is likely to experience as a result of population growth, and refer to parts of the world that might suffer more than others.
- You make some simple suggestions about how the issues surrounding population growth could be tackled in different countries.

Level 7
- As well as level 6, you are confident with all the key terminology and with handling data from the graph.
- You understand the global implications of population growth for both developed and less developed countries.
- Your letter is written clearly and has well-expressed ideas about the problems we may face in the future. You relate many of the issues to real examples and explain clearly how the problems are caused.
- You make some good suggestions about how these issues could be tackled, showing evidence of good research skills.
- High level literacy is demonstrated throughout.

Level 8
- In addition to level 7, you describe fully the growth of the world's population and project how this is due to change in the future.
- You make highly effective use of research opportunities to illustrate the problems of population growth in countries at different stages of development.
- Your examples also illustrate how the problems are being addressed and how effective the measures taken have been.
- A high level literacy is demonstrated throughout.

Exceptional performance

In addition to Level 8…

- You apply your work to appropriate models of population change.
- You make comparisons between these models of change and the material provided in this assessment.

Figure 1 The population explosion!

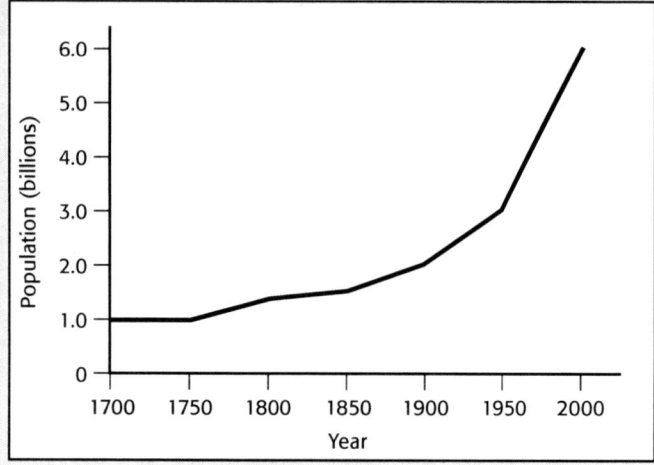

Figure 2 Population data for the UK and Mali, for 2003

Country	UK	Mali
Birth rate (per 1000 people)	11	47
Death rate (per 1000 people)	10	19
Infant mortality (per 1000 live births)	5	118
Life expectancy (years)	78	45

© OUP: this may be reproduced for class use solely within the purchaser's school or college

People and resources

Name   **Class**   **Date**

World population growth

Assessment task

A series of questions about world population growth, including a letter to the World Health Organisation expressing concern about the effects of this rise.

Level awarded:

Teacher's comments:

Targets for improvement:

- Describe ideas in greater detail. ❏
- Suggest more reasons/processes to explain geographical ideas. ❏
- Try to use more geographical words and terms in your writing. ❏
- Try to support your writing with further, researched ideas. ❏
- Improve accuracy and/or presentation skills. ❏
- Use a greater range of presentation styles/techniques in your work. ❏
- Improve personal organisation and homework to raise your achievement level. ❏
- Ask for help about ideas you don't understand. ❏

Student's comments:

People and resources Test

| Name | Class | Date |

1   The **population** of the world is changing, but how is it changing? Tick the correct box in this list.   *[1 mark]*

❑   The population has stayed the same

❑   The population has gone up a lot

❑   The population has gone up a little

❑   The population has gone down

2   The population changes because of the number of people who are born and the number who die in a year. The terms that geographers use are birth rate, death rate, and natural increase. Match up the terms with the correct definition.   *[3 marks]*

Birth rate   *the number of people who die in a year divided by the number of thousands of people in the population.*

Death rate   *the number of people who are born in a year divided by the number of thousands of people in the population.*

Natural increase   *the difference between the birth rate and the death rate.*

3   Now you are going to work out the missing statistics for the countries in this table.   *[3 marks]*

Country	Birth rate per 1000	Death rate per 1000	Natural increase
A	2.0	1.6	0.4
B	4.6	3.2	
C	7.3		2.3
D		0.8	0.2

4   People are spread out around the world. In some places there are very few people, and in other places there are lots of people.

a   Give TWO reasons to explain why few people live in the Sahara desert.   *[2 marks]*

_____

_____

b   Give TWO reasons to explain why lots of people live in South East England.   *[2 marks]*

_____

_____

5 a People need **resources** to live. This paragraph tells you about resources but some words are missing. Choose from the words below to fill in the gaps.   *[3 marks]*

basic   natural   manufactured

> People need _____ resources, which they get from the earth or the atmosphere. Without _____ resources people would die. Sometimes people make things they need; these are _____ resources.

b Resources can be **renewable** (which means we can recycle them or grow more), or **non-renewable** (which means they will be used up one day). Find FOUR resources in this wordsearch and put them in the right column of the table.   *[4 marks]*

L	Q	R	C	T	D
C	A	E	R	Z	G
K	O	T	T	H	E
J	Y	A	E	Y	T
D	E	W	L	M	N
C	R	O	P	S	L

Renewable	Non-renewable

c You use lots of resources indirectly every day. Say what resources are needed for each of these household items? One has been done for you.   *[4 marks]*

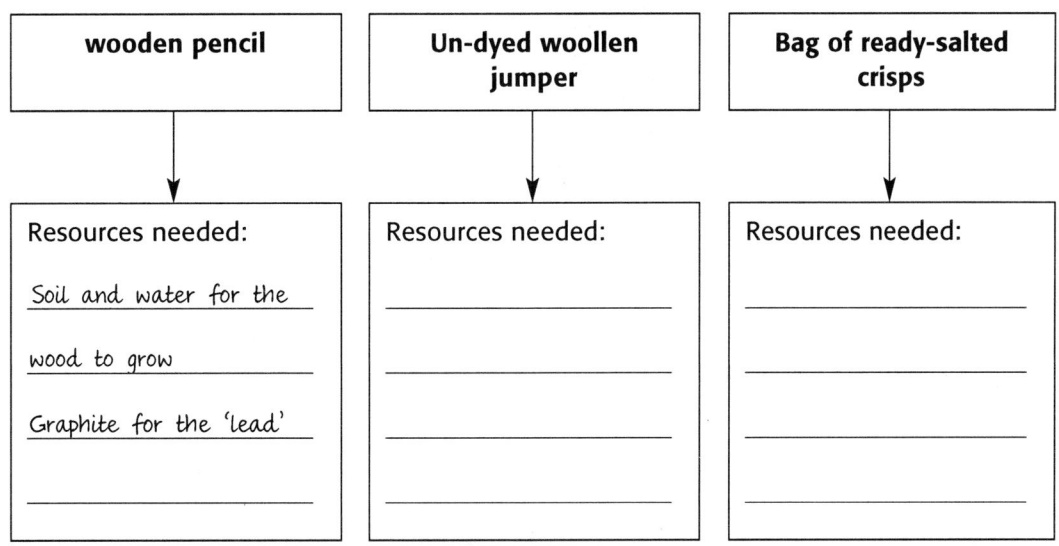

wooden pencil	**Un-dyed woollen jumper**	**Bag of ready-salted crisps**
Resources needed:	Resources needed:	Resources needed:
Soil and water for the wood to grow	_____	_____
Graphite for the 'lead'	_____	_____
_____	_____	_____

d We all use a lot of resources that we don't really need. Suggest TWO things that you have used today that you could have done without. One example has been done for you.

[4 marks]

Example Petrol in the car when I could have walked

---

6 Different countries use different amounts of resources. **Energy** is an example of a resource. This data table tells you how much energy each person uses on average per year, in eight different countries.

Country	Ethiopia	Chad	India	Egypt	Bulgaria	UK	Saudi Arabia	USA
Kg of energy used per year	20	16	250	600	2400	3700	4500	7800

a Complete the numbering on this axis. *[1 mark]*

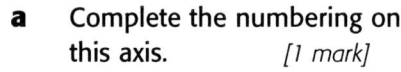

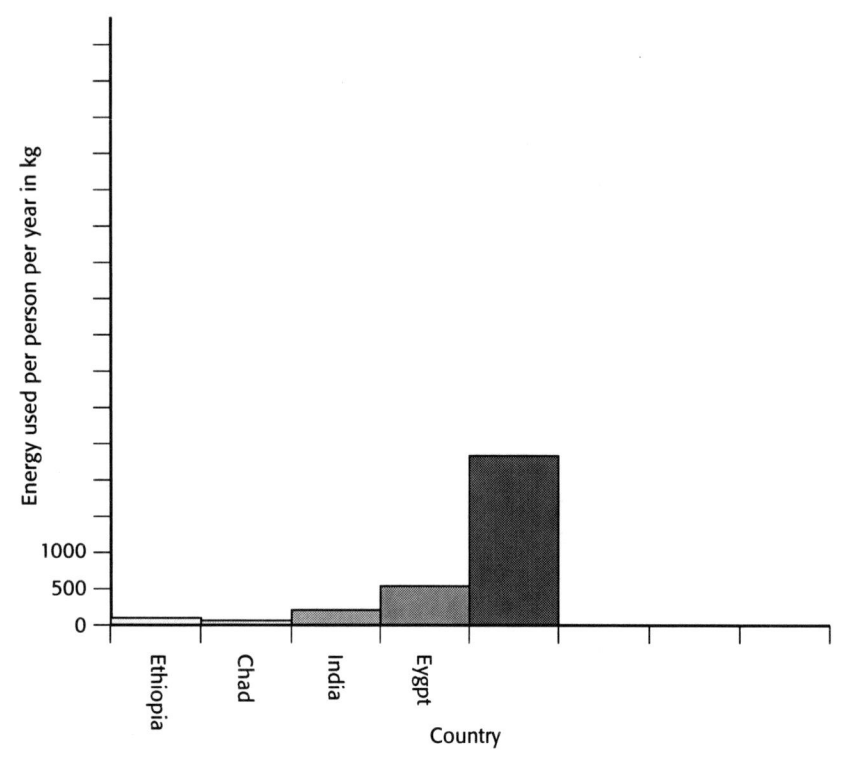

d Write a title on this line. *[1 mark]*

c The first 5 bars have been done for you. You need to finish the last 3 bars. *[4 marks]*

Energy used per person per year in kg

1000
500
0

Ethiopia   Chad   India   Eygpt

Country

b Finish labelling the countries on this axis. *[1 mark]*

e Which two countries have the least energy use? *[2 marks]*

_____

_____

f Which country has the highest energy use? *[1 mark]*

_____

g Suggest two problems that could be caused in the poorer countries because of their low energy use. *[2 marks]*

_____

_____

4   Food is another type of resource that people need. This map shows the amount of food eaten in a day by the average person in the countries of North and South America. Some of the countries have been labelled for you.

   a   What patterns can you see in the amount of food eaten by people over this continent?

   [4 marks]

Key
Average daily food intake
in calories per person

over 3000		2000-2500	
3000-3500		less than 2000	
2500-3000		data not available	

   b   Why do you think that there are these differences? Think about climate, income, population density, farm machinery and chemicals, differences in wealth, education, and other factors.

   [8 marks]

Total marks: 50   **Total score:**   /50

1 The population has gone up a lot (1 mark).

2 1 mark for each correct line.

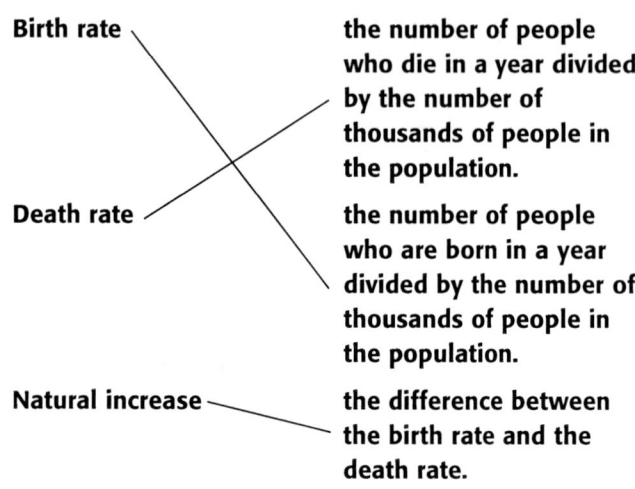

Birth rate — the number of people who are born in a year divided by the number of thousands of people in the population.

Death rate — the number of people who die in a year divided by the number of thousands of people in the population.

Natural increase — the difference between the birth rate and the death rate.

3 1 mark for each correct number (underlined numbers show where gaps were).

Country	Birth rate per 1000	Death rate per 1000	Natural increase
A	2.0	1.6	0.4
B	4.6	3.2	1.4
C	7.3	5.0	2.3
D	1.0	0.8	0.2

4 a 1 mark for each sensible reason (e.g. too dry to grow crops; no water supply). Maximum of 2 marks.
b 1 mark for each sensible reason (e.g. lots of jobs; flat land for easy building). Maximum of 2 marks.

5 a 1 mark for each correct word placement.

People need **natural** resources, which they get from the earth or the atmosphere. Without **basic** resources people would die. Sometimes people make things they need, these are **manufactured** resources.

b 1 mark for each correct word in the table.

Renewable	Non-renewable
crops	metal
water	coal

c 1 mark for each resource, up to a maximum of 4 over both boxes (although pupil may have more than 4 resources).

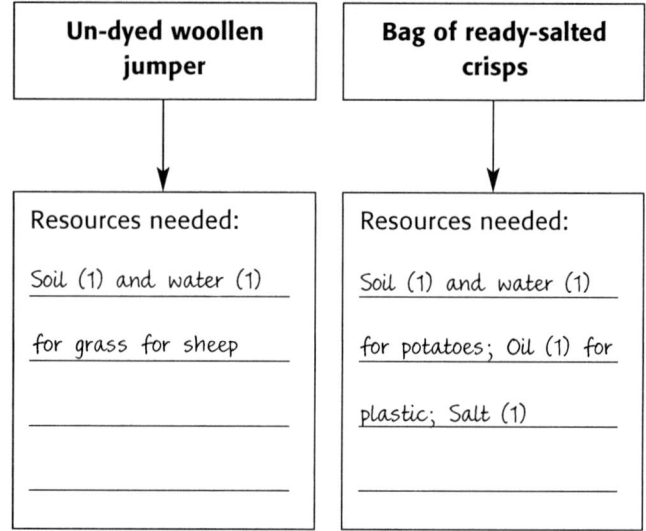

Un-dyed woollen jumper	Bag of ready-salted crisps
Resources needed: Soil (1) and water (1) for grass for sheep	Resources needed: Soil (1) and water (1) for potatoes; Oil (1) for plastic; Salt (1)

d 1 mark for stating the first resource, 1 mark for expanding.
1 mark for stating the second resource, 1 mark for expanding.

6 a 1 mark for labelling numbers on energy use axis.
b 1 mark for labelling countries in the right order.
c 1 mark for each bar (up to 3 marks) fourth mark for using a ruler and shading correctly.
d 1 mark for a sensible title.
e Chad and Ethiopia (2 marks).
f USA (1 mark).
g 1 mark for each sensible reason (e.g. have to collect firewood; can't work after dark). Maximum of 2 marks.

7 a People in North America have more food than people in countries in South America (1 mark), then up to 3 marks for naming countries.
b 1 mark for up to four simple explanations, with a second mark in each case for elucidation – up to a maximum of 8 marks.
For example, lower income means less money to spend on food (1 mark), but also less to invest in health and education, so income doesn't rise and malnutrition continues.

People and resources

Name   **Class**   **Date**

Now I've reached the end of the People and resources chapter:

	Yes	Think so	No
◆ I can give reasons why the Earth's population has risen so fast.			
◆ I know some of the factors that affect a country's birth and death rates.			
◆ I know how we are spread or distributed around the world.			
◆ I can describe some of the ways in which population density is linked to climate.			

◆ I know what these terms mean:

birth rate ❑   death rate ❑   natural increase ❑   resource ❑   natural resource ❑

The part of this topic that I enjoyed most or found most interesting was:

Energy: a key resource 5

Photocopiable worksheets

Learning activities

Assessment materials

[W] indicates material provided as editable Word files, as well as in PDF format, on the CD-ROM.

On the CD-ROM: pupil profile sheet; course theme, and lesson planning documents.

Name   **Class**

Many of the world's common sources of energy have a long history.

1 Read the text below which describes some of the main events in the history of energy.

2 Then complete the timeline to show these events. (One has been put in for you.)

Steam is one of the oldest sources of power used in industry and transport. A Greek called Hero designed a model of a steam turbine around 2000 years ago. But he didn't bother pursuing it, and the first working steam engine was not invented until 1712, by the Englishman Thomas Newcomen. Richard Trevithick later converted a steam engine to power the first ever steam locomotive.

The oldest recorded dam was built in 300 BC in China. For centuries, the water held in the reservoirs behind dams was used only for drinking and irrigation. Then, in 1869, Aristide Berges managed to convert the energy from a waterfall in the Alps into electrical energy. Hydroelectric power was born.

Oil did not become important as a source of energy until the 19th century. In 1840, in Scotland, James Young discovered that a colourless liquid distilled from crude oil would burn in a lamp. In 1859, the American Edwin Drake marketed another liquid distilled from crude oil, called kerosene, for lamps. In that year he became famous as the first person to drill successfully for oil. By this time petrol had also been discovered. It was used to remove stains, and was considered of little value – until the first petrol-driven car was developed in 1886 by the German Karl Benz.

The first nuclear power station to produce electricity was built in the USA in 1951.

Today, many alternative sources of energy are being developed – but they are not really new! The first wind engine was developed in 1850. The first commercial use of geothermal energy was in 1818. Solar energy got going in the 1950s during the space race. The power of the sea's tides was first harnessed to give electricity in 1966, by a barrage built across the River Rance in northern France.

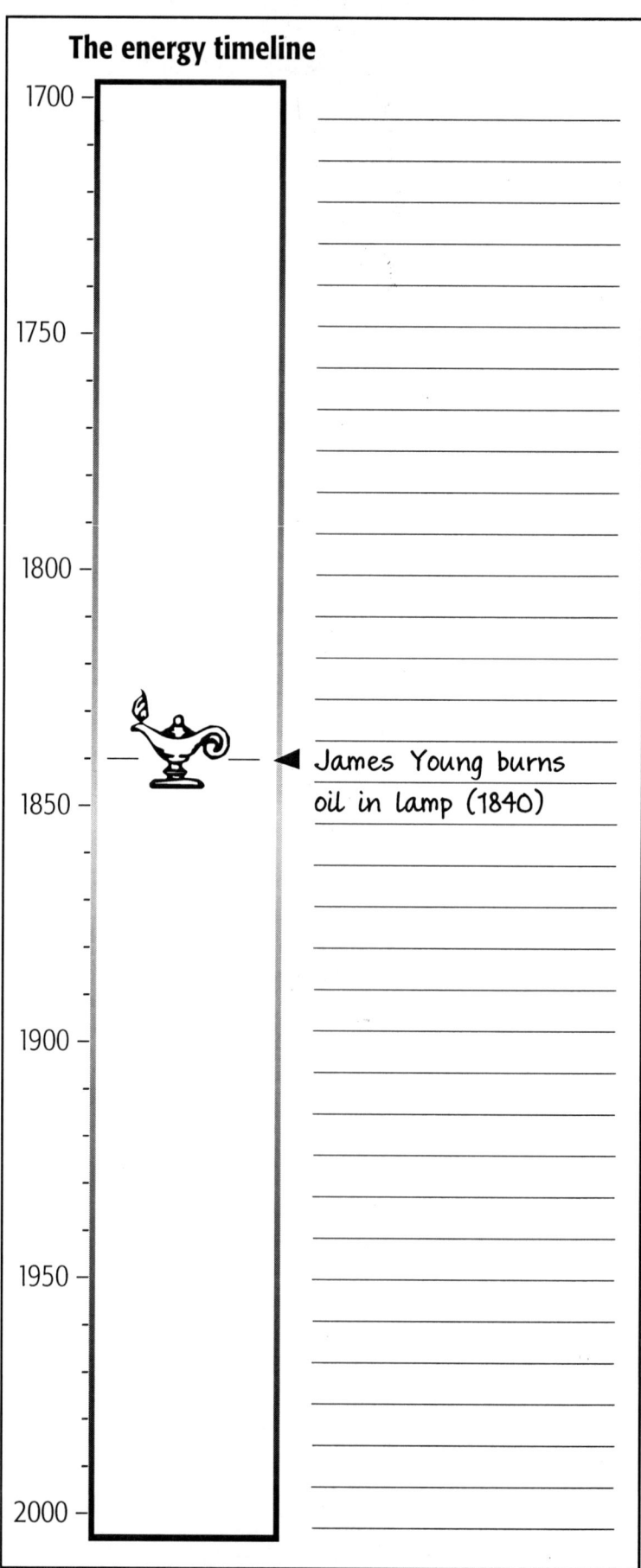

The energy timeline

1700 —

1750 —

1800 —

◄ James Young burns oil in lamp (1840)

1850 —

1900 —

1950 —

2000 —

Name   **Class**

Meet Michael! He recently had a strange dream. This is how it started:

"Help!! I woke up, and looked at the electric alarm clock. It was blank! Grabbed my watch – 8.30 – late for school. Mum, dad and my sister Claire were all still asleep.

Went to switch on the light – it didn't work! Radio dead as well. What am I going to do? The electrics don't seem to be working. No coffee or toast for breakfast. No hot water!"

Now write Michael's diary for the rest of the 'dream' day. What difficulties do you think he faced without electricity? Use the headings in the boxes to help you.

Getting to and from school
During the day at school
At home in the evening

Name   Class

1 List ways in which energy is used around your school.

for electric lights

_____   _____   _____

_____   _____   _____

_____   _____   _____

2 Now write how and where energy is wasted at school.

_____

_____

_____

3 Working in a small group, discuss your answers. Choose two main ways
in which energy is wasted in your school.

a _____   **b** _____

4 Suggest steps to prevent energy being wasted in these two ways.

a _____

_____

_____

b _____

_____

_____

Your school has written guidelines about how to make the school a safe
and attractive environment. They are called **policies**. You will have seen
notices about what to do in case of fire, for example.

5 On the back of this sheet, write an **energy policy** for your school with:

   a written guidelines on how to save and use energy sensibly

   b illustrations which reinforce your message.

You can work with your group to develop the policy.

Name   Class

This diagram explains how the world is slowly getting warmer.
Read the seven labels below and write them in the correct boxes.

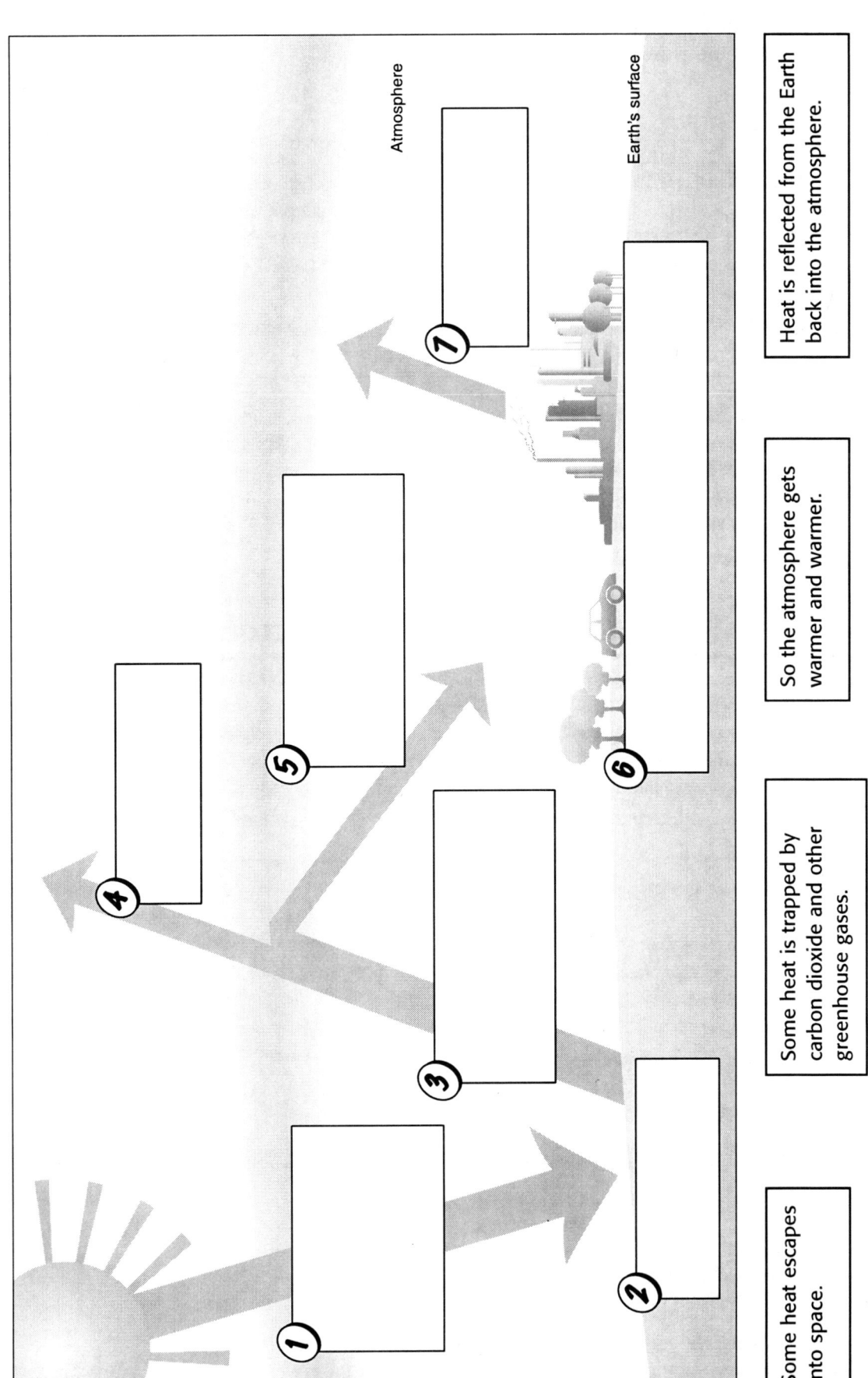

Atmosphere

Earth's surface

1

2

3

4

5

6

1

Heat is reflected from the Earth back into the atmosphere.

The sun's rays pass through the atmosphere to the Earth's surface.

So the atmosphere gets warmer and warmer.

Burning fossil fuels and removing forests increases the level of carbon dioxide.

Some heat is trapped by carbon dioxide and other greenhouse gases.

Some heat escapes into space.

The Earth's surface gets warmed.

Name   **Class**

Scientists agree that the Earth will continue to grow warmer during the 21st century.
But they do not agree about the causes, or possible effects.

Read these extracts.

A

The sun is blamed for global warming

Scientists have dismissed claims that we can halt global warming by drastically cutting our consumption of fossil fuels. New evidence has shown that the main cause of global warming is in fact the Sun.

The temperature rise, previously blamed on fossil fuels, is mainly due to an increase in the Sun's energy output. This increases periodically, making the Earth warmer. An increase of just 0.2% in solar output has the same affect as doubling the amount of carbon dioxide in the atmosphere.

B

Disaster ahead, warns UN

The United Nations has warned of global environmental disaster if rich countries do not cut back on their fossil fuel consumption. The increase in carbon dioxide from burning fossil fuels is mainly responsible for global warming. Industrialised nations such as Britain could have to cut back on their use of oil by as much as 90% to help avert catastrophic flooding and storms around the world.

C

Global warming is natural, say industrialists

An American report has concluded that global warming is almost entirely natural, and will happen anyway, no matter how little fossil fuel we burn. The amount of carbon dioxide added to the atmosphere by industry makes virtually no difference.

Environmentalists say they expected the report to reach this conclusion, since the research was paid for by American industrialists. The USA produces over 20% of the world's carbon dioxide, although it has only 5% of the world's population.

D

Global warming – cooler Britain?

Scientists in Britain are sharply divided over the possible effects of global warming on our islands. Some say that global warming will mean a rise in temperature of about 3°C by the end of the 21st century. An alternative viewpoint indicates that the opposite may happen, as the northern polar ice cap begins to melt. A vast surge of cold water from the North Pole could replace the warm North Atlantic Drift. The overall effect of this would be that temperatures in Britain could fall by 3°C.

Now answer these questions in your exercise book.

1 Summarise the viewpoint on global warming outlined in each extract.

2 Why do you think experts can't agree about the causes or effects of global warming?

3 Why might some groups of people, for example industrialists, want to argue that global warming is a natural process?

4 What is your own opinion? Do you think global warming is a major problem? Is it important to you? Who should be responsible for dealing with the problem? Justify your viewpoint.

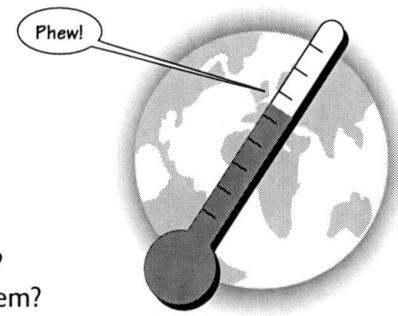

Name _____ Class _____

All of the answers to the puzzle are key words to do with energy.

1 Use the clues to complete the puzzle.

Clues

1 Using energy straight from sunlight (2 words)

2 A store of energy

3 Where the energy in almost every fuel comes from

4 Where fuel is burned to give electricity (2 words)

5 The Earth is warming up! (2 words)

6 The man who discovered electricity

7 The main polluting gas that forms when fossil fuels are burned (2 words)

8 The most important fuel in the world, at present

9 Describes electricity made in a way that does not harm the environment

Now answer these questions.

2 What word do the letters in the shaded boxes form? _____

3 What does this word mean? _____

4 Give two examples of this type of energy.

a _____ b _____

5A Energy timeline **

2
1712	steam engine;
1818	geothermal energy;
1840	distilled oil used as fuel;
1850	wind engine;
1859	first drilling for oil, kerosene marketed;
1869	hydroelectric power;
1886	first petrol-driven car;
1951	first nuclear power station;
1950s	solar power for satellites;
1966	tidal barrage.

5B What – no electricity? **

Answers will vary according to pupils' powers of imagination!

5C Does your school waste energy? **

You may need to research this one before sending the pupils out. Answers will vary according to ways of use and wastage suggested. Expect answers referring to heating, lighting, open doors, draughts, photocopiers and computers on standby, etc.

5 If possible provide pupils with examples of policies that are already in operation in the school. An anti-bullying policy is something that is of direct relevance to pupils; a policy taken from the school's staff handbook would offer a contrast.

5D What is global warming? *

1 Correct order is:

1 The sun's rays pass through the atmosphere to the Earth's surface.

2 The Earth's surface gets warmed.

3 Heat is reflected from the Earth back into the atmosphere.

4 Some heat escapes into space.

5 Some heat is trapped by carbon dioxide and other greenhouse gases.

6 Burning fossil fuels and removing forests increases the level of carbon dioxide.

7 So the atmosphere gets warmer and warmer.

5E How will global warming affect us? **

1
A The main cause of global warming is an increase in the Sun's energy output, not people.

B The richer countries must cut back on burning fossil fuels, to avoid environmental disaster.

C According to industrialists, industry is not to blame for global warming.

D Nobody really knows the effects of global warming. Some experts predict the UK will get warmer, others say it will get cooler.

2 Data has to be collected over many years to see what the trends are, and what might be causing them – and we still do not have enough data. Different experts make different assumptions, and use different computer models, to predict what will happen – and they could all be wrong. We still do not understand enough about how the atmosphere and oceans interact, for example, to creat accurate models. Some people also have vested interests in supporting certain views.

3 Relates to the final point in 2 above. For example oil companies want to keep on selling oil and petrol. Car companies want to keep on selling petrol-driven cars. Factory owners and power stations want to keep on burning oil or gas or coal in their furnaces. If it is proved beyond doubt that fossil fuels cause global warming, all these businesses will suffer.

5F An 'energetic' crossword *

1
① Solar power
② Fuel
③ Sun
④ Power station
⑤ Global warming
⑥ Faraday
⑦ Carbon dioxide
⑧ Oil
⑨ Green

2 Renewable
3 It means we will not run out of this source of energy.
4 **a, b** Choose from solar, geothermal, tidal, wind, wave, hydro, biomass, wood.

Kyoto!

***

Aims

- Pupils understand the implications of global warming for various countries of the world
- Pupils make sense of the complexities of The Kyoto Conference on Climatic Change
- Pupils appreciate the merits of the various options available

Introduction

This activity addresses Unit 14 of the QCA Scheme of Work (*Can the Earth cope? Ecosystems, population and resources*) and follows on from unit 5.6 of **geog.2** on pages 82-83.

Activity

The activity should take two lessons; one lesson for preparation and familiarization with roles, and one lesson for the simulation.

Lesson one – role development

1   Divide the class up into the following delegations:
    1   Alliance of Small Island States
    2   OPEC
    3   Large less developed countries with large populations and rapid industrial growth – China, India, Brazil, and Indonesia
    4   The least developed countries with minimal contributions to carbon dioxide emissions
    5   The European Union
    6   Australia
    7   Japan
    8   The USA

2   Issue each group with a set of group instructions (pages 167-168) and the relevant role card (pages 164-166).

3   Instruct the groups to read their role card and prepare a speech for the Conference. Each group will need to appoint a spokesperson.

Lesson two - The Kyoto Conference on Climatic Change

(In order to accommodate the role play in two lessons this activity may be started during lesson one.)

1   You should act as Chairman of the Conference. A spokesperson from each delegation should present their case and outline their proposal. Each presentation should be limited to three minutes, and two minutes should then be allowed for any questions from other delegates.

2   Voting on the proposals should then take place. Each delegation has one vote, and, in the event of a tie, the Chairman has the casting vote. Three options should be written on the board (page 163). All delegations should be encouraged to vote for one of these options, which in most cases will mean that they will almost certainly have to modify their original demands.

3   When voting is completed, the option receiving the fewest votes should be discarded and a second vote taken between the two remaining options. The option receiving the most votes will be that adopted by the whole Conference. It should be stressed that it is most important in terms of both world opinion, and future progress, that the Conference should end with a definite proposal that has been agreed by all those present.

Kyoto!

***

Between the two votes, you may wish to hold a brief debate during which representatives of the different delegations could attempt to persuade other delegations to vote for particular opinions.

Follow-up

1 The Kyoto Protocol

When the role play is completed, you should provide details of the proposals which were, in reality, adopted at The Kyoto Conference:

- Europe must, by 2010, cut carbon dioxide emissions by an average of 8%, when compared to 1990 levels
- The USA must cut emissions by 7%
- Japan must cut emissions by 6%
- Australia was regarded as a special case, and was permitted to increase emissions by 8%

No cuts were imposed on any of the other groups, but all were encouraged to make every effort to control, and, where possible, to reduce emissions. The USA was persuaded to drop its demand that cuts should be imposed on less developed countries with large industrial outputs.

During the Conference the less developed countries, known as the G-77 Group, in coalition with China, voted as a single delegation. This included the first four groups listed in the lesson one text. There were very considerable differences of opinion within this group, so it has been subdivided for this role play.

It was estimated that the cuts agreed by the Conference, once they had been ratified by individual governments and then carried out, would reduce world carbon dioxide emissions by 5.4%.

2 Problems with implementation

You may wish to discuss the problems of implementing such a major international agreement.

Despite the agreement, signed by all delegates, little progress was made towards implementation in the years following the Conference:
- Very few national governments ratified the agreement.
- There was no agreement about the most efficient method of monitoring progress by individual countries.
- There was no agreement about the nature of sanctions that could be imposed on countries that failed to carry out the terms of the agreement.
- It has proved to be very difficult to measure the precise effects of the planting of new forests – 'carbon sinks' – on carbon dioxide levels.
- The most serious blow came in 2001 when President George Bush withdrew the USA from the agreement. As yet this major problem has not been resolved during future meetings.

Evaluation

A series of questions is provided on page 168. These questions could be used either to initiate a class discussion or be completed as a homework.

Kyoto!

The proposals

It is suggested that you write these up on the board after all the delegations have finished speaking.

Proposal one

By 2010, all countries must reduce carbon dioxide emissions to a level which is 10% below the 1990 level.

Proposal two

By 2010, all developed countries (5-8 inclusive) must reduce carbon dioxide emissions to a level which is 8% below the 1990 level.

All developing countries (1-4 inclusive) must keep to present, 1995, carbon dioxide emission levels.

Proposal three

By 2010, developed countries, such as the USA, members of the EU and Japan, should reduce their carbon dioxide emissions to a level which is 7% below the 1990 level.

The developing countries must keep to present, 1995, levels and should make every effort to achieve reductions.

Countries with special needs, such as Australia, should be permitted to increase emissions slightly.

Name   **Class**

Alliance of Small Island States

The average rise in sea level during the last 100 years has been 10 to 25 cm. It's been estimated that there could be an average rise of 50 cm above present levels by 2050. In your alliance there are many low-lying coral islands, such as Tuvalu in the Pacific Ocean. Some of these islands could completely disappear, both because of rising sea levels and because coral will no longer be formed.

You want all other countries to be aware of how serious this threat is. It isn't only small islands that will suffer from sea-level rise: many continental cities and heavily populated areas are also situated on low-lying coasts. They, too, would be devastated by rising sea levels.

Your alliance urges a return to 1990 levels of carbon dioxide emissions by 2005.

Organisation of Petroleum Exporting Countries (OPEC)

You depend heavily on the export of oil. You are against any measures that would lead to the demand for oil dropping and oil prices falling. These would both happen if countries around the world had to reduce their carbon dioxide emissions. It would mean your standard of living would go down.

In particular, Kuwait and Saudi Arabia, two of the world's major oil producers, are against reducing carbon dioxide emissions. They say they would demand compensation if this happened.

You propose that oil-producing countries receive compensation for any loss of income caused by reductions in carbon emissions.

Large less developed countries: China, India, Brazil, and Indonesia

Between you, you have some of the largest and most rapidly growing populations in the world. You are trying to develop your industries quickly so you can create jobs and raise the standard of living. You think that it would be unfair if the more developed countries were to demand that you should reduce carbon dioxide emissions at this stage. These developed countries have benefited most from the high standards of living produced by industrialisation.

You agree that there is a problem, but feel strongly that the main priority is to reduce emissions in the major industrialized nations of the developed world. These countries, including the USA, Japan, and the EU are responsible for 85% of the increased carbon dioxide at present in the atmosphere.

You will not agree to reduce emissions in your own countries, and wish to continue to expand manufacturing industry. You will, however, make every effort to introduce pollution-free technology in future and reduce pollution from existing industry.

Kyoto!

Name   **Class**

The least developed countries

You have very little manufacturing industry, so are only responsible for a tiny amount of the world's carbon dioxide emissions. However, you're extremely concerned about global warming and its likely environmental effects.

The countries of sub-Saharan Africa (countries south of the Sahara, including Chad, Niger, and Sudan), are worried about increasing drought and desertification (the spread of deserts). These things are a result of global warming. Also, countries like Bangladesh are very low-lying and feel that any rise in sea level would be disastrous for them.

You think that the major producers of carbon dioxide emissions should reduce their emissions by moving factories to less developed countries. Alternatively, they should pay you compensation.

You propose a reduction of carbon dioxide emissions to 35% below 1990 levels by the year 2020. If developed countries do not reach this target, they should pay compensation to less developed countries.

The European Union

Climatic change is taken very seriously in the EU, particularly in Germany, France, The Netherlands and Scandinavia, where Green Parties are strong. Many low-lying parts of the EU are already at risk from flooding. Also, high pollution levels are causing environmental damage, such as damage to the ozone layer and destruction of forests by acid rain.

You think that all industrial countries should reduce carbon dioxide emissions immediately. You hope that industrial countries elsewhere, such as Japan and the USA, will agree to this. If they fail to do so, it could put your industries at a disadvantage. They would be forced to install expensive new technology designed to reduce carbon dioxide emissions.

You propose a 15% reduction of emissions of greenhouse gases to 1990 levels by the year 2010. All industrial countries should reduce their emissions starting from now. However, the EU would be reluctant to reduce emissions by as much as this unless other major industrial countries, such as the USA and Japan, reduce them by similar amounts. If the EU acted alone it could make its industries uncompetitive in world markets.

geog.2: 5 Energy: a key resource

Australia

You specialize in the production of energy. You are the world's biggest exporter of coal and rely heavily on this fuel for domestic energy. You also depend heavily on the export of manufactured goods such as high-quality steels, the production of which produces high levels of carbon dioxide emissions.

Australia makes a lot of money by exporting coal. It also relies on coal for domestic energy. It has a small population for its size and so features quite highly on the amount of CO_2 production per head. A big reduction in emission levels would have a devastating effect on Australia.

You feel that you are a special case and that you should be allowed some increase in carbon dioxide emissions in the future. You feel that different countries have different circumstances and different abilities to make carbon dioxide emission reductions. Each developed country should set a different target.

Japan

You have very few natural resources. You have to import most of the raw materials and a lot of the fuel that you use. A network of 52 nuclear power stations now provides a high proportion of your energy.

Although there is still environmental pollution from heavy industry, you feel that you are an efficient user of energy. You think the potential for the future reduction of carbon dioxide emissions is small.

You resent accusations that your policies have not always been seen as friendly to the environment. You are keen to see a reduction in world carbon dioxide emissions.

You feel there should be an overall, world, reduction of 5% in carbon dioxide emissions by 2012. However, as you're already very efficient, you think there should be some exemptions. You propose a target of only a 2% reduction for Japan, as compared to 1990 levels, by 2012.

The USA

You are, at present, the world's greatest producer of carbon dioxide emissions. However, you're not convinced that this is causing much harm to the environment. You worry that if you have to cut your carbon dioxide emissions it might harm your economy.

You feel strongly that any agreement made should apply to all countries. If you have to reduce emissions, you think that the larger developing countries should have to too. These countries increased their emissions by 25% between 1990 and 1995 and may contribute as much as 50% of total world emissions by 2010.

As a world leader you would like to be able to sign any agreement. However, you will not sign anything that will damage American industry. You will only sign if the target date is a long way ahead and if all countries are involved in the reductions. You would also like to trade off increased carbon dioxide emissions by industry against the growth of forests that absorb more carbon dioxide.

Kyoto!

Name   **Class**

Group instructions

In this activity you will be holding a conference to decide what to do about climate change. Between you, you need to try to come to an agreement about how to cut carbon dioxide emissions.

The class will be divided into the following groups:
1   Alliance of Small Island States
2   OPEC (The Organization of Petroleum Exporting Countries)
3   Large less developed countries: China, India, Brazil, and Indonesia
4   The least developed countries
5   The European Union (EU)
6   Australia
7   Japan
8   The USA

Each group will want different things.

1   Read the background information about climate change in the box below.

Background information

The world is warming up. Graph A shows that the average temperature around the world has been increasing.

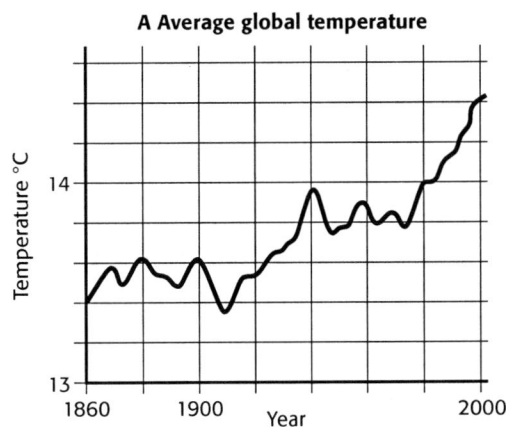

A Average global temperature

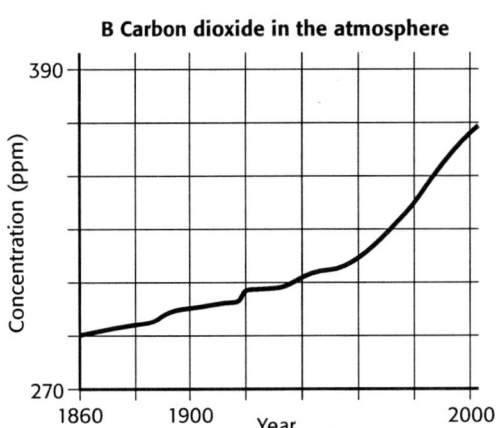

B Carbon dioxide in the atmosphere

Why is this happening? Well the major culprit is carbon dioxide. It's called a greenhouse gas because it traps heat in the Earth's atmosphere. The problem is that we keep burning fossil fuels and, when this happens, more and more carbon dioxide is released into the atmosphere (see Graph B). The result – **global warming**.

Scientists have made many predictions about how global warming will affect us. They include:

■   the polar ice caps will melt, so sea levels will rise
■   islands and low-lying coasts will disappear below the sea
■   climates around the world will change
■   crops and pasture will be ruined by climate change, which could result in famine
■   species of plants and animals that cannot adapt to the climate change will die out. Already coral reefs throughout the world are dying out, largely because of warmer seas created by global warming. As climates become warmer, pests and diseases will spread to new areas.

---

geog.2: 5 Energy: a key resource

2   Read the role card for your group.

3   Between you, write a speech to be given at **The Kyoto Conference on Climatic Change**. (Your speech should last about 3 minutes.)

4   Choose a spokesperson for your group. They will be responsible for speaking at the Conference on behalf of your country or group of countries.

5   Your spokesperson will deliver your speech at the Conference and answer any questions from other delegations.

6   After all the delegations have spoken, it will be time to vote. Firstly, you will have to choose from a list of three proposals. The proposal receiving the fewest votes will be discarded. Then you will have to vote again for one of the remaining two proposals.

It is unlikely that the demands that your delegation has made will be completely met by any one of the proposals. So you will need to compromise!

7   Between the two votes, you may wish to talk to other delegations, attempting to persuade them to vote for a particular opinion. At the actual Conference in 1995, different delegations argued for many hours before an agreement was reached!

Note: It is most important that every delegation should vote for one of the proposals during each voting session. This will show world opinion that some progress has been made, and may open the door to further improvements at future conferences.

Evaluation

After the role play has been completed, your teacher will outline the actual agreement which was signed as the Kyoto Protocol in 1995.

1   **a** How far did the actual agreement satisfy the needs of the country, or group of countries, which you represented?
   b Do you think the outcome of the Conference was satisfactory?
   c Do you think that it will have any real impact on carbon dioxide emissions and the problem of global warming?

2   **a** How close was the actual agreement to the final proposal voted for by the delegates at your conference?
   b What are the problems in reaching a sensible agreement when a large number of delegates are present? (There were 174 countries at the 1995 Conference!)

3   **a** What are some of the problems that might arise when countries attempt to carry out the proposals that have been voted for?
   b Is there any way of checking that individual countries are implementing the proposals?
   c How can countries that fail to carry out the terms of the agreement be punished?

Windfarm

***

Aims

- Pupils are able to carry out a geographical enquiry into resource planning and management
- Pupils understand how different groups of people in the area are affected
- Pupils are able to explain how and why people attempt to manage environments
- Pupils are able to deliver and argue a case in a public enquiry

Introduction

This activity provides extension material for chapter 5 'Energy: a key resource' in **geog.2**. It addresses Unit 14 of the QCA Scheme of Work (*How can a resource be planned and managed?*).

The activity is in three parts. In part one pupils will carry out a series of tasks to familiarise themselves with the subject matter and plan their debate. Part two is a public enquiry. Pupils will take on the role of interested parties to discuss the planning application for a windfarm. In part three pupils will write a newspaper article reporting on the public enquiry.

This activity could be carried out over three lessons, or two lessons and a homework.

Resources needed:

Lesson one:
- Pre-prepared packs for each group, containing slightly different information. Each pack will consist of:
  - information sheet 1 (page 171) - which is the same for each group
  - map of the area (page 172)
  - two other sheets specifically labelled for that group (pages 173-184)
  - developing your argument sheet - which is the same for each group (page 185). 'Advice about drawing cross sections will be useful to two groups – The St Wenn Parish Residents' Association and the local environmentalists.
- Each pack in a labelled folder.

Lesson two:
- Pre-prepared classroom, maybe with rules on the board, scrap paper and pens on five desks, a space at the front for each group to move into when they make their speeches, even a banner!
- Sticky labels for pupils to write their character names on and stick on their tops if they wish.

Lesson three or homework:
- Writing frames if you want to use them (pages 186-187).
- ICT facilities if you wish, or plain and lined paper instead.

Windfarm

***

Activity

Lesson one – familiarisation with roles

1 Discuss renewable energy and wind power as a whole class.

2 Divide the class into groups of 3-5 pupils, depending on the size of the class. Assign each group a role from the following list:

- Residents of Higher Ball Farm
- Cornwall Archaeological Unit
- WindWatts Ltd. - the company which wants to develop the windfarm
- St. Wenn Parish Residents' Association
- Local environmentalists
- Representatives for the Ministry of the Environment

In a mixed-ability class, the roles could be assigned on an ability basis. The harder characters to work on are the local environmentalists and WindWatts. Easier characters are local residents and the Ministry of the Environment.

3 Issue each group with a pre-prepared information pack.

4 Tell the class how long they have to complete the series of tasks on their instruction sheets. These will help them to develop their case for the public enquiry.

Lesson two – public enquiry

In the second lesson the whole class will debate the issues and come to a decision.

1 Start by lining up the class outside the classroom and telling them that when they enter they will be in character, and that the room is the Parish Hall in St. Wenn. They will need to group themselves into their roles before they go in.

2 When they enter they should sit in their groups around desks. Each group will need their notes and scrap paper and a pencil to jot down any points raised by other groups. These could have been laid out beforehand.

3 Introduce yourself as the Chairperson for the meeting and welcome the interested parties. You will need to remind them of the rules (these could be written on the board beforehand). Suggested rules are:
- no talking unless given permission by the Chairperson
- no rudeness to other groups
- each group has a turn to speak uninterrupted before questions are asked
- hands up if they want to ask a question.

4 Call on WindWatts to outline the plan for the windfarm. Do not let the other groups ask WindWatts any questions yet, or it will descend into a brawl!

5 Then call on the other groups to speak, in any order. They may be asked questions at the end of their speeches, as may all the other groups if a point is raised. WindWatts may be asked questions by the other groups during these slots.

6 At the end there will be a vote, in role, for or against the windfarm, but WindWatts may not vote!

Lesson three – report on public enquiry

Instruct pupils to prepare an article reporting on the public enquiry for a local newspaper. This could be a third lesson or a homework. It could be word-processed, written using a desktop publishing package, or use pages 186-187.

Windfarm

Name   **Class**

Information sheet 1

> PUBLIC ENQUIRY
> **ST. WENN PARISH HALL**
> TO DISCUSS THE PROPOSED
> WINDFARM ON
> ST. BREOCK DOWNS

A planning application has been made to develop a windfarm near Wadebridge in Cornwall. Whenever a planning application is made for a big project there is a public meeting where people can give their views. After this it is decided whether or not the development can go ahead.

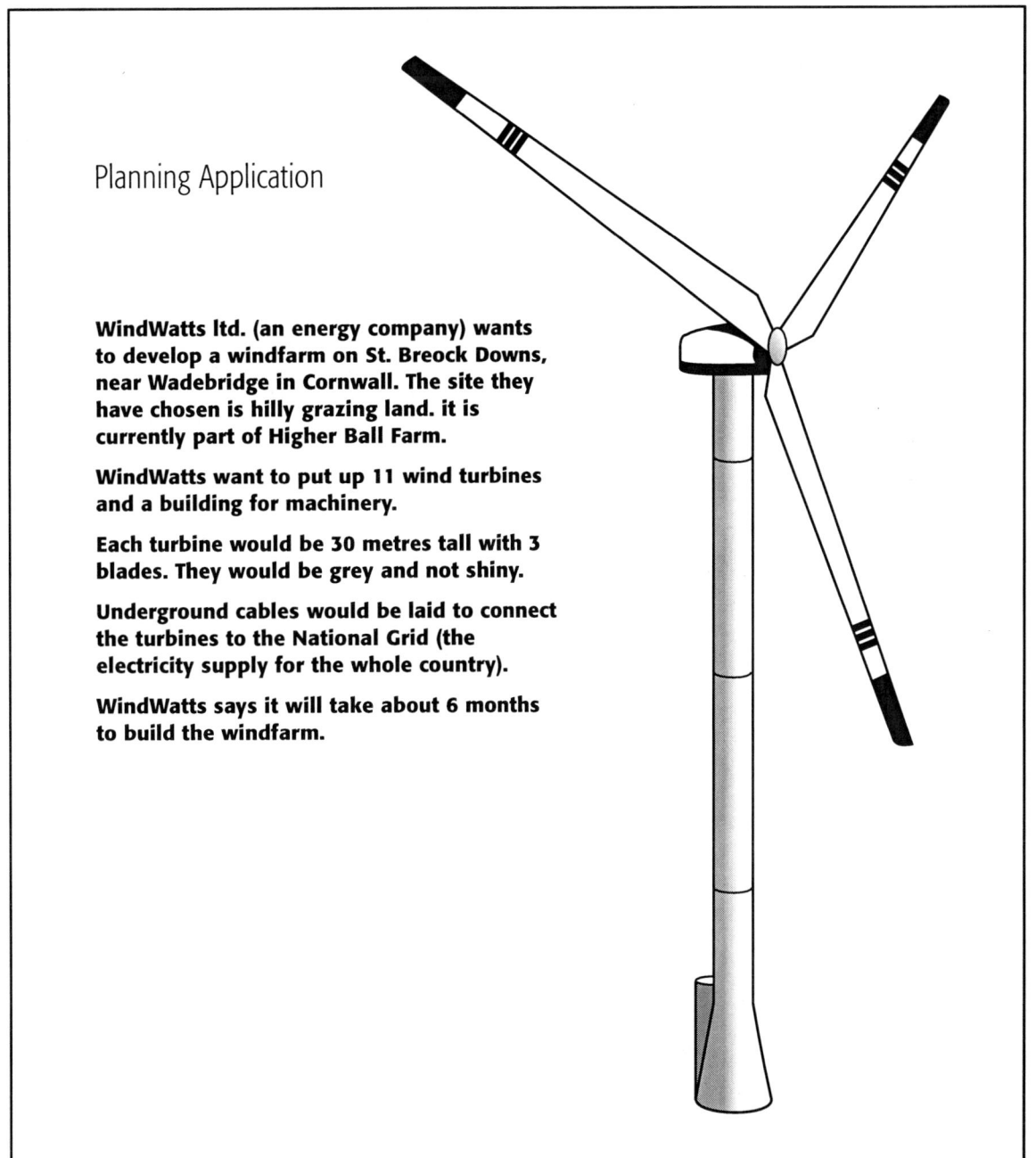

Planning Application

WindWatts ltd. (an energy company) wants to develop a windfarm on St. Breock Downs, near Wadebridge in Cornwall. The site they have chosen is hilly grazing land. it is currently part of Higher Ball Farm.

WindWatts want to put up 11 wind turbines and a building for machinery.

Each turbine would be 30 metres tall with 3 blades. They would be grey and not shiny.

Underground cables would be laid to connect the turbines to the National Grid (the electricity supply for the whole country).

WindWatts says it will take about 6 months to build the windfarm.

     geog.2: 5 Energy: a key resource

Name   Class

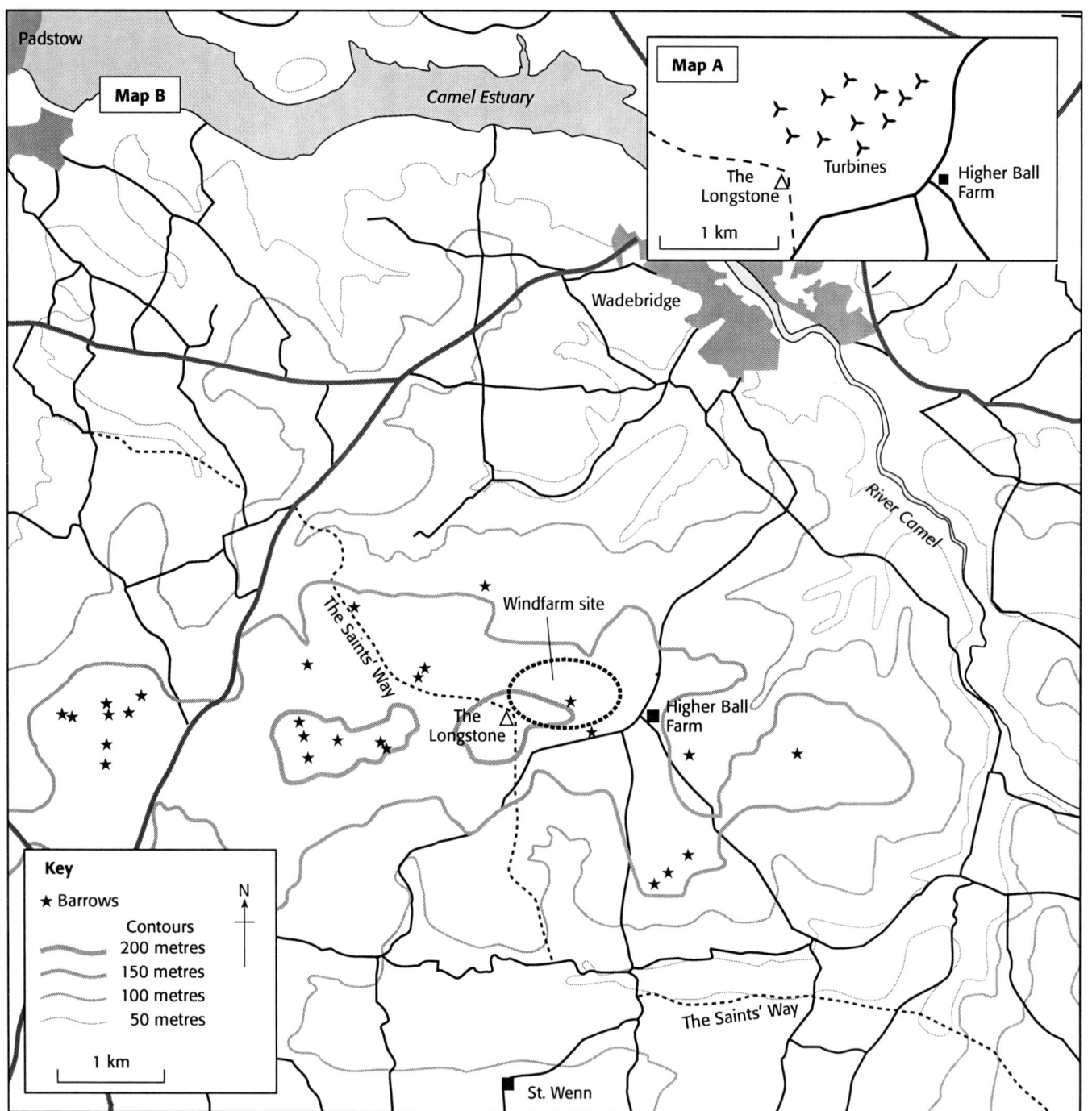

Map B

Padstow

Camel Estuary

Wadebridge

River Camel

The Saints' Way

Windfarm site

The Longstone

Higher Ball Farm

The Saints' Way

St. Wenn

Map A

Turbines

The Longstone

Higher Ball Farm

1 km

Key

★ Barrows

N

Contours
200 metres
150 metres
100 metres
50 metres

1 km

Name   Class

Information sheet 2 for the residents of Higher Ball Farm

Here is some information that you will find useful when preparing your debate.

What is a windfarm?

Most scientists agree that using fossil fuels is causing global warming. We need more sustainable ways to get energy. Wind is one way. We can put wind turbines in windy areas. The wind turns the turbine and this generates electricity. A wind farm is an area with lots of these turbines in it.

Traffic

The roads near the site are minor roads, so they're very narrow. You already have problems driving big farm machinery down these roads. The company say there will be two cranes and 12-15 other vehicles at the site whilst the windfarm is being built. Afterwards there will be the cars of the people who work there.

Leasing the land

You own the land that WindWatts want to build a windfarm on. At the moment you use it to graze cows. The government is trying to encourage farmers to use some of their land for other things, because we are producing too much food. You could make more money by leasing some of your land to the wind turbine company (£1000–£2000 per year, per turbine).

Noise

Wind turbines make a humming noise when they spin. The present noise level at the farm (from wind and local traffic) is 32 decibels. Noise levels are expected to go up to about 35-45 decibels when the windfarm is built. People living near other windfarm sites have found the constant noise irritating. You worry it will disturb both you and your animals.

TV and radio

Windfarms can disrupt TV and radio receptions. In other places where windfarms have been built, residents living up to 10 km away have had reception problems.

Employment

The wind turbine company, WindWatts, claim that 20 people will be needed to help build the windfarm. Afterwards 10 people will be needed to run it. Jobs are hard to find in this area and this could benefit your family.

Windfarm

***

Name _____   Class _____

Instruction sheet for the residents of Higher Ball Farm

These tasks will help you to develop your argument for the public enquiry.
Cross off each task as you complete it. Your teacher will tell you what time you
need to have finished by.

1 Write the names of the pupils in your group here: _____

_____

2 Write the time you need to have finished these tasks by here: _____

3 Read Information sheet 1 and look at the map.

4 What do you use the land for at the moment? _____

5 How many turbines do WindWatts want to build? _____

6 What would the turbines look like? _____

_____

7 What feelings do you have about the appearance of the windfarm? _____

_____

8 Use the map to work out how far the nearest wind turbine is from your farm. _____

9 How long do WindWatts say the building work will take? _____

10 Read Information sheet 2.

11 What problems could the traffic cause?
Complete this brainstorm together.

12 What problems might the noise from the windfarm cause?

_____

13 Are there any other problems the windfarm might cause? _____

_____

14 What positive things could the windfarm bring for you? _____

_____

15 Now you are going to develop your argument. You should use the
'Developing your argument' sheet.

geog.2: 5 Energy: a key resource

Name   **Class**

Information sheet 2 for the St. Wenn Residents' Association

Here is some information that you will find useful when preparing your debate.

What is a windfarm?

Most scientists agree that using fossil fuels is causing global warming. We need more sustainable ways to get energy. Wind is one way. We can put wind turbines in windy areas. The wind turns the turbine and this generates electricity. A windfarm is an area with lots of these turbines in it.

Traffic

The roads near the site are minor roads, so they're very narrow. The company say there will be two cranes and 12-15 other vehicles at the site whilst the windfarm is being built. Afterwards there will be the cars of the people who work there. The route for traffic will be through St. Wenn then north towards Higher Ball Farm, turning left just before the farm.

The view from your village

The site is an Area of Great Landscape Value (AGLV). This means that it is recognised by the government as a beautiful natural area. There are hedges, woods, and a few scattered traditional buildings.

Each wind turbine would be the size of a 10-storey office block. It's possible that having a windfarm within view of the village could lower property values.

Economy

Tourists bring a lot of money into Cornwall. In this area many people come to enjoy the peaceful countryside and see some of the ancient sites. Some tourists might think the windfarm is noisy and ugly and stop coming to the area. Other tourists might come especially to see the windfarm.

TV and radio

Windfarms can disrupt TV and radio receptions. In other places where windfarms have been built, residents living up to 10 km away have had reception problems.

Employment

The wind turbine company, WindWatts, claim that 20 people will be needed to help build the windfarm. Afterwards 10 people will be needed to run it. Unemployment has been a problem in this area for some time.

geog.2: 5 Energy: a key resource

Windfarm

***

Instruction sheet for the St. Wenn Residents' Association

These tasks will help you to develop your argument for the public enquiry.
Cross off each task as you complete it. Your teacher will tell you what time you
need to have finished by.

1   Write the names of the pupils in your group here: _____

   _____

2   Write the time you need to have finished these tasks by here: _____

3   Read Information sheet 1 and look at the map.

4   What is the land being used for at the moment? _____

5   How many turbines will there be? _____

6   Use the map to work out how far the windfarm will be from your village. _____

7   Are there any slopes or hills between your village and the windfarm that
   would hide it from your view?
   (Hint: use the contour lines.)_____

   _____

8   Read Information sheet 2.

9   Use the map to work out the route that the vehicles will take.
   Draw it on your map.

10   What problems could the traffic cause?
   Complete this brainstorm together.

11   What does your view of the site from the
   village look like now?

   _____

   _____

12   What feelings would you have about the appearance of the windfarm? _____

   _____

13   What positive things could the windfarm bring for you? _____

   _____

14   Now you are going to develop your argument. You should use the
   'Developing your argument' sheet.

Name   **Class**

Information sheet 2 for Cornwall Archaeology Unit and English Heritage

Here is some information that you will find useful when preparing your debate.

> Cornwall Archaeology Unit is a group interested in finding out about and preserving ancient sites. English Heritage is another group that protects historic places for the public. You are working together in this debate as you have similar opinions.

What is a windfarm?

Most scientists agree that using fossil fuels is causing global warming. We need more sustainable ways to get energy. Wind is one way. We can put wind turbines in windy areas. The wind turns the turbine and this generates electricity. A windfarm is an area with lots of these turbines in it.

Nearby historic sites

A small part of the site proposed for the windfarm is in an Area of Great Historic Value (AGHV). Nothing of historic interest has been found on the site itself but nearby are:

▪ 'The St. Breock Downs Monolith' – an upright stone put there by Bronze Age people
▪ barrows (old burial mounds)
▪ 'The Longstone', a standing stone that was used as a meeting place for villagers in the Middle Ages.

Also, you think there may be a Neolithic tomb in the area but you haven't found it yet.

Many tourists come to see these ancient sites. In the future the windfarm could be part of the landscape and would be visible from any of the ancient sites.

The Saints' Way

This is an ancient route that pilgrims from Ireland and Wales travelled in the centuries before the Normans came to England. This route is now part of the road to the south of the windfarm.

Windfarm

***

Name _____   **Class** _____

Instruction sheet for Cornwall Archaeology Unit and English Heritage

These tasks will help you to develop your argument for the public enquiry.
Cross off each task as you complete it. Your teacher will tell you what time you
need to have finished by.

1   Write the names of the pupils in your group here: _____

_____

2   Write the time you need to have finished these tasks by here: _____

3   Read Information sheet 1.

4   What is the land being used for at the moment? _____

5   How many turbines will there be? _____

6   Read Information sheet 2 and look at the map.

7   How close is the nearest turbine to The Longstone? _____

8   Highlight all the barrows and The Saints' Way on your copy of the map.

9   What will the turbines look like from The Longstone? _____

_____

10 WindWatts have argued that the
wind turbines will add to the look
of the area because they are elegant.
They say they are a part of the
continuation of history. Fill in all the
good and bad points about the
windfarm being near these historic
sites on this brainstorm. Write the
good points in red and the bad
points in black.

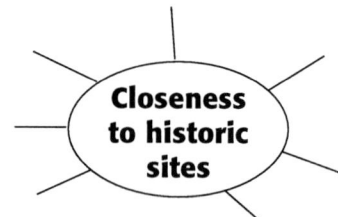

11 The area has already been affected
by modern life. What modern things
would there be in this area?
(Think about tarmac roads, buildings…) _____

_____

_____

12 Now you are going to develop your argument. You should use the
'Developing your argument' sheet.

Information sheet 2 for local environmentalists

Here is some information that you will find useful when preparing your debate.

What is a windfarm?

Most scientists agree that using fossil fuels is causing global warming. We need more sustainable ways to get energy. Wind is one way. We can put wind turbines in windy areas. The wind turns the turbine and this generates electricity. A windfarm is an area with lots of these turbines in it.

Natural views

The site is an Area of Great Landscape Value (AGLV). This means that it is recognised by the government as a beautiful natural area. There are hedges, woods, and a few scattered traditional buildings. Near the site is the Camel Estuary Special Area of Great Landscape Value.

The Saints' Way

This is an ancient route that pilgrims from Ireland and Wales travelled in the centuries before the Normans came to England. This route is now part of the road to the south of the windfarm.

Environmental benefits

Burning fossil fuels to make electricity is causing global warming.
This means sea levels will rise, some areas will flood, our climate will change - and these are just some of the problems!

Windfarms don't cause global warming – no fossil fuels are burnt. Over its lifetime, WindWatts estimate that the windfarm will save 11 745 tonnes of coal. It will make enough electricity for 2500 houses.

Wildlife

Migrating birds like strong winds. Windfarms are built in the windiest places. The fast-moving blades would kill any bird that flew into them.

Traffic

The roads near the site are minor roads so are very narrow. During the construction period there will be 12-15 vehicles a day at the site, as well as two cranes. Afterwards, there will be the cars of the people working there. The route for traffic will be through St. Wenn, then north towards Higher Ball Farm, turning left just before the farm.

Noise

The company has worked out how much noise similar turbines make. The noise at Higher Ball Farm is expected to be a continual hum at about 35–45 decibels. The present noise level at the farm is 32 decibels.

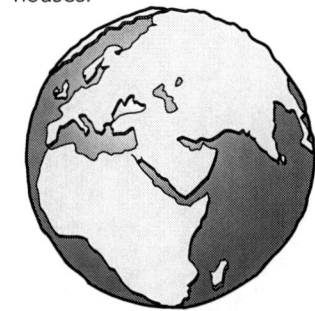

Windfarm
***

Name   Class

Instruction sheet for local environmentalists

These tasks will help you to develop your argument for the public enquiry.
Cross off each task as you complete it. Your teacher will tell you what time you
need to have finished by.

1 Write the names of the pupils in your group here: _____

_____

2 Write the time you need to have finished these tasks by here: _____

3 Read Information sheet 1 and look at the map.

4 What is the land being used for at the moment? _____

5 How many turbines will there be? _____

6 You like to walk along The Saints' Way path. Mark this on the map.

7 What would your feelings be about the windfarm when you are walking

along The Saints' Way? _____

_____

8 You're keen to protect the Camel Estuary Special Area of Great Landscape
Value. How far is this from the windfarm? (measure in a straight line from

the nearest turbine) _____

9 Are there any slopes or hills that will hide the turbines from view at the

Camel Estuary? (Hint: use the contour lines) _____

10 What would the turbines look like from the Camel Estuary? _____

_____

11 Read Information sheet 2.

12 Use the map to work out the route that the vehicles will take. Draw it on your map.

13 You are concerned about your local area,
but also about the whole environment.
What things will happen if we continue to
rely on fossil fuels.
Complete this brainstorm together.

Using
fossil fuels

14 How could the windfarm help to stop global warming? _____

_____

15 Now you are going to develop your argument. You should use the
'Developing your argument' sheet.

Information sheet 2 for WindWatts Ltd

Here is some information that you will find useful when preparing your debate.

What is a windfarm?

Most scientists agree that using fossil fuels is causing global warming. We need more sustainable ways to get energy. Wind is one way. We can put wind turbines in windy areas. The wind turns the turbine and this generates electricity. A windfarm is an area with lots of these turbines in it.

Environmental benefits

Over its lifetime the windfarm will make enough electricity for 2500 houses. WindWatts estimate that it will save 11 745 tonnes of coal. Carbon dioxide from burning coal and other fossil fuels is causing serious problems for the environment. Wind power doesn't give off any gases – nothing gets burned.

Wildlife

A small number of birds have been injured by wind turbines. There is some evidence that the noise from the turbines may scare many birds away.

Noise

Modern wind turbines are designed to be quiet. They can't be heard more than 350 m away. At other windfarms the noise hasn't disturbed farm animals.

On some of the older windfarms noise has been a big problem. Some people are against windfarms because of this. To keep people happy you could put up a screen of trees to block all noise. You don't think this is necessary so don't offer to do this unless you are forced to.

Economy

The windfarm will create jobs – 20 whilst it is being built, and 10 to run it.

Cornwall spends the same amount importing energy as it earns from tourism. It can save money by making some of its own energy.

Traffic

The roads near the site are minor roads so are very narrow. During the construction period there will 12-15 vehicles a day at the site, as well as 2 cranes. Afterwards there will be the cars of the people working there.

The route for traffic will be through St. Wenn, then north towards Higher Ball Farm, turning left just before the farm.

The site for the windfarm

For a windfarm you need lots of wind, so it has to be built on high ground. This site is the windiest in this part of Cornwall.

A small part of the site is in an Area of Great Historic Value (AGHV). WindWatts will work with local archaeologists and English Heritage to make sure that no ancient sites are damaged by the windfarm.

TV and radio

At some windfarms people living nearby have had problems with their TV and radio receptions. At St. Breock Downs you intend to use modern turbines, made from fibre glass. These turbines are designed to cut down on interference with TV and radio receptions.

The area doesn't look like it did in the past because of modern buildings and roads. Wind turbines are elegant and look dramatic so you feel they would blend in with the landscape well. They may even attract tourists.

Name   **Class**

Instruction sheet for WindWatts Ltd

These tasks will help you to develop your argument for the public enquiry.
Cross off each task as you complete it. Your teacher will tell you what time you
need to have finished by.

1   Write the names of the pupils in your group here: _____

_____

2   Write the time you need to have finished these tasks by here: _____

3   Read Information sheet 1.

4   What is the land being used for at the moment? _____

5   How many turbines will there be? _____

6   What will they look like? _____

_____

7   Read Information sheet 2.

8   Why did you choose this site?_____

_____

9   Why are windfarms good for the environment?_____

_____

10   What benefits could the windfarm
have for the local area? Fill in this
brainstorm together.

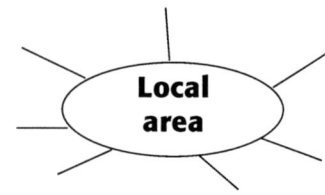

11   How are you trying to prevent noise problems? _____

_____

12   Work out how close the nearest turbine is to Higher Ball Farm (the nearest

building to the site). Will the residents of the farm be able to hear the turbines? _____

13   Some people will say that your windfarm will spoil the landscape. What features

of the turbines add to the landscape value of an area? _____

14   There are many historical sites in this area, but is the area just like it was in the Bronze Age?

_____

15   Now you are going to develop your argument. You should use the
'Developing your argument' sheet.

Name   **Class**

Information sheet 2 for the Ministry of the Environment

Here is some information that you will find useful when preparing your debate.

What is a windfarm?

Most scientists agree that using fossil fuels is causing global warming. We need more sustainable ways to get energy. Wind is one way. We can put wind turbines in windy areas. The wind turns the turbine and this generates electricity. A windfarm is an area with lots of these turbines in it.

Global warming

When fossil fuels like coal, oil, and gas are burnt, they release carbon dioxide. This goes into the atmosphere and traps heat. The atmosphere gets warmer – we get global warming. This means:

- the polar ice caps will melt so sea levels will rise around the world.
- coastal areas will get flooded. This could include parts of East Anglia, London, Essex, and the North East, in Britain.
- climates will change so crops won't be able to be grown where they are now, causing problems with food supply. This could affect Britain.
- there will be more storms and perhaps even more droughts, in Britain.
- tropical diseases will spread to Britain.

Greenhouse gases are causing serious problems for the environment and, if we want to reduce these, people need to use alternative sources of energy. Wind power doesn't give off any gases.

Acid rain

All rain is slightly acidic. But sulphur dioxide and nitrogen oxides react with rain to make it much more acidic. This acid rain attacks buildings and metal structures such as bridges and railings. It releases aluminium from the soil and this can kill plants and trees. Some forests in places like Scandinavia have been destroyed by acid rain. It can get carried into rivers and lakes and poison fish. All this damage can cost a great deal of money.

Wind power does not give off any gases that can lead to acid rain.

Government policy

The government has signed treaties to reduce greenhouse gas emissions and acid rain. They want people to use renewable sources of energy like wind, solar, and wave power.

Over its lifetime, WindWatts estimate that the windfarm will save 11 745 tonnes of coal. It will make enough electricity to supply 2500 houses.

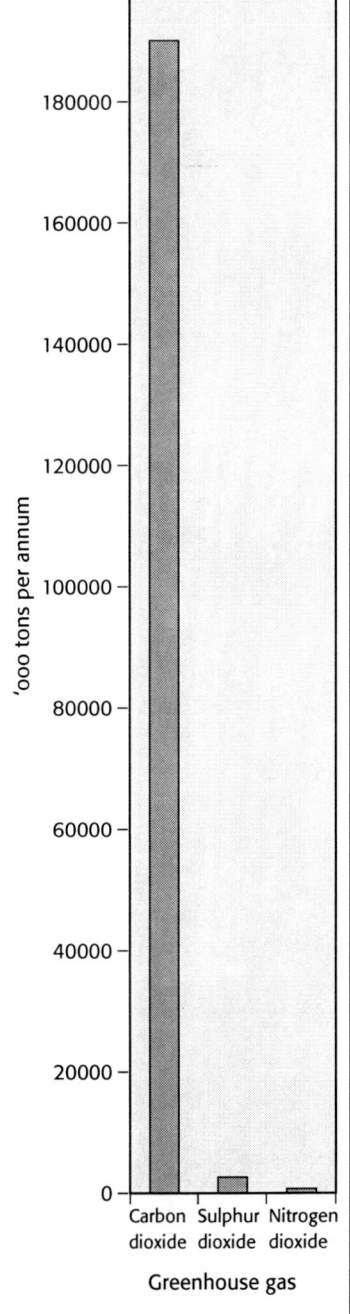

This graph shows how much of each gas comes from British power stations using fossil fuels.

Greenhouse gas (Carbon dioxide, Sulphur dioxide, Nitrogen dioxide)
'ooo tons per annum

Windfarm

***

Name   Class

Instruction sheet for the Ministry of the Environment

These tasks will help you to develop your argument for the public enquiry.
Cross off each task as you complete it. Your teacher will tell you what time you
need to have finished by.

1   Write the names of the pupils in your group here: _____

_____

2   Write the time you need to have finished these tasks by here: _____

3   Read Information sheet 1.

4   What type of energy will be used to make electricity here?_____

5   Read Information sheet 2.

6   Name three fossil fuels. _____

7   Why does burning fossil fuels lead to global warming (also called the

greenhouse effect)? _____

8   What things might happen because
of global warming? Fill in this
brainstorm together.

9   How much of each gas is released
by British power stations using fossil

fuels each year?_____

_____

10 How can using wind power reduce this? _____

_____

11 What is acid rain? _____

_____

12 Why is it bad? _____

_____

13 How can using wind power reduce it? _____

_____

14 Now you are going to develop your argument. You should use the
'Developing your argument' sheet.

Name   Class

Developing your argument

This writing frame will help you to develop your argument for the public enquiry. When it is complete, work out who is going to say what and practice making your speeches.

When people ask you questions during the public meeting you will need to think on your feet. Use the information sheets to help you with your answers.

We are: (fill in your character role here)
We are interested in the windfarm debate because:
We would like to make these points at this meeting: (make a list of your points)
Point 1 (in these boxes expand your arguments for each point, you might not need every box)
Point 2
Point 3
Point 4
Point 5
We would like to summarise our argument as:
Questions we want to ask the other groups: Group to ask   Question   Answer given

Windfarm

Name   **Class**

Writing frame

Now you are going to write a newspaper report about the public enquiry. First complete the tasks below. They will help you to sort out what information you need for your report.

1   Think of a headline and write it here

2   Write today's date here _____

3   Write the date that the class did the debate here _____

4   Fill in this box to say what the meeting was all about.

The meeting was about a proposed windfarm. A windfarm is _____

_____

_____

A company called WindWatts want to _____

_____

_____

5   In this box write down all the groups and what their feelings were about the windfarm.

Groups	Feelings about the windfarm
Residents of Higher Ball Farm	
St. Wenn Parish Residents' Association	
Cornwall Archaeology Unit and English Heritage	
Local environmentalists	
Ministry of the Environment	

6   At the end of the debate you had a vote. Write the result in this box.

***

Name   **Class**

7   Now you are going to make your neat report. You will need to use all the
information you have written onto this writing frame and put it into a
format like this one:

Today's date

Headline

There was a public meeting at St. Wenn Parish Hall on (write the date of the meeting here). The meeting was about…	The people at the meeting were…
	(write about the feelings of the groups here).
	If you have time and space you could put a picture of one of the characters here.
Maybe you could put a map of the site or a diagram of a turbine here.	
	There was a vote after the meeting. The result was…

geog.2: 5 Energy: a key resource

Energy: a key resource

The assessment opportunities for Energy: a key resource are as follows:

▮ The **level-marked assessment** 'Does global warming really matter?' on pages 189-191.

In this assessment pupils need to consider the causes and effects of global warming. They are presented with a series of conflicting viewpoints, which they need to evaluate, drawing on their prior knowledge and understanding of the topic. As a conclusion, pupils need to think about possible positive, as well as negative consequences of global warming.

A **feedback form** for the level-marked assessment is provided on page 192.

▮ The **scored test** on pages 193-196.

▮ Opportunities for interim assessments provided by **geog.2**:

Kyoto! (a role play, with the opportunity or pupils to work in groups) on pages 161-168 of this file.

Windfarm (a public enquiry role play, with the opportunity for pupils to work in groups) on pages 169-187 of this file.

Activities 9, 11, 13, 14, 15, 16, 20, 25, 27, 29, 32, 35, and 37 in the *Further suggestions for class and homework* section on pages 114-115 of the *geog.2 teacher's handbook*.

Worksheet A: Front page news for *The Piper Alpha disaster* (a webfile) in *geog.2, Energy: a key resource* on *geog.world*.

Worksheet B: UK oil refineries for *The Piper Alpha disaster* (a webfile) in *geog.2, Energy: a key resource* on *geog.world*.

▮ The **self-assessment form** for the whole Energy: a key resource chapter on page 197.

Energy: a key resource

Name   **Class**   **Date**

Does global warming really matter?

The level at which I am currently working is ☐

so my target level for this assessment is ☐

because

Assessment task

In this assessment, you will write a report or PowerPoint presentation with the title 'Does global warming really matter?'. To help you answer this question, you will first read some background information on the subject, including:

- opinions of people who believe that global warming is a natural process;
- opinions of others who believe that humans are to blame for global warming;
- some views on what global warming will mean to us.

You will also need to do some extra research, and re-read any work you have done in class or for homework on the topic.

Most scientists agree that global warming is really happening. It's thought that, by the end of the 21st century, the world will be a much warmer place than it is now. What they can't agree on, however, is what causes global warming, or what the effects are.

Read through the newspaper extracts and quotes about global warming, they give some very different viewpoints! Think about what you know on the subject (have you learnt about global warming in science as well as in geography?). Do some extra research on the topic (Hint: try searching for articles on news sites on the Internet).

When you've completed your research, you can start writing your report or PowerPoint presentation. It should include:

- a summary of the arguments that global warming is a natural process;
- a summary of the arguments that humans are the cause;
- an evaluation of these arguments, and your own opinion;
- a summary statement to answer the question: 'Does global warming really matter?'.

Before you start work, make sure you understand the task and what you have to do. And look at the **success criteria** on the next page, so that you know how to achieve your target level – or better.

Level 3
- You show some understanding of global warming.
- You give a brief statement to say whether you think global warming matters.

Level 4
- You write about either how global warming is caused by people, or how it is the result of natural processes.
- You write a statement about the impact of global warming, giving your own opinion.

Level 5
- You write about how global warming is caused by both natural and human processes.
- You make a detailed statement about the impact of global warming, giving simple justification to your statement.

Level 6
- You evaluate the arguments about how global warming is caused, and come to an overall conclusion.
- You make an overall statement about the impact of global warming that is justified and supported by some evidence.

Level 7
- You evaluate the possible causes of global warming, come to an overall judgement, and give your own opinion.
- Your statement about the impact of global warming is backed up by detailed evidence, which is evaluated.

Level 8
- You evaluate the possible causes of global warming, and make your own judgements based on information provided and from your own research.
- Your statement regarding the impacts of global warming is balanced, fully justified, and uses a range of appropriate information.

Exceptional performance

In addition to Level 8…
- You evaluate critically the sources of evidence given, and draw on information beyond this assessment to inform your conclusion.
- You illustrate your work with a range of examples that support your conclusions effectively.

Scientists have dismissed the claim that we can stop global warming by cutting back on our use of fossil fuels. New evidence has shown that the main cause of global warming is, in fact, the sun. The temperature rise is simply due to an increase in the sun's energy output, which, it is claimed, happens quite regularly.

The United Nations has warned that we are heading for a global environmental disaster if we do not cut back on our use of fossil fuels. The increase in carbon dioxide from burning fossil fuels is mainly responsible for global warming. Rich countries such as the UK could be forced to cut back their use of oil by as much as 90% to help avoid flooding and storms around the world.

An American report has concluded that global warming is entirely natural, and will happen regardless of how much carbon dioxide we add to the atmosphere. Environmentalists say that they are hardly surprised that the report reached this conclusion, as the USA produces over 20% of the world's carbon dioxide.

Scientists in Britain just cannot agree over the effects of global warming. Some say that it will make the country warmer. Others state that the melting of the north polar ice cap, leading to a rush of cold water, will in fact make it cooler!

Global warming will make huge areas of the world into deserts. Crop yields are predicted to drop dramatically in places like central USA where it is likely to become warmer and drier.

By the end of the 21st century, it will be warm enough in the south of England to have large-scale vineyards! Sounds good to me.

Are we seriously saying that, with all of our technology, we can't cope with climate change. If it gets drier, so what? Irrigate more land. Plenty of land is artificially farmed anyway – we don't exactly fit in entirely with what mother nature wants now, do we?

Who said a change in climate won't affect us?! That's ridiculous. What about all the animal and plant species that have become extinct because of climate change? What about the dinosaurs?

Energy: a key resource

Name   **Class**   **Date**

Does global warming really matter?

Assessment task
A report summarising some of the different facts and opinions about the causes and effects of global warming.

Level awarded:

Teacher's comments:

Targets for improvement:

- Describe ideas in greater detail. ❏
- Suggest more reasons/processes to explain geographical ideas. ❏
- Try to use more geographical words and terms in your writing. ❏
- Try to support your writing with further, researched ideas. ❏
- Improve accuracy and/or presentation skills. ❏
- Use a greater range of presentation styles/techniques in your work. ❏
- Improve personal organisation and homework to raise your achievement level. ❏
- Ask for help about ideas you don't understand. ❏

Student's comments:

Energy: a key resource Test

Name   **Class**   **Date**

Read these instructions carefully before you start:
✓ Write your name, class, and the date in the spaces above.
✓ Your teacher will tell you how long you have to complete this test.
✓ Start time _____ End time _____
✓ Read the questions through before you start.
✓ Check your answers at the end.

1   Fuel is a store of energy. Tick all the things that are fuels in this list.   *[3 marks]*

     ❑   Coal   ❑   Iron   ❑   Wood   ❑   Petrol   ❑   Soil

2   This paragraph tells you how **coal** was made, but there are gaps in it. Use the words below to fill in the gaps. Be careful – you don't need to use all the words!   *[3 marks]*

       tens   **water**   **sunlight**   **millions**   **buried**

> Plants that live in swamps use _____ to make their food. When the plants die they are _____. They get squashed and over many _____ of years coal is made.

3   **Fossil fuels** are the world's main fuels. Unscramble these words to find THREE types of fossil fuels.   *[3 marks]*

     oacl   1. _____

     lio   2. _____

     sga   3. _____

4   **a**   People often turn fossil fuels into **electricity**. These boxes explain how electricity is made. You need to work out what order they should go in, and put the correct number in the circle in each box.   *[4 marks]*

◯ The turbine turns in a generator.	◯ This makes electricity, which then goes down wires to homes, schools, offices, and factories.
◯ The steam forces a turbine to go round.	◯ The fossil fuel is used to heat water to make steam

     b   If a country finds fossil fuels under the ground or in the sea, they are very happy. Give TWO reasons why it is good for a country to have fossil fuels.   *[4 marks]*

_____

_____

---

     geog.2: 5 Energy: a key resource

c Using fossil fuels can cause damage to the environment. In the table below are some activities that use fossil fuels. Give one example of damage caused by each activity.

[4 marks]

Activity	Example of damage caused
Digging coal from the ground	
Transporting oil in a ship	
Burning fossil fuels	
Using petrol in cars and lorries	

5 When fossil fuels are burned, a gas called **carbon dioxide** is released into the atmosphere. This table shows the amount of carbon dioxide in the air in different years. Follow the instructions to turn these figures into a line on the graph below. The graph already has a line on it showing the average global temperature.

Year	1860	1880	1900	1920	1940	1960	1980	2000
Concentration of carbon dioxide (in ppm)	290	295	305	310	320	330	350	370

a Complete the numbering on this axis *[1 mark]*

e Write a title on this line. *[1 mark]*

c Plot the numbers in the table as crosses on the graph. The first three have been done for you. *[5 marks]*

d Now join up the crosses with a smooth line (no ruler). *[1 mark]*

b Finish labelling the years on this axis. *[1 mark]*

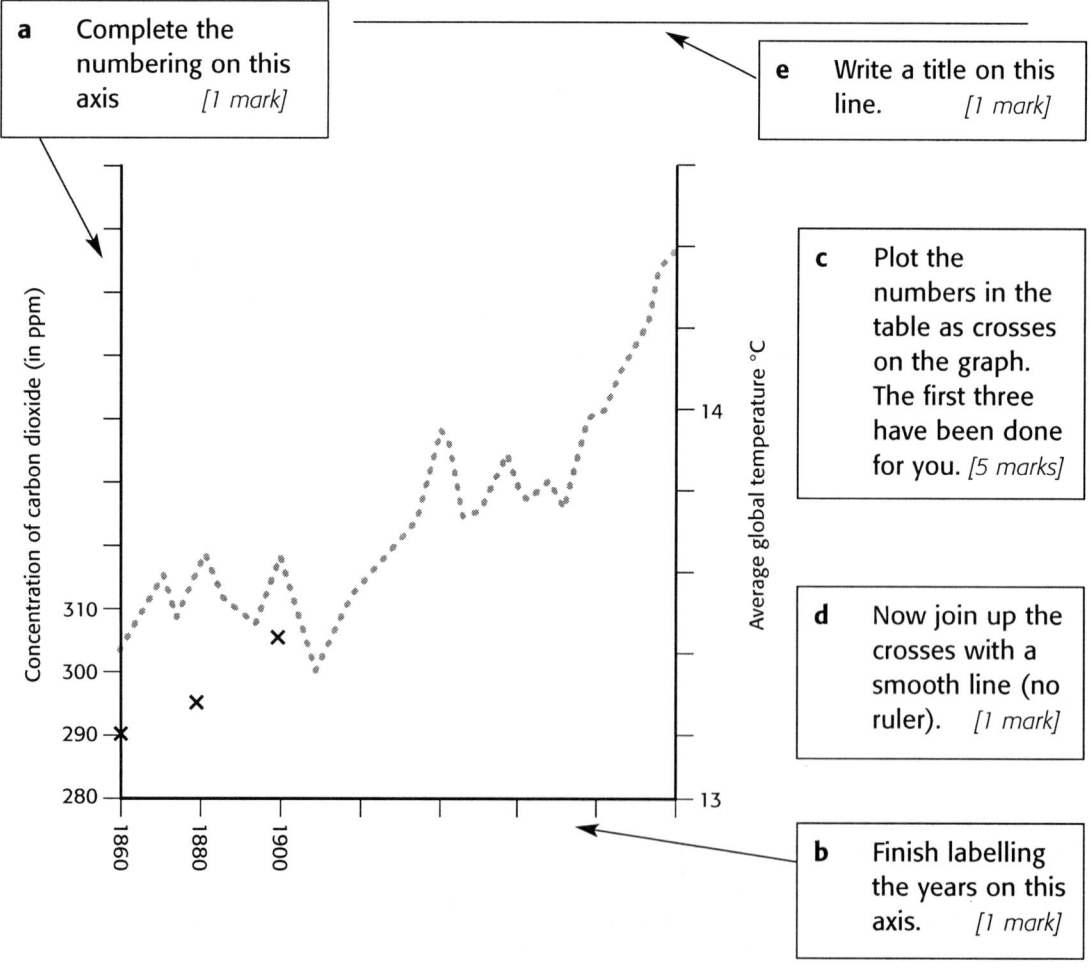

f What has happened to the amount of carbon dioxide in the air? *[1 mark]*

g What link can you see between the carbon dioxide line and the temperature line?

[1 mark]

_____

h Why do you think this link has happened?   *[3 marks]*

_____

_____

_____

_____

6 **Global warming** will cause many problems around the world. One of the effects of the rise in temperature is that ice will melt in the Arctic and the Antarctic.

a What will this do to sea levels around the world?   *[1 mark]*

_____

b There will be many other problems. Fill in one possible problem for each of the areas in the table.   *[8 marks]*

Animals living in the Arctic	
Small islands which are not far above sea level now	
Farming in Britain	
Ski resorts in the Alps in Europe	

7 One way to help prevent the problems caused by using fossil fuels is to use green energy.

a Name one type of green energy.   *[1 mark]*

_____

b Suggest THREE advantages of using this kind of energy.   *[3 marks]*

_____

_____

_____

c Suggest TWO problems there might be in using this type of energy.   *[2 marks]*

_____

_____

Total marks: 50   Total score: /50

1   1 mark for each correct tick.
   ✓ Coal
   ✓ Wood
   ✓ Petrol

2 a   1 mark for each correct word placement.

> Plants that live in swamps use <u>sunlight</u> to make their food. When the plants die they are <u>buried</u>. They get squashed and over many <u>millions</u> of years coal is made.

3   1 mark for each correct fuel.
   coal
   oil
   gas

4 a   1 mark for each correct number placement.

③ The turbine turns in a generator.	④ This makes electricity, which then goes down wires to homes, schools, offices, and factories.
② The steam forces a turbine to go round.	① The fossil fuel is used to heat water to make steam

b   1 mark for each sensible reason, a second for amplification (e.g. can sell the fossil fuels -1 mark - to make money -1 mark -; can develop industry using cheap power). Maximum of 4 marks.

c   1 mark for each sensible suggestion in the table. Maximum of 4 marks. Must be relevant to the activity (e.g. burning fossil fuels releases carbon dioxide).

5 a   1 mark for labelling the carbon dioxide axis.
   b   1 mark for labelling the years on the horizontal axis.
   c   5 marks for accurate crosses (1 mark lost for each cross plotted inaccurately).
   d   1 mark for joining up the line (no marks if a ruler used).
   e   1 mark for a sensible title.
   f   increased (1 mark).
   g   as one increases so does the other (1 mark).
   h   the carbon dioxide in the air traps heat (1 mark), so the atmosphere gets warmer (1 mark), so the average temperature goes up (1 mark).

6 a   They will rise (1 mark).
   b   1 mark for a simple statement in each box, second mark for expansion. (e.g. polar bears will not be able to travel on the ice (1 mark), so they will not be able to get their food (1 mark). Maximum 8 marks.

7 a   1 mark for any one of: tidal, solar, wind, biomass, wave.

   b   Advantages could include: no release of greenhouse gases; sustainability; cheaper fuel costs (after set-up costs); renewable; no release of gases that could lead to acid rain – 1 mark for each advantage given up to a maximum of 3 marks.

   c   Problems / disadvantages could include: high set-up costs; tidal power works best where there's a high tidal range; solar power doesn't work well in high latitudes or cloudy areas; wind power depends on wind; spoiling the view (wind power) – 1 mark for each problem given up to a maximum of 2 marks.

Energy: a key resource

Name   Class   Date

Now I've reached the end of the Energy: a key resource chapter:

	Yes	Think so	No
◆ I know why we like electricity so much, as a form of energy.			
◆ I can describe how electricity is made.			
◆ I know why fossil fuels are so important, and why oil is the most important.			
◆ I know that having a natural resource – such as oil – can change a country, and how.			
◆ I know what global warming is, and how it is affecting our Earth.			
◆ I know that the wind is likely to be the UK's biggest source of renewable energy in the coming years.			
◆ I understand how the wind can be used to generate electricity.			

◆ I know what these terms mean:

fossil fuel ❑   *a renewable source of energy* ❑   *a non-renewable source of energy* ❑

The part of this topic that I enjoyed most or found most interesting was:

Crime

Photocopiable worksheets

Learning activities

Assessment materials

[W] indicates material provided as editable Word files, as well as in PDF format, on the CD-ROM.

On the CD-ROM: pupil profile sheet; course theme, and lesson planning documents.

Name   **Class**

Study this flow diagram.

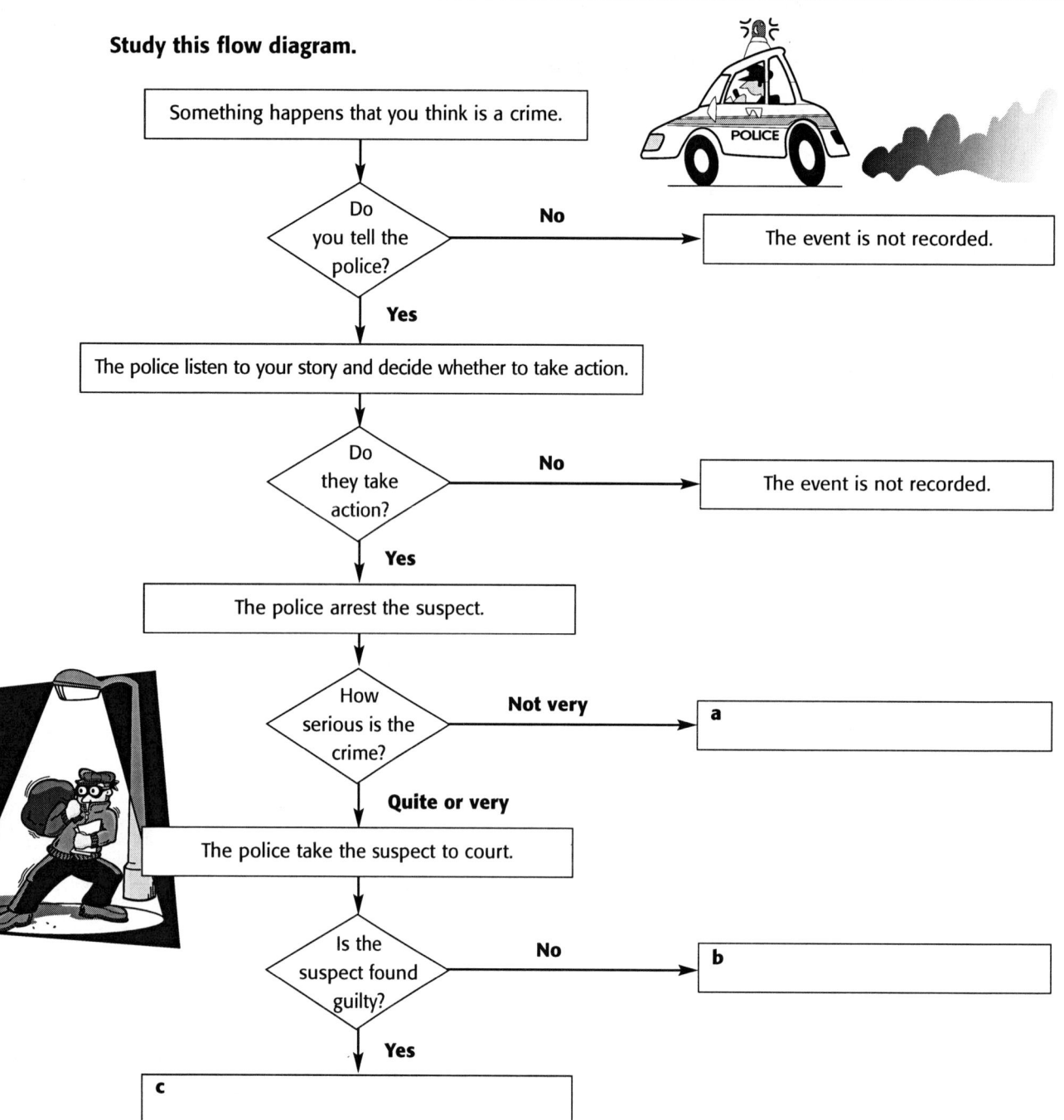

Something happens that you think is a crime.

Do you tell the police? — **No** → The event is not recorded.

Yes

The police listen to your story and decide whether to take action.

Do they take action? — **No** → The event is not recorded.

Yes

The police arrest the suspect.

How serious is the crime? — **Not very** → **a**

Quite or very

The police take the suspect to court.

Is the suspect found guilty? — **No** → **b**

Yes

c

1 Now fill in the gaps in the flow diagram using these text boxes.

| The suspect is freed. | The suspect is punished. | The suspect is cautioned (warned). |

2 Cut out the flow diagram and stick it in your exercise book. Give it a title.

3 For each of these crimes, use the flow diagram to help you decide what might happen if:
   a a Year 10 boy steals 50p from his sister in Year 7
   b a woman is caught shoplifting in a very posh perfume shop
   c a murderer is caught because he left his fingerprints at the murder scene
   d two men are fighting outside a pub on a Saturday night; one is bleeding heavily.

Name   Class

Each time Fred's Foods is burgled Fred's insurance company pays him for the stolen stock. So does anyone lose out?

Answer the questions to find the hidden costs of burglary.

COME ON, MATE ~ IT'S OK TO NICK FROM STORES, THEY CAN AFFORD IT! THE INSURANCE WILL PAY!

1 In his first year Fred paid an insurance premium (charge) of £200 a month. He was burgled three times that year and each time it cost the insurance company £2300 to replace his stock.

  a How much money did Fred pay the insurance company that year? _____

  b How much did the insurance company lose that year on Fred's insurance? (the amount they paid out minus the amount he paid them)

  _____

  c How do you think the insurance company feels about this loss?

  _____

2 Because of the burglaries, the insurance company raises Fred's premium to £350 a month. What do you think will happen to the price of food in his shop? Why?

  _____

  _____

3 The burglaries make the insurance company think the whole area is high risk, so they increase the premiums for everyone living there.
  How do you think people feel about this? _____

  _____

4 Mrs Rajput is elderly and can't walk far. So she shops only at Fred's.
  After rent she has only £40 a week left for food, clothes and presents.
  Her food used to cost £34 a week at Fred's. Now it costs £36.

  a How much less does she have each week, to buy clothes and presents?_____

  b How do you think Mrs Rajput feels about this? _____

  _____

  _____

5 On the back of this sheet, list all the people who have lost out, because of the burglaries at Fred's shop.

6 Look at the picture of Fred's shop.

  a What security precautions can you see?

  _____

  _____

  b What else could Fred do to deter burglars? _____

  _____

  _____

Looking after your neighbourhood

*

Name _____ **Class** _____

A lot of crime occurs in this street, especially vandalism, mugging and fighting.

The Neighbourhood Residents' Association is very worried about the crime. This is Mr Antoine, their leader.

> The graffiti, vandalism and litter make the street look really rough. It looks like no-one cares. No wonder there's so much crime! And there are not enough street lights, and too many dark alleys. We must make the street safer.

1 First identify the street's problems.

   a Write the title 'Looking After Your Neighbourhood' in your exercise book.

   b Cut out the picture of the street and stick it in your book.

   c Colour in the picture and label all the things you think would encourage crime.

2 Now help Mr Antoine to improve the street.

   a Make a list of all the things that could be done to make the street safer. (You can work on your own or with a partner.) Write the list in this box.

   b In your exercise book, use your list to help you draw the street as it could look after it has been improved.

   c Write about the changes you have made and why you have made them.

The street needs:

The police are investigating a recent spate of local burglaries.

1 Read the police report.

2 On the map, mark each burglary site with a red star.

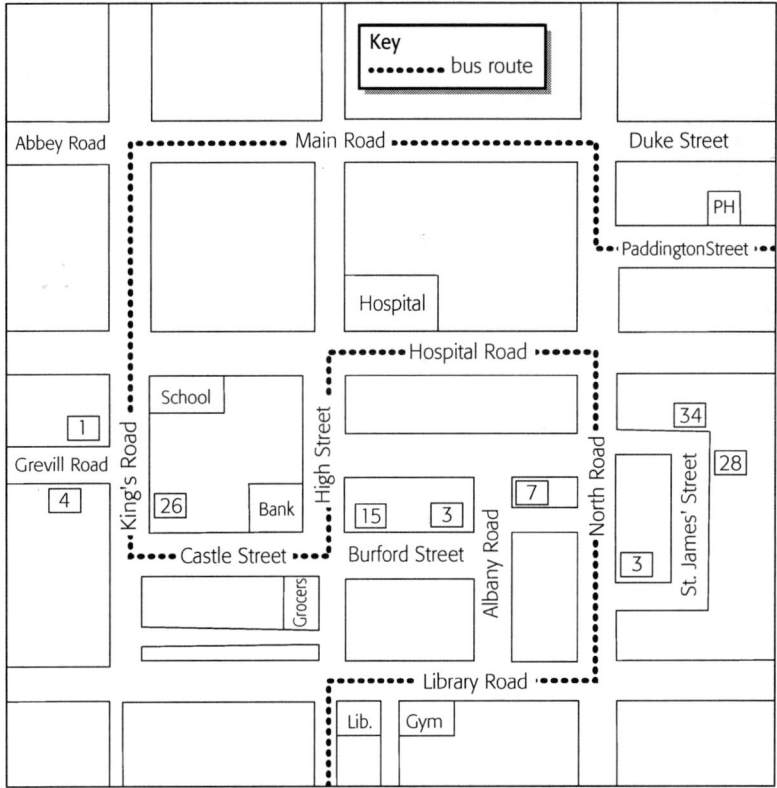

POLICE REPORT

Over the last few months there have been 13 burglaries in the district. These are the addresses at which burglaries occurred, in the order in which they happened:

① 15 Burford Street   ⑧ 1 Grevill Road

② 26 King's Road   ⑨ 28 St. James' Street

③ 3 St. James' Street   ⑩ Grocer's, High Street

④ 34 St. James' Street   ⑪ City Hospital

⑤ 3 Burford Street   ⑫ 4 Grevill Road

⑥ City Hospital   ⑬ 7 Albany Road

⑦ County Library

The police have interviewed three suspects and listed the places each one visits.

Suspect A

- Used to work at the City Hospital. (Lost his job two months ago.)
- Used to walk to work by the shortest route from Paddington Street, where his home is.
- One evening a week goes to classes at the school, by bus.
- At weekends visits his mother in Abbey Road, travelling as far as he can by bus.

Suspect B

- Works at the school.
- Catches the bus to work at the nearest stop to Duke Street, where he lives.
- In the evenings goes running down North Road and Library Road to the gym next to the library.
- At weekends goes off to stay with his girlfriend, driving straight out of the city along Duke Street.

Suspect C

- Works at the County Library.
- Gets the bus to work from the stop nearest Grevill Road, where he lives.
- Spends a lot of evenings with friends in St. James' Street, walking there by the shortest route from his home.
- His girlfriend works in the bank in the High Street.
- Meets her after work every Friday, walking there from the library.

3 Read each profile. Mark lines on the map showing the routes each suspect uses. Use a different colour for each suspect.

4 Burglars often operate in areas they are familiar with, where they can spot opportunities. On that basis, which of the three suspects appears most likely? _____

Why?_____

_____

Now answer these on the back of this sheet.

5 Is there anything in the profiles that makes you think: **i** A might be guilty?   **ii** B could be the one?

6 Geography can give clues. But the police also need to collect **evidence**. List some types of evidence you think they'll look for, in this case.

What causes crime?

Name   **Class**

Welcome to the Crime Squad!

The table below shows data for one year for some London boroughs. You will use it to check if there are links between unemployment, GCSE pass rates and crime!

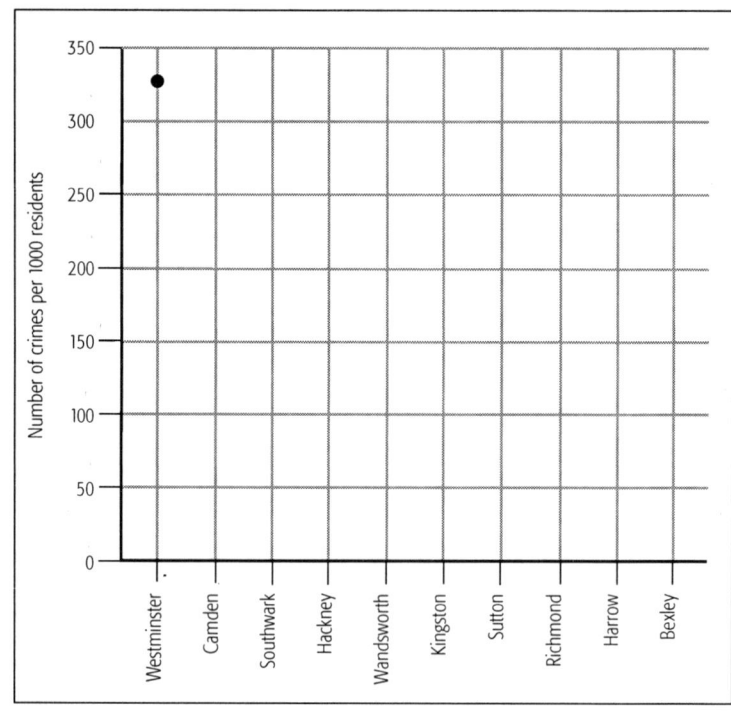

London borough	Number of crimes per 1000 residents	% of people unemployed	% of pupils with 5 GCSEs at A–C
Westminster	332	12	29
Camden	209	15	42
Southwark	187	19	22
Hackney	171	22	24
Wandsworth	133	13	30
Kingston	97	7	56
Sutton	84	8	53
Richmond	81	7	48
Harrow	77	8	53
Bexley	75	9	43

1 First, draw a crime graph like the one started above.

   a Use a large piece of graph paper. Draw and label the axes as above.

   b Mark in the crime rate for each borough (as for Westminster).

   c Now join your dots with a smooth line (no rulers!).

   d Give your graph a title.

2 On a large piece of tracing paper, draw a graph for unemployment.

   a Draw the axes exactly the same length as for your crime graph.

   b Name the places along the horizontal axis, exactly as before.

   c Show % unemployed on the vertical axis, going up to at least 22%.

   d Now plot the points just as you did for crime, and give your graph a title.

3 On a second piece of tracing paper, draw a graph for the GCSE results, in exactly the same way. The vertical axis should show % of pupils, and go up to 60%.

4 Place the unemployment graph over the crime graph. Compare the two. Are they the same shape? What differences can you see? Note down the similarities and differences on scrap paper.

5 Repeat step 4 for the graphs of exam results and crime.

6 Now present your findings as a piece of neat written work.

   a First stick the crime graph into your book with the overlays as flaps on top.

   b Describe the shape of the crime graph, saying where crime is highest and lowest.

   c Now say how the overlay graphs match (or not) the crime graph.

   d Is there a link between crime and unemployment, or crime and exam results? Write down your conclusions, and try to give reasons. Explain anything unusual.

   e Suggest other data that might help to explain the variation in crime.

I only wish I'd worked harder at Geography.

6A Reporting a crime *

1.
   a. The suspect is cautioned (warned).
   b. The suspect is freed.
   c. The suspect is punished.
3.
   a. The theft will not be reported to the police.
   b. The shop is very likely to report the crime to the police. So the police will arrest the shoplifter. They will probably let her off with a caution, and record the crime. But if she is a persistent shoplifter, or the shop insists on pressing charges, she may be brought to court. She is likely to receive a (light) punishment, for example community service.
   c. The murderer is punished – perhaps given a life sentence.
   d. If the police are called (or happen to pass by) the men will be arrested. The assault seems serious so one or both may be brought to court and receive a prison sentence.

6B Burglary – who pays? **

1.
   a. £2400   b. £4500
   c. determined to make up for this loss
2. Prices will go up, because Fred has to earn extra money to pay the insurance company.
3. annoyed
4.
   a. £2   b. upset
5. Fred, Fred's customers, the householders in the area, and, initially, the insurance company (but they will make up for it in the end, unless the raised premiums put their customers off).
6.
   a. an external light, metal bars, burglar alarm, door lock
   b. install a security camera, get a security guard (although it is unlikely his business could afford that), install metal shutters on the window and door

6C Looking after your neighbourhood *

1.
   c. Pupils should label the litter, graffiti, broken windows and so on.
2.
   a. Suitable ideas include removing the old car and other dumped rubbish, repairing the street light, pavement and potholes, restoring the vandalised houses so that people can live in them, lighting the alley way (or closing it off).

6D Mapping crime **

4. Suspect C. He is the only one of the three who passes all the burglary sites during his routine weekly trips.
5.
   i. Suspect A has lost his job. Maybe he is desperate for money? One of the places that was burgled (twice) was the City Hospital, where he worked.
   ii. A car would be an advantage to a busy burglar. B seems to be the only one with a car.
6. Fingerprints at the sites, stolen goods in the suspects' homes, evidence of any witnesses, evidence from CCTV cameras, evidence from the suspects' bank accounts where unexplained sums of money (from selling stolen goods?) may appear.

6E What causes crime? ***

1.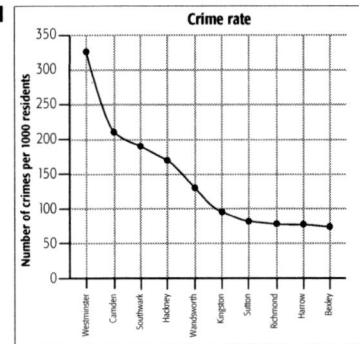

2.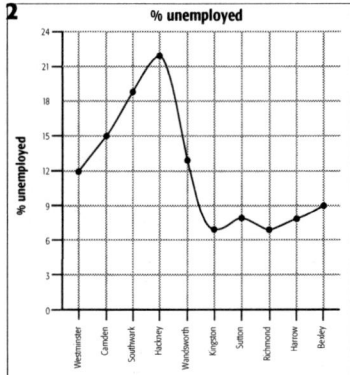

3.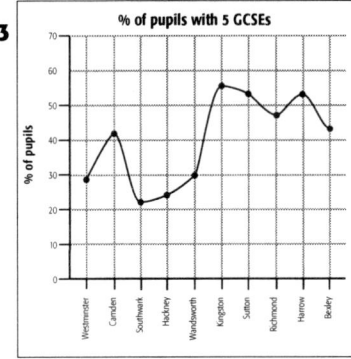

4. In general there appears to be a correlation between unemployment and crime rate. The five areas with lowest unemployment also have the lowest crime rates. Westminster appears to be the odd one out, with the highest crime rate but not the highest unemployment rate.
5. There also appears to be a general (inverse) correlation between crime rate and GCSE pass rates. The five boroughs with the highest pass rates have the lowest crime rates. There is a little trough in pass rate at Southwark and Hackney corresponding to a little peak in crime rate. However the correlation is not as obvious as it was for unemployment. Camden is the worst fit.
6.
   b. Westminster has the highest crime rate, Bexley the lowest. The graph zig zags but overall it slopes downwards from left to right.
   c. See the answers for 4 and 5.
   d. There appears to be a link between all three.
      The five boroughs on the right, with lowest unemployment, are probably the most affluent overall. There may be more security systems in homes, and fewer local criminals. The residents may also have higher expectations of their children and the local schools. Schools in affluent areas with a low crime rate will also find it easier to attract and keep teachers.
      Where unemployment is higher, a borough is likely to be poorer. People may be tempted into crime because they need money. People may also have lower expectations of their children and their local schools, and not push their children to study. The crime rate will also affect schools, as it may be hard to attract and keep teachers. Westminster appears to be a misfit. It is a central London borough so one reason could be that a lot of outsiders travel into and through it every day.
   e. Data on the type and quality of housing, house prices, average earnings, average distance from the centre of London, incidence of transport routes, number of daily commuters into the borough, number of police stations and pubs per thousand people, and the ethnic and cultural makeup could all be useful.

Who killed Colonel Protheroe?   **

This activity is intended as a lesson- or topic-starter to capture pupils' interest in the topic of crime.

Aims

- Pupils understand the use of logical inference
- Pupils revise bearings and scale

Introduction

This activity addresses Unit 15 of the QCA Scheme of Work (*Crime and the local community*), and the logical processes of induction as part of pupils' development of thinking skills. It also provides some relief from the otherwise relentless doom and gloom often associated with the topic of crime!

Activity

This game works best with groups of 4-6 players.

Tell each group to follow the instructions on page 207.

The winner is the first player to work out:
- who murdered Colonel Protheroe;
- how they did it;
- where they committed the crime.

You will need to cut up the cards provided on page 208. You may want to photocopy or print these onto stiff card and laminate them.

Each player should also be given a checklist with all the suspects, weapons, and places on page 209.

Extension exercise

This short exercise requires pupils to find out the real name of the village of Silverley, where Colonel Protheroe was murdered. Pupils will need to use their atlases for this activity.

The answer is the village of Capel St. Mary in Suffolk.

Name   **Class**

Poor Colonel Protheroe has been murdered in the village of Silverley.
He was found dead yesterday at midnight. Who did it? How? Where?
It's up to you to solve the mystery.

You are going to play this game with 4-6 players, using the game cards given
to you by your teacher. The winner is the first player to work out:
I   who murdered Colonel Protheroe;
I   how they did it;
I   where they committed the crime.

Your teacher will give each of you a check list of all the suspects, weapons, and
places. Put a tick in the box beside each one when you know they **weren't**
involved in the murder. Make sure you keep your list covered during the game.

Activity

1   First sort all the game cards into three groups: suspect (**who**), weapon
        (**how**), and place (**where**).

2   Shuffle each group face down. Then take the top card from each group
        and secretly place it in an envelope. The cards in this envelope hold the
        clues to Colonel Protheroe's murder.

3   Deal out the cards that are left (it doesn't matter if you don't all have the
        same number of cards). Don't let the other players see your cards!

4   Cross off the places, weapons, and suspects that are in your hand. You
        know they aren't the cards in the envelope.

5   Now take it in turns to ask questions. You want to find out what the cards
        in the envelope are, so ask: "Was it … (**name**), with the … (**weapon**) in
        the … (**place**)?" You can only question one person during your turn.

6   The person asked shows the questioner if any of the cards are in their
        hands. They should be careful not to reveal their cards to the other
        players. The questioner then ticks off his or her list. Next person's turn!

7   If you think you have worked out who did it, where, and how, write down
        your answer and place it face down.

8   Then look in the envelope. If you are right you have won.
        If you are wrong, you're out of the game. Put the cards back in the
        envelope. Then keep quiet and let the other players carry on until
        someone guesses correctly.

Extension exercise

Colonel Protheroe was murdered in the village of Silverley. But where is
Silverley? Well, actually Silverley isn't the village's real name. So what is? Read
the description below and then see if you can work out the real name of the
village. You will need to use your atlas.
*'It is 54 miles north east of the London suburbs. Cambridge is 40 miles from
the village. Aldeburgh is on the coast 26 miles from the village. Aldeburgh is
63 miles from Cambridge. The coastal village of Jaywick is 16 miles south of
the village. 12 miles east is the village of Falkenham.'*

Name   Class

RAILWAY STATION	MRS AMELIA BONNINGTON	POISON
VICARAGE	CHARLES SMYTH	CANDLESTICK
OLD HALL	DR ROSCOE	PISTOL
POST OFFICE	MRS DUPONT	KITCHEN KNIFE
CHURCH	LETITIA HOPPER	ROPE
THE ANCHOR INN	REV. ALBERT SALT	HAMMER

Name   **Class**

Who killed Colonel Protheroe? How? Where?

Who?
Mrs Amelia Bonnington ☐
Charles Smyth ☐
Dr Roscoe ☐
Mrs Dupont ☐
Letitia Hopper ☐
Rev. Albert Salt ☐

How?
Poison ☐
Candlestick ☐
Pistol ☐
Kitchen knife ☐
Rope ☐
Hammer ☐

Where?
Railway station ☐
Vicarage ☐
Old Hall ☐
Post Office ☐
Church ☐
The Anchor Inn ☐

Who killed Colonel Protheroe? How? Where?

Who?
Mrs Amelia Bonnington ☐
Charles Smyth ☐
Dr Roscoe ☐
Mrs Dupont ☐
Letitia Hopper ☐
Rev. Albert Salt ☐

How?
Poison ☐
Candlestick ☐
Pistol ☐
Kitchen knife ☐
Rope ☐
Hammer ☐

Where?
Railway station ☐
Vicarage ☐
Old Hall ☐
Post Office ☐
Church ☐
The Anchor Inn ☐

Who killed Colonel Protheroe? How? Where?

Who?
Mrs Amelia Bonnington ☐
Charles Smyth ☐
Dr Roscoe ☐
Mrs Dupont ☐
Letitia Hopper ☐
Rev. Albert Salt ☐

How?
Poison ☐
Candlestick ☐
Pistol ☐
Kitchen knife ☐
Rope ☐
Hammer ☐

Where?
Railway station ☐
Vicarage ☐
Old Hall ☐
Post Office ☐
Church ☐
The Anchor Inn ☐

Who killed Colonel Protheroe? How? Where?

Who?
Mrs Amelia Bonnington ☐
Charles Smyth ☐
Dr Roscoe ☐
Mrs Dupont ☐
Letitia Hopper ☐
Rev. Albert Salt ☐

How?
Poison ☐
Candlestick ☐
Pistol ☐
Kitchen knife ☐
Rope ☐
Hammer ☐

Where?
Railway station ☐
Vicarage ☐
Old Hall ☐
Post Office ☐
Church ☐
The Anchor Inn ☐

Home design and crime

**

Aims

- Pupils are aware of the importance of design on vandalism and crime
- Pupils can evaluate their local area
- Pupils are aware of correlation
- Pupils are aware of hypothesis testing

Introduction

This exercise is linked to Unit 15 of the QCA Scheme of Work (*Would a better understanding of the geography of crime help people reduce its occurrence?*). It is linked to unit 6.5 on pages 100-101 of **geog.2**.

Pupils should grasp the idea of a disadvantagement score (here called a D-score) and how it can be calculated for a house or for a block of flats. They then apply it in theory, before carrying out fieldwork to test the hypothesis that D-scores are related to high levels of litter, graffiti, and vandalism.

Activity

For the first part of this activity you will need to photocopy a property page from a local newspaper. Make sure you have enough copies for work in pairs.

1 Give each pair the following:
   - activity sheet (page 211)
   - 'Building survey tables' sheet (page 212)
   - 'Abuse level tables' sheet (page 213)
   - a copy of the property page from a local newspaper.

2 Each pair of pupils should attempt to calculate a D-score for each of the houses/flats on the property page. This stage is intended to familiarise pupils with the scoring system. They are unlikely to be able to attach a score to every feature of every house or flat.

3 The pairs should then test Dr Coleman's hypothesis and scoring system out on the area around their school. Ideally this will be an area with a range of housing types.

4 The pairs should collate their fieldwork data on a scattergraph. The D-scores should be plotted on the horizontal axis, the abuse scores on the vertical. According to Dr Coleman's hypothesis, the points on this graph should join together to form an upwards sloping line. This shows a correlation between poor design and crime.

5 Initiate a class discussion about whether Dr Coleman's hypothesis works for the area tested? Do areas with the highest D-score have the highest levels of graffiti, vandalism, and litter?

At each stage, pupils should be thinking of ways in which the disadvantagement score could be lowered.

Home design and crime

Name   **Class**

Dr Alice Coleman is a geographer. She came up with a hypothesis about crime (a hypothesis is when you make a statement and then you investigate it to see if it is true). She said that houses and flats that are badly designed are more likely to be targeted by criminals.

She said that houses and the land around them should look neat and tidy. They should look as if somebody owns and looks after them. They should also look as if the owner can watch over them easily. If a house is overlooked, criminals will probably steer clear. They'll be scared of being caught in action!

To test her hypothesis, Dr Coleman came up with a list of things that might affect levels of crime. These factors can be used to work out a score for a house or block of flats. The score is called a D-score or 'disadvantagement' score.

The higher the D-score, the higher the danger of disadvantage.
The higher the D-score, the more likely it is that the area will have problems of litter, graffiti, vandalism, or other crime.

You're going to find out if Dr Coleman's hypothesis works.

Activity

Use the tables to help you collect data to answer the questions below:

1   **a** Look at the houses (and/or flats) on the property page given to you by your teacher. Working in pairs, see if you can use the tables to give each property a D-score. (You won't be able to give a score for everything, so don't panic!)
  b What can be done to improve the D-score for each of these properties?

2   **a** Now try Dr Coleman's system out in an area near your school. For each house or block of flats, try to calculate both a D-score and an abuse level score.
  b What could be done to improve the situation?

3   **a** Draw a scattergraph to show the results collected by the class. Put the D-scores on the horizontal (x) axis, and the abuse scores on the vertical (y) axis.
  b Does Dr Coleman's idea work for your area? Do areas with the highest D-score have the highest levels of graffiti, vandalism, and litter?

Name   Class

Building survey tables

HOUSES

Part of house	Description	How to calculate the D-score
Front garden	3-4 metres	If shorter, score 2 If longer, score 1
Fences/hedges	Waist high	If higher, score 1 If none, score 2
Front gate		If none, score 1
Front windows	Overlooking garden	If frosted or high up, score 1 If none, score 2 If part of house blocks view, score 1
Front door facing the road	Overlooking garden	If facing the side, score 1
Secure back garden	Private, no gate	If shared, score 1 If communal, score 2
Rear	Back or side alleys	If either, score 1 If both, score 2
End house	Blank side wall	If present, score 1
Looks	Paintwork, curtains, front door	If one is poor, score 1 If more than one, score 2

Highest possible score = 14   TOTAL SCORE: _____

FLATS

Description	How to calculate the D-score
More than 12 homes per block	Score 1
More than 6 homes per entrance	Score 1
More than 3 storeys per block	Score 1
Any overhead walkways	Score 1
More than 1 interconnecting exit	Score 1
More than 1 vertical route	Score 1
More than 4 dwellings per corridor	Score 1
Any entrance not facing the street	Score 1
Any ground floor entrance without a front garden	Score 1
Any garages below the block	Score 1
More than 1 block per site	Score 1
More than 1 gate or gap in perimeter fence	Score 1
Any play areas	Score 1
Any public areas in grounds	Score 1

Highest possible D-score = 14   TOTAL SCORE: _____

Home design and crime

Name   Class

Abuse level table

Sign of crime	How to calculate the abuse score
Litter	None score 0 Clean and casual score 1 Dirty and decayed score 2
Graffiti	None score 0 Inside or outside score 1 Inside and outside score 2
Vandalism	Score 1 point each for damage to: fence, shed, window, door, stairs, lift, garage, walls, electrical fittings, refuse bins or shutes 10

Maximum abuse score = 14   TOTAL SCORE: _____

Crime

The assessment opportunities for Crime are as follows:

▪ The **level-marked assessment** 'How secure is your school?' on pages 215-218.

In this assessment pupils need to record security information around their school. This is followed by an evaluation of the security measures, and suggestions for ways to improve security in one area of the school.

A **feedback form** for the level-marked assessment is provided on page 219.

▪ The **scored test** on pages 220-224.

▪ Opportunities for interim assessments provided by **geog.2**:

Home design and crime (fieldwork, with the opportunity for pupils to work in pairs) on pages 210-213 of this file.

Activities 5, 11, 14, 21, 26, 27, and 29 in the *Further suggestions for class and homework* section on pages 130-131 of the *geog.2 teacher's handbook*.

Worksheet A: Plan a route for the night patrol for *Crimebusters!* (a webfile) in *geog.2, Crime* on *geog.world*.

Worksheet B: CCTV – good or bad? for *Crimebusters!* (a webfile) in *geog.2, Crime* on *geog.world*.

▪ The **self-assessment form** for the whole Crime chapter on page 225.

Crime

Name	Class	Date

How secure is your school?

The level at which I am currently working is ☐

so my target level for this assessment is ☐

because

Assessment task

This assessment is about the security of your school. You will:

a record information about any security measures in your school;

b say how effective you think these measures are;

c choose one aspect of security in your school and suggest how it could be improved.

Walk around your school and make a note of any security features you see. For each feature, write down how effective you think it is. Are there any places where there is no security, or where you think security measures could be improved?

If you want, you can record your notes in the 'Security measures' table (write your school's name at the top). Note: you don't have to fill in every box, and even if somewhere has good security, it doesn't mean it can't be improved!

When you've finished this task, decide on one aspect of your school's security that you think could be improved. Think of as many ways as you can of improving the situation. Make sure your suggestions are practical, and not too expensive!

If you want, you can record your notes in the grid provided. You can include diagrams in your answer if you wish.

Before you start work, make sure you understand the task and what you have to do. And look at the **success criteria** on the next page, so that you know how to achieve your target level – or better!

Level 3
- You record at least one piece of information about security in your school.
- You choose one area for improvement.

Level 4
- You record several pieces of information about security in your school.
- You choose one area for improvement and give reasons for your choice.

Level 5
- You record security information from all around your school.
- You choose one area for improvement and suggest some ways in which the area could be improved.

Level 6
- You record security information from all round your school, and make a judgement about the effectiveness of security in most locations.
- The suggestions for improving your chosen area are generally appropriate.

Level 7
- You record security information from all round your school, and make a judgement about the effectiveness of security in all locations.
- The suggestions for improving your chosen area are generally appropriate and are supported by plans (perhaps including diagrams or maps).

Level 8
- Your judgements about all of the security measures in your school are valid and are based on appropriate information.
- The suggestions for improving your chosen area are entirely appropriate and are realistic in terms of cost.

Exceptional performance

In addition to Level 8...
- You evaluate the relative positive and negative points of your chosen location.
- You understand that problems might still exist after improvements have been made.
- You relate your findings to examples in different contexts and locations from beyond the activity in order further to justify your choices and plans.

Security in _____

Location	Security measure (or lack of!)	Good points	Bad points	Improvements

Improving security in _____

My chosen location:
The problem is:
My suggested solutions are:

Crime

Name   **Class**   **Date**

How secure is your school?

Assessment task
An evaluation of school security measures, with suggested improvements for one aspect of the security.

Level awarded:

Teacher's comments:

Targets for improvement:

- Describe ideas in greater detail. ❏
- Suggest more reasons/processes to explain geographical ideas. ❏
- Try to use more geographical words and terms in your writing. ❏
- Try to support your writing with further, researched ideas. ❏
- Improve accuracy and/or presentation skills. ❏
- Use a greater range of presentation styles/techniques in your work. ❏
- Improve personal organisation and homework to raise your achievement level. ❏
- Ask for help about ideas you don't understand. ❏

Student's comments:

Crime Test

Name   **Class**   **Date**

1   There are lots of types of crime. Put a tick next to the things in the list that are crimes.

[3 marks]

❏   Taking someone's pen and keeping it without their permission

❏   Lying to your teacher

❏   Riding your bike on the pavement

❏   Leaving all the lights on in your classroom when there's no-one there

❏   Beating up another pupil

2   When a crime is committed, lots of people can be affected. Read the text in the box below and then list all the victims of the crime.   *[3 marks]*

> Mr Smith was taking his earnings from his taxi to the bank. On the way he was mugged. The muggers took all his money. Mrs Manani saw the mugging and now she's too scared to go out of her house alone in case it happens to her.
>
> When Mr Smith got home, his wife asked him for money to pay the milkman, but he didn't have any money so she couldn't pay the bill. Mr Smith's daughter wanted to go to a friend's birthday but she couldn't have her pocket money to buy a present.

Victims:

_____   _____

_____   _____

_____   _____

3   **a**   Crimes can happen in urban (city) or rural (countryside) areas, and some crimes can happen in both. Put these crimes into one of the three columns in the table.   *[6 marks]*

- People getting on a bus without paying for their tickets
- Shoplifting in a large department store
- House burglary
- Farmer dumping chemicals by the road
- Bank raid
- Stealing sheep from a field

Urban crimes	Rural crimes	Crimes that could happen in both areas

b More crimes tend to happen in urban areas. Suggest TWO reasons for this.   *[4 marks]*

_____

_____

_____

_____

4   Criminals usually commit crimes in areas that they know well. This mental map shows where a criminal is likely to operate.

Key
- knows this area well
- opportunities for crime
- area of crime

home

shopping and entertainment

work or school

a   Where do you think this criminal is likely to shoplift?
Mark the place on the map with an **A**.
[1 mark]

b   Where do you think this criminal is likely to steal money from someone he knows?
Mark the place on the map with a **B**.   *[1 mark]*

c   Where do you think this criminal is likely to steal a car?
Mark the place on the map with a **C**.   *[1 mark]*

5   Areas with high **physical disorder** attract criminals. Suggest TWO things that you might find in an area with high physical disorder.   *[2 marks]*

_____

_____

_____

6   Crime can be prevented if an area is well designed or has crime prevention measures added.

a   Suggest TWO things a shopkeeper could do to stop criminals targeting his shop.
[2 marks]

_____

_____

_____

b A new housing estate has been built. It has <u>burglar alarms on every house</u>, <u>window locks</u>, <u>only one entrance</u> to the estate and <u>all the houses face each other</u> with car parking in the middle.

For each underlined item explain how it protects against crime.   *[8 marks]*

burglar alarms on every house	
window locks	
only one entrance	
all the houses face each other	

7 The heroin trade is an example of **organized crime**. Look at this diagram.

opium farmer   local opium dealer   area drug dealer   Afghan drug boss   drug smuggler   drug smuggler   UK drug boss   area drug dealer   street dealer   addict

money

a Which two criminals make the most money?   *[2 marks]*

_____

_____

b All the people involved in this chain are responsible for destroying the addict's life. Give ONE reason why heroin destroys people's lives.   *[1 mark]*

_____

_____

c What punishment do you think convicted drug dealers should be given? Give ONE reason for your decision.   *[2 marks]*

_____

_____

8 On this map you are going to plot the locations of house burglaries.

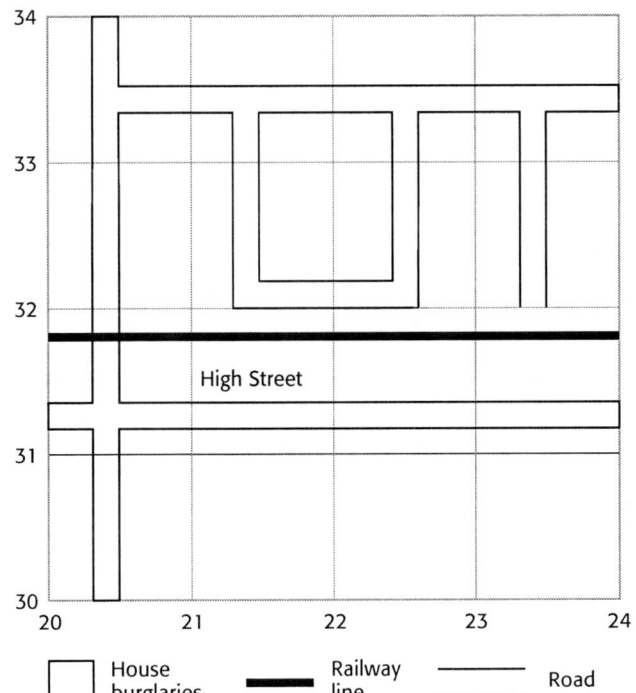

High Street

| | House burglaries | | Railway line | | Road |

a Choose a symbol for house burglaries and add it to the key.
[1 mark]

b Plot these house burglaries on the map (remember to read along the bottom numbers first). [5 marks]

235 321
202 314
236 322
236 327
202 339
216 321
224 321
234 327
214 321
234 325

c What pattern can you see in the location of the house burglaries? [2 marks]

_____

_____

d Why do you think this pattern exists? [6 marks]

_____

_____

_____

_____

_____

_____

_____

_____

_____

_____

_____

_____

Total marks: 50   Total score: /50

1   1 mark for each correct tick.
  ✓ Taking someone's pen and keeping it without their permission
  ✓ Riding your bike on the pavement
  ✓ Beating up another pupil

2 $\frac{1}{2}$ mark for each victim.
  Mr Smith
  Mrs Manani
  Mrs Smith
  Milkman
  Daughter
  Daughter's friend

3 a   1 mark for each correct entry in the table.

Urban crimes	Rural crimes	Crimes that could happen in both areas
Bank raid	Farmer dumping chemicals by the road	People getting on a bus without paying for their tickets
Shoplifting in a large department store	Stealing sheep from a field	House burglary

   b   1 mark for simple first reason, second mark for expansion. 1 mark for simple second reason, second mark for expansion (e.g. people in urban areas earn more money (1 mark), so they have more to steal (1 mark)).

4 a   1 mark for label near shopping/entertainment area.
   b   1 mark for label near work/school.
   c   1 mark for label near shopping/entertainment area (due to more car parks and people leaving cars for a period of time).

5   1 mark for any sensible point (e.g. broken windows). Maximum 2 marks.

6 a   1 mark for any sensible point (e.g. fix alarm). Maximum 2 marks.
   b   1 mark for each simple reason, second mark for expansion (e.g. alarms put burglars off (1 mark) because they will go off and attract attention (1 mark)). Maximum 8 marks.

7 a   UK drug boss (1 mark) Afghan drug boss (1 mark).
   b   1 mark for a sensible reason (e.g. damages brain).
   c   1 mark for a punishment, 1 mark for a reason (no right or wrong here).

8 a   1 mark for a symbol (can be anything).
   b $\frac{1}{2}$ mark for each correct plot, up to a maximum of 5 marks.

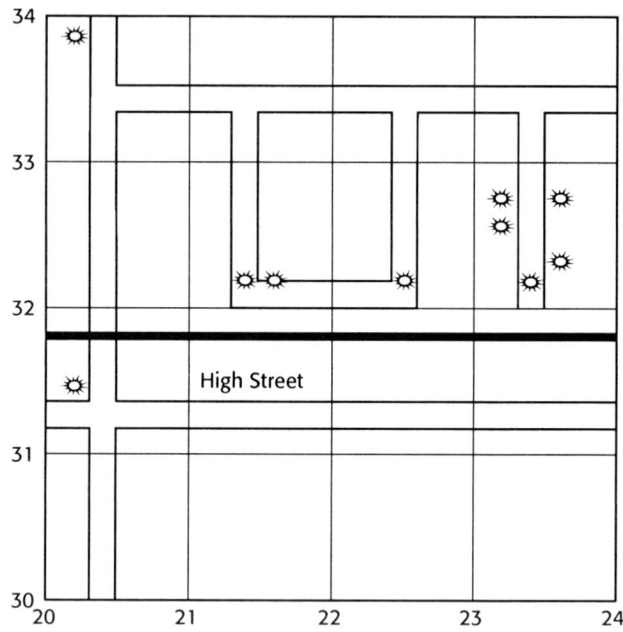

   c   Near railway line (1 mark) and down quieter streets (or dead-ends and cul-de-sacs) (1 mark).
   d   Up to 6 marks awarded as follows:

marks	description
1-2	Simple explanations of pattern.
3-4	More complex explanations of pattern.
5	Complex explanations of pattern with some idea of interactions between factors.
6	Complex explanations of pattern with clear exemplification of interactions between factors.

Crime

Name   **Class**   **Date**

Now I've reached the end of the Crime chapter:

	Yes	Think so	No
◆ I can describe how crime can affect all of us – not just the victims.			
◆ I can give reasons why many crimes are not reported to the police.			
◆ I know some of the things we can do to cut burglaries, and street crime.			
◆ I know that Afghanistan is the world's top producer of heroin, and why. I know how heroin is linked to crime.			

◆ I know what these terms mean:

crime ❑   victim ❑   offender ❑   sentence ❑   secure accommodation ❑

fraud ❑   burglary ❑   vandalism ❑   domestic violence ❑   assault ❑

environmental crime ❑   terrorism ❑   crime hotspot ❑

The part of this topic that I enjoyed most or found most interesting was:

Photocopiable worksheets

Learning activities

Assessment materials

[W] indicates material provided as editable Word files, as well as in PDF format, on the CD-ROM.

On the CD-ROM: pupil profile sheet; course theme, and lesson planning documents.

Name   Class

Many of the main features of Brazil are included in this crossword.

1 Use an atlas and the map below to help you complete the crossword.

1 City on the north-east coast of Brazil

2 The second largest river in the country

3 The largest river in Brazil

4 One of the world's ten largest cities, in the south-east of Brazil

5 The old capital city

6 City at approximately 20° S, 44° W

7 The main mountains, the Brazilian …

8 The ocean to the east of Brazil

2 The letters in the shaded boxes spell the name of the capital. What is it?

_____

3 Now locate and label the features in the crossword on the map.

4 Lightly shade the area that represents Brazil.

N

0   500   1000   1500   2000 km

Name　　　　　　　　　　　　　　　　　Class

Use a library book or search Chapter 7 of geog.2 to help you answer these.

1 Colour in the Brazilian flag. Use the correct colours.

2 Complete the factbox below, using the list of missing words.

3 Find three other facts about Brazil and add them to the factbox.

4 Draw an image (a picture) of Brazil.

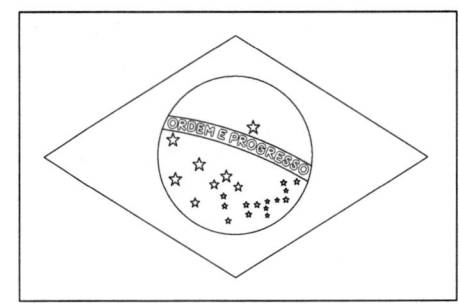

Missing words:
Brasilia
São Paulo
fifth
Amazon
180
Highlands
south-east
fifth
100
three

Factbox

- Brazil is the _____ largest country in the world.

- About _____ million people live in Brazil. This is around _____ times the population of the United Kingdom.

- The capital city is _____ . Brazil also has one of the world's largest cities, _____ _____ .

- The River _____ flows through Brazil. It is an enormous river, carrying over one _____ of the world's fresh water. Where it reaches the Atlantic Ocean, it is over _____ miles wide.

- The Brazilian _____ are the main mountains in Brazil. They are in the _____ _____ of the country.

_____

_____

_____

_____

Image

Name **Class**

These graphs are population pyramids.

What you have to do …

1 Divide the graphs for 2000 and 2025 into three age groups: children, adults, the elderly. To do this draw two lines across each graph, along the tops of the rows marked 10–14 and 60–64.

2 Now colour in the two graphs. Use a different colour for each age group but the same colours on both graphs.

3 Next, on the outline graph below right, draw a population pyramid for 2050, using the table below for the figures.
Label and shade the graph like the other two. Give your graph a title.

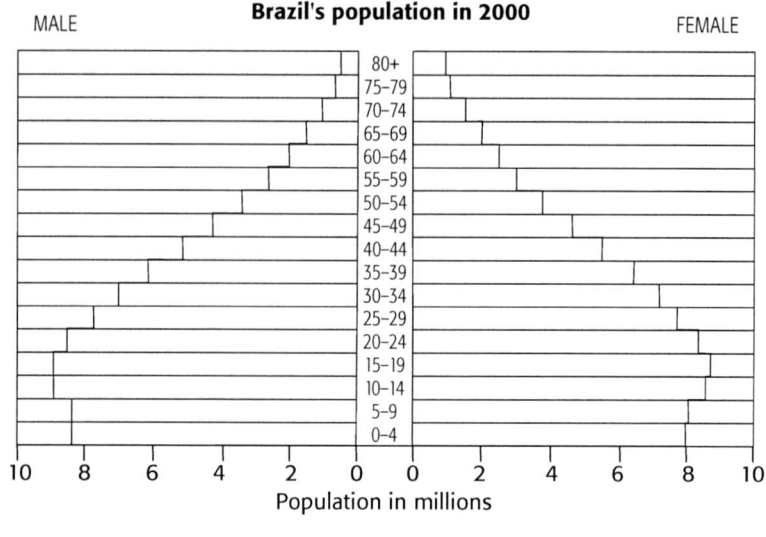

Brazil's population in 2000

Age range	Males (millions)	Females (millions)
0–4	5.5	5.7
5–9	5.8	5.8
10–14	5.9	5.9
15–19	6.0	6.0
20–24	6.2	6.1
25–29	6.3	6.2
30–34	6.4	6.3
35–39	6.5	6.4
40–44	6.5	6.6
45–49	6.4	7.3
50–54	6.6	7.0
55–59	6.0	7.0
60–64	6.0	7.2
65–69	5.8	6.7
70–74	3.9	5.9
75–79	3.2	5.1
80+	4.3	5.9

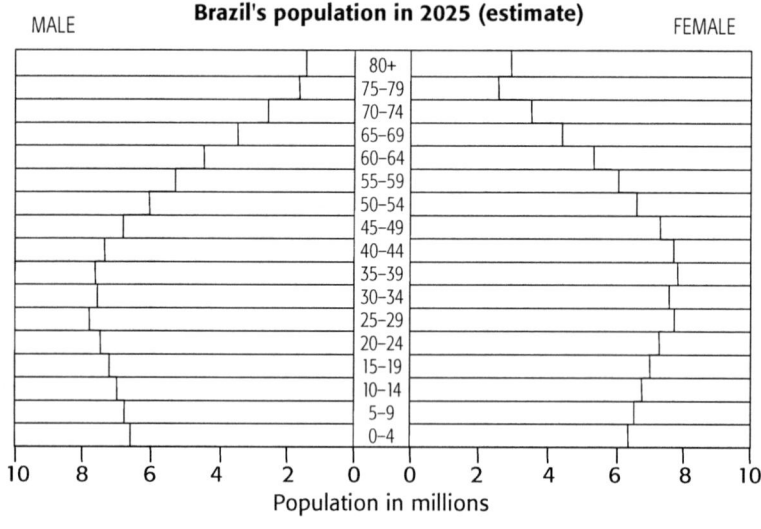

Brazil's population in 2025 (estimate)

Answer these questions in your exercise book.

4 In 2000, about how many people were:

   a males aged 35 to 39?

   b females aged 4 and below?

5 Brazil in 2000 was described as a 'country of young people'. Do you think this was true? Give reasons for your answer.

6 How will Brazil's population change between:

   a 2000 and 2025?   **b** 2025 and 2050?

7 Will Brazil still be a country of young people in 2050?

8 How do you think these changes will affect the people of Brazil?

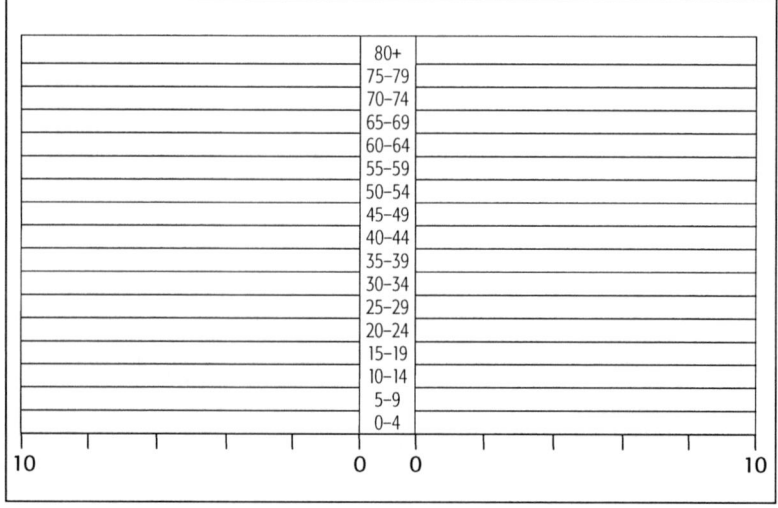

How developed is Brazil?

**

Name   **Class**

Gross Domestic Product (GDP) is the total wealth a country produces in a year – the total value of its goods and services.

We use GDP per person, or per capita, as a measure of development.

GDP per capita =

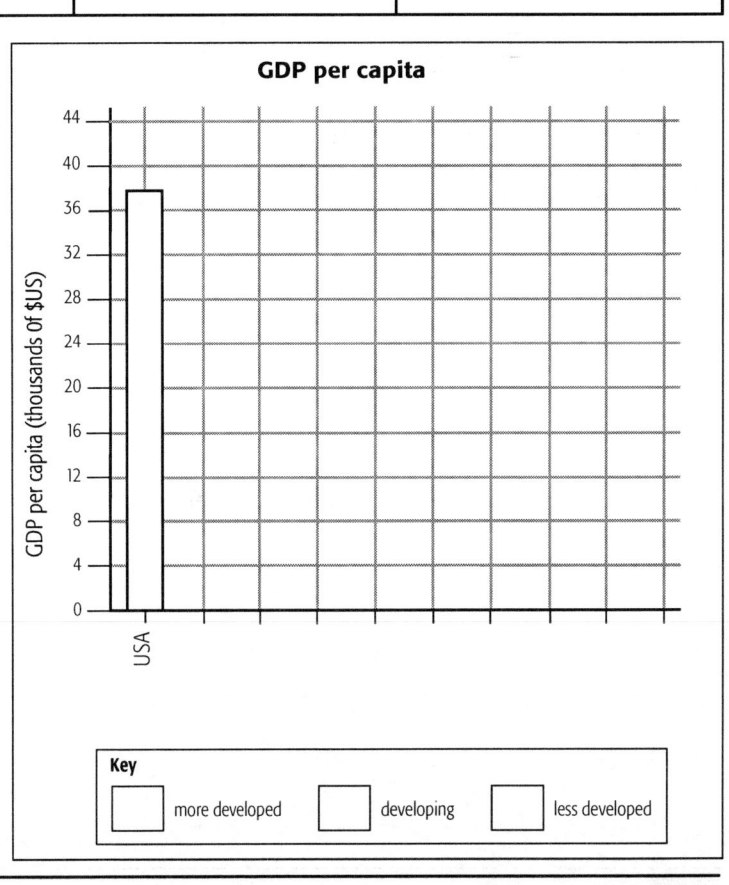

1 Complete the table on the right, putting the countries into rank order, with the highest GDP per capita first.

Country	GDP per capita (US dollars)
Japan	28 200
India	2 900
Brazil	7 600
Kenya	1 000
UK	27 700
Mexico	9 000
USA	37 800
South Korea	17 800
Bangladesh	1 900
Greece	19 900

Rank	Country	GDP per capita
1		
2		
3		
4		
5		
6		
7		
8		
9		
10		

2 On the outline on the right, draw a bar graph for GDP per capita. Plot the data in rank order.
Draw a thin outline bar for each country, as shown for the USA.

3 Now divide the countries into three groups:
a more developed
b developing
c less developed
Do this by colouring in the bars.
Use a different colour for each group.
Fill in the key to match.

In your exercise book:

4 Using the graph to help you, write a paragraph about how developed Brazil is compared with other countries.

5 Explain why GDP per capita is not always the best measure of development.

GDP per capita

GDP per capita (thousands of $US)

44
40
36
32
28
24
20
16
12
8
4
0

USA

Key

☐ more developed   ☐ developing   ☐ less developed

geog.2: 7 Oi Brazil!

Name   Class

How does Brazil compare to the United Kingdom?
Larger or smaller? More crowded or less? How do its cities
compare in size with UK cities? How does its standard
of living compare with the UK's?

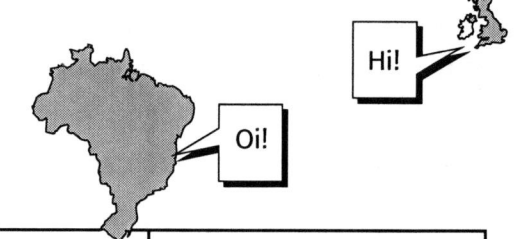

Oi!

Hi!

1 Find the facts and fill in the table below.

	Brazil	The UK
How large is it? (Find out the **area** in square kilometres.)		
How many people live there? (Find out the **population** in millions.)		
How crowded is it, on average? (Work out the **population density**.)		
What is the capital city, and how many people live there?		
What other large cities are there? (Give the **names** and **populations** for three other cities.)		
How many people live in towns and cities? (Find out the **percentage** of urban population.)		
How much food do people have, on average? (Find out the daily **calorie consumption**.)		
How long do people live for, on average? (Find out the **life expectancy**.)		
How rich are people, on average? (Find out the **Gross Domestic Product** per capita.)		

2 Now write a paragraph to say how Brazil compares with the UK.

_____

_____

_____

_____

_____

_____

_____

Name   Class

You are an economist working for the Brazilian government.

Transbank, a European banking company, lends money to people setting up new industries. It is keen to develop in areas outside Europe, and it is looking at Brazil as a possible location.

Transbank has asked you to provide a brief report on Brazil's economy.

It should be based on the information below.

It should not exceed 200 words in total and should be word-processed.

Population
- 178 million
- 79% live in urban areas
- 80% live within 200 miles of the Atlantic coast
- Largest city — São Paulo
- Capital city — Brasilia

Economy
Once dominated by agriculture, Brazil has recently undergone rapid industrial expansion. It now has a diverse modern economy. Conditions are excellent for foreign investment, as Brazil has numerous natural as well as human resources - for example iron ore and coal. But rising prices (inflation) remain a problem, and make it hard for new businesses to get established.

The primary sector
- Brazil produces 25% of the world's coffee, is the world's leading producer of orange juice, and the second largest exporter of cocoa beans.
- The logging industry has huge potential, but is under increasing pressure from environmental groups.
- Mining is developing rapidly as transport systems improve, and offers great potential for the future.

Manufacturing
- Developing rapidly as the Brazilian economy expands.
- The São Paulo region is the main manufacturing centre.
- Main products are textiles, chemicals, and transport equipment.

Culture
Brazil has a wide and lively ethnic mix.
40% of the population is of African extraction.
A large proportion is decended from European settlers: Portuguese, Italian, German and Spanish.
Cultural ties with the United States are increasing. Foreigners settling in Brazil find the people friendly and accommodating.
The cost of living is much lower than in Western Europe.

7A Brazil: what do you know? *
1   1 Belem, 2 Parana, 3 Amazon, 4 São Paulo, 5 Rio de Janeiro, 6 Belo Horizonte, 7 Highlands, 8 Atlantic.
2   Shaded boxes spell BRASILIA.

7B What is Brazil like? *
2   Brazil is the **fifth** largest country in the world.
About **180** million people live in Brazil. This is around **three** times the population of the United Kingdom.
The capital city is **Brasilia**. Brazil also has one of the world's largest cities, **São Paulo**.
The River **Amazon** flows through Brazil. It is an enormous river, carrying over one **fifth** of the world's fresh water. Where it reaches the sea, it is over **100** miles wide.
The Brazilian **Highlands** are the main mountains in Brazil. They are in the **south-east** of the country.
The remaining facts will vary from pupil to pupil.

7C How is Brazil's population changing? **
3

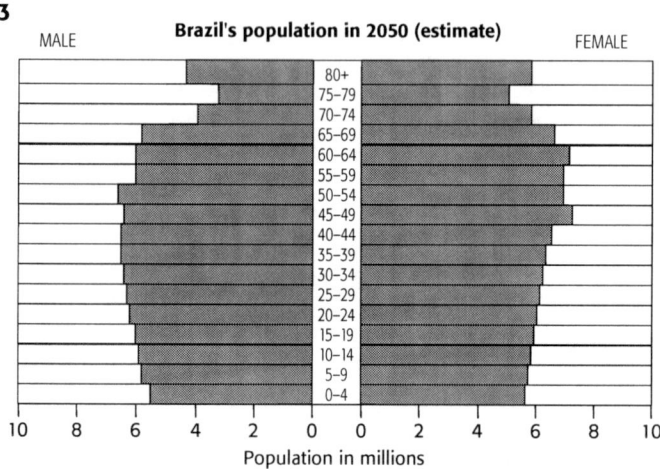

Brazil's population in 2050 (estimate)
MALE   FEMALE

80+
75–79
70–74
65–69
60–64
55–59
50–54
45–49
40–44
35–39
30–34
25–29
20–24
15–19
10–14
5–9
0–4

10 8 6 4 2 0   0 2 4 6 8 10
Population in millions

4   **a** 6 million   **b** 8 million
5   Brazil is a 'young country' because of the large proportion of people aged under 20, as shown on the pyramid.
6   **a** The 'bulge' at the bottom of the graph for 2000 will have moved higher up the pyramid by 2025. So the number of people of working age will increase. The number of young people will decrease, and the number of elderly increase.
b The 'bulge' will have moved even higher, towards the elderly. The number of elderly people will increase while the number of young people decreases even further. The population is now ageing. (The total population does not appear to have changed much between 2025 and 2050. You could ask pupils to find rough totals from the graph and table to check this.)
7   No, Brazil will no longer be a country dominated by young people.
8   As time goes on there will be fewer working people supporting an ageing population. So there will be more pressure on working people to produce, so that the country has the money to look after its elderly. Working people may have to pay higher taxes to support the elderly.

7D How developed is Brazil? **
1   The rank order is: **1** USA, 37 800   **2** Japan, 28 200   **3** UK, 27 700   **4** Greece, 19 900   **5** S. Korea, 17 800   **6** Mexico, 9 000   **7** Brazil, 7 600   **8** India, 2 900   **9** Bangladesh, 1 900   **10** Kenya, 1 000

2, 3

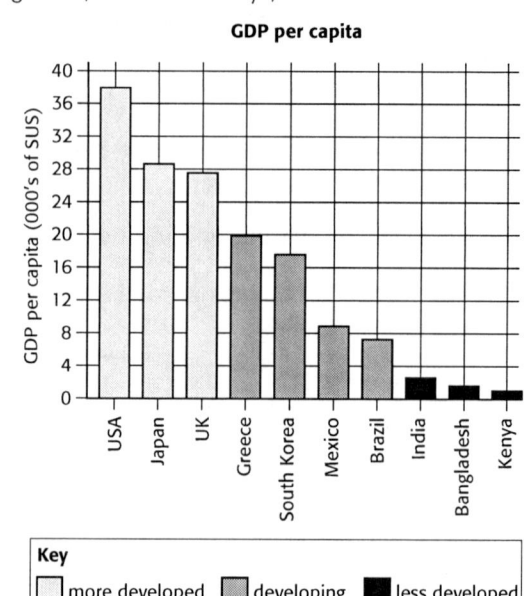

GDP per capita

GDP per capita (000's of $US)

40
36
32
28
24
20
16
12
8
4
0

USA Japan UK Greece South Korea Mexico Brazil India Bangladesh Kenya

Key
☐ more developed   ▨ developing   ■ less developed

4   From the graph, Brazil is shown to be in the middle section – it is a developing country.
5   GDP is based solely on wealth creation, and does not tell you about people's quality of life. It does not tell you whether money is being spent on the services people really need, like a clean water supply, a stable food supply, health care, education, an electricity supply and so on.
6   Measures include adult literacy rate, infant mortality rate, % with access to safe water, number of people per doctor, and so on.

7E Comparing Brazil and the United Kingdom **
Point out that data will vary a little from source to source.

	Brazil	The UK
Area	8.5 million sq km	0.24 million sq km
Population	178 million	60 million
Population density	20.9 people per sq km	250 people per sq km
Capital and its population	Brasilia 2.2 million	London 7.01 million
Three other cities and their populations (for example…)	São Paulo 10.3 million	Birmingham 0.97 million
	Rio de Janeiro 6.2 million	Leeds 0.42 million
	Belo Horizonte 2.4 million	Manchester 0.40 million
% urban population	80.7	89.4
Average daily calorie consumption	2974 calories	3276 calories
Life expectancy	68	78
GDP per capita	7 600	27 700

7F Brazil: the place for new industry! ***
Answers will need to be marked against information boxes.

Brazil by rail

***

Aims

■ Pupils are able to understand the history of the growth of Brazil's railway network
■ Pupils can relate the history of the growth of Brazil's railways to a general model of transport network growth
■ Pupils can relate this to environmental issues

Introduction

This activity addresses Unit 11 of the QCA Scheme of Work (*Investigating Brazil*).

It also provides extension material for unit 7.3 on pages 110-111 of **geog.2**. It uses the map of Brazil's natural resources on page 109 of **geog.2**.

Activity

Initially pupils should put the five descriptions of the stages of growth of Brazil's railway network (page 237) into the correct order (d, a, e, b, c) and place them on the time-line (pages 238-239).

They should then compare the growth of Brazil's railway network with the model provided on page 236. This model, by Taaffe, Morrill, and Gould, links the growth of transport networks to economic development.

Pupils should note that different parts of Brazil's railway network have developed to different stages, and explore why this might be.

In questions 6 and 7 pupils then consider the likely future of Brazil's railway network. These questions require pupils to draw on their prior learning about Brazil. Less-able pupils may require some help with these questions.

In a whole-class session, you could use this as a verbal (discussion) activity; then, using groups, you could get pupils to write up their answers.

Name   **Class**

Development of a transport network

(a)

(b)

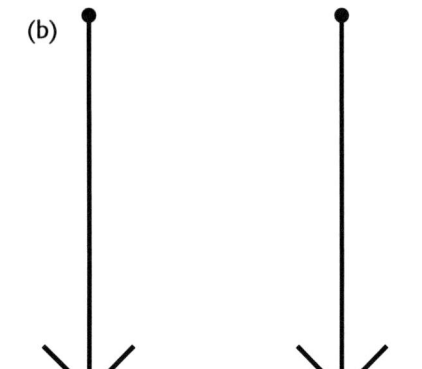

(c)

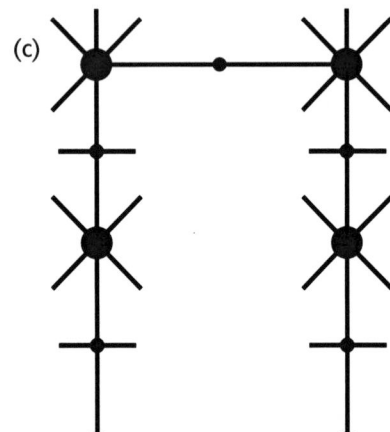

(d)

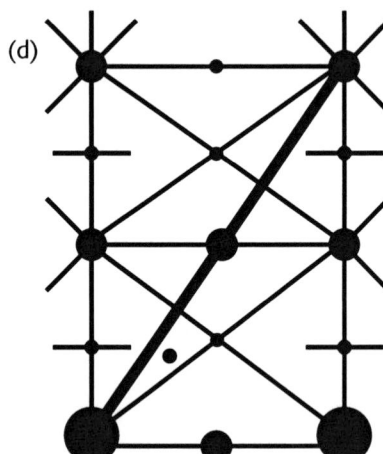

This model suggests that transport networks tend to develop in four stages:

A   The first stage shows small ports and trading stations along the coast of an undeveloped region. Local tracks lead inland for a short way to supply the ports with goods and food, but there is little contact along the coast between one port and the next.

B   Stage 2 shows the development of main routes inland with small settlements growing up at the inland ends of these routes. The coastal ports with inland routes grow because of the increased trade they carry.

C   The third stage consists of the growth of links between the coastal ports and of other routes connecting the inland towns.

D   In stage 4 all the towns develop links with each other, and the biggest roads and the busiest railways or air routes connect the most important towns.

Name   **Class**

A good railway network is a sign of a highly developed country. How good is Brazil's railway network? How and why did it grow to its current state? What is its future? You are going to do an activity to try to answer these questions.

Tasks

1   Have a look at the five boxed labels below. They fit into the five gaps on 'The development of Brazil's railways' timeline. You need to work out which label goes where.

2   Now look at your 'Development of a transport network' page. This model has four stages. Which stage or stages do you think are shown by each map of Brazilian railways?

3   The 1987 map seems to show that different parts of Brazil are at different stages of development. Which stages would you say have been reached by the railways near:
   a   Belém?
   b   Fortaleza?
   c   Porto Alegre?

4   Look at the map on page 109 of **geog.2**. What goods do you think are carried on the railways near Belem, Fortaleza, and Porto Alegre?

5   Do you think that railways are likely to be **more** or **less** harmful to the environment than roads? (Hint: which has more engines; 1 passenger train, or the buses or cars that carry that number of people?)

6   Do you think that Brazil's railway network is likely to grow or shrink?

7   **a**   What do you think ought to happen in the future?
   b   What do you think is most likely to happen in the future?
   c   If you were the Brazilian Government, what would you do?

Labels to be sorted and inserted in the correct blank spaces on the time-line

> **a** São Paulo to Santos rail link is built. A system using cables and cogs is used to climb the steep slope between the two places.

> **b** The rail system grows with many branches. Inland and cross links are added to form an 'iron quadrilateral'.

> **c** Most railways suffer from old equipment and poor maintenance, and are losing money. Only the Madeira to Mamore sightseeing train and Victoria to Minas to Tubarao railways remain profitable.

> **d** The first railway in Brazil is built by Dr Thomas Cochrane, linking Rio with Petropolis in the mountains.

> **e** Two main railways are linked by a coastal route. Branch lines are often narrow gauge (this means they are small-scale railways and can't take full-sized trains).

geog.2: 7 Oi Brazil!

Name   Class

The development of Brazil's railways

1854

1867

1869

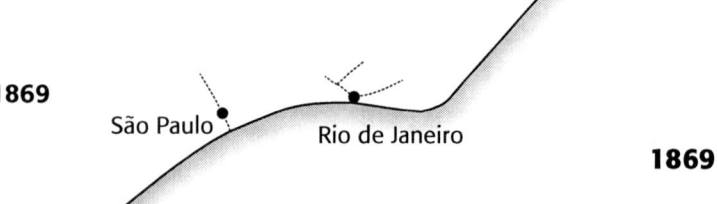

1869

1869 – 1889

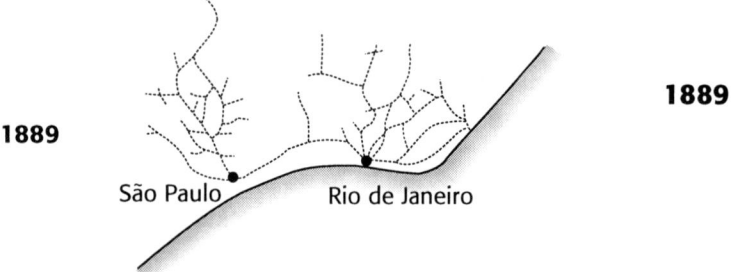

1889

1889

1890 – 1955

Brazil's railways are run by 22 private companies, many using different gauges
(having different gauges means not all trains can travel on all lines).

1955

1955

1957   The Brazilian Government nationalises 17 of the 22 railway companies (this means the government takes control of most of the railways). It begins to close lines that aren't making money. The Government says that all railways must be standard gauge (meaning all trains run on one type of track).

The São Paulo railways are still run by five private companies.

1971   São Paulo State Railways is created through merging the five private companies.

1987

Locating a car plant in Brazil

**

Aims

- Pupils learn about the geography of Brazil
- Pupils can locate and describe key features of Brazil's natural and human environment
- Pupils are able to work as a group and make and justify decisions

Introduction

This activity addresses Unit 11 of the QCA Scheme of Work (*What is it like? Are there differences within the country?*). It is a decision-making exercise that can be done after unit 7.10 on pages 124-125 of **geog.2**.

Pupils will take on the role of the senior management of a car manufacturer. It will be their job to find the optimum location for a new car assembly plant.

Pupils will gain experience in decision making and presenting a case in public using whatever techniques are available, from designing a poster to using PowerPoint.

Activity

1   Divide the class into groups of four, or slightly more depending on the class size.

2   Give each group an information sheet (page 241) and a set of role sheets (pages 242-245). Instruct the groups to decide between them who should take on each management role.

3   Pupils should work on their own (or in pairs depending on the size of the group) to complete the tasks on their individual role sheets.

4   The pupils within each group should compare their findings and discuss which region they should build their car factory in.

Presentation

Each management team should prepare a poster to present their conclusions. There is an opportunity to use ICT here. Pupils could design their poster using a word processing programme or a desktop publishing package. They could also graph some of their individual findings using a spreadsheet programme. Alternatively, pupils could present their findings in a short PowerPoint presentation.

Pupils may find the map of Brazil in the Outline maps section of this resource file helpful.

Pupils should present their finished posters (or PowerPoint presentations) to the class, briefly explaining how and why they chose their factory site.

It is expected that the groups will select the South East as the optimum region to build their factory in.

Name   Class

Information sheet

As you have read, Brazil is a country with a lot of variety.

It has several different ecosystems and its climate varies depending on where you are. It is rich in natural resources but not every area has the same resources.

There is also variety in **where** and **how** people live. Some areas have a very high population density but others are nearly empty. Some people live in luxurious conditions but others are very poor indeed.

In this activity you will be finding out more about the differences between Brazil's regions.

Activity

You are on the management board of a firm that makes cars. Your firm has decided to manufacture a new ethanol-powered car. It has been decided that the assembly plant will be built somewhere in Brazil. But which region is best? You are going to decide.

First you need to think of a name for your car, and a trademark or logo.

Then, within your group, decide who is going to take on each role. Each board should have the following:

- **Personnel Manager**   Responsible for finding a cheap but educated workforce.
- **Transport Manager**   In charge of getting raw materials to the factory and distributing the finished cars.
- **Production Manager**   In charge of supplying power to the factory and making sure production is as efficient as possible.
- **Sales Manager**   Responsible for finding a good market for the finished cars.

Follow the instructions on your individual role cards.

Name   Class

Personnel Manager

As Personnel Manager you are looking for a region with lots of cheap labour. The higher the population density, the cheaper the labour should be. This is because there will be many people in a small area needing jobs. It would also be good to find a region where lots of people go to school, so that you have educated workers.

1 Look at this table. You need to put the regions into rank order of population density, with the densest first and the least dense fifth. Write the rank number for each region in the third column.

Region of Brazil	Average number of people per square km	Rank
North	2.9	
South	39.5	
North East	28.3	
South East	70.1	
West Central	6.1	

2 Now look at the table below. You need to rank the regions in order of education. The region that has the lowest percentage of children **not** in school should go first and the highest fifth. Write the rank number for each region in the third column.

Region of Brazil	% of children in urban areas who *don't* go to school	Rank
North		
South		
North East		
South East		
West Central		

3 Add the ranks for each region together. As Personnel Manager you are looking for the region with the lowest total.

Write the region here: _____

4 Compare your results with the rest of your group. Which region is the best for you to build your factory in? Be prepared to compromise!

Write the region here: _____

5 Now you are going to present your findings. Still working in your group, design a poster explaining where you think the factory should be built. You need to say why you have decided on this region.

Remember to put your company logo on the poster.

6 Show your poster to the other groups. Be prepared to explain why you chose the region you did. Which region did they decide on?

Locating a car plant in Brazil ✱✱

Name _____   Class _____

Transport Manager

You are looking for a region that has plenty of the natural resources that you need. If your car factory is in this region you won't have to pay high transport costs.

1   Look at this map. It shows how much iron, copper, and nickel each region has. These are the raw materials that your factory will need most. Put the regions in rank order. The one with the most iron, copper, and nickel should go first. Write your rank numbers in the table.

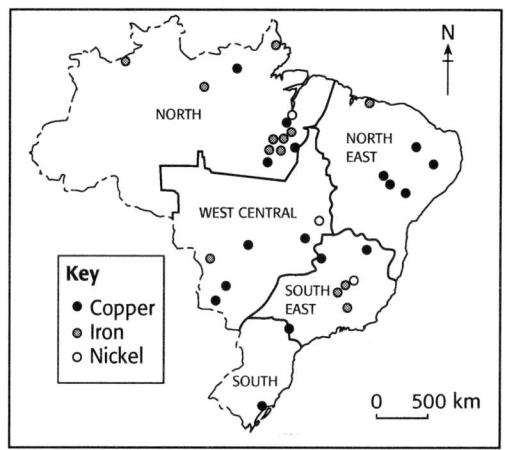

Region of Brazil	Rank
North	
South	
North East	
South East	
West Central	

2   The government says it will give you a development grant if you distribute your cars by rail. Look at this railway map. Which region has the densest rail network? Put the regions in rank order with the densest first. Write your rank numbers in the table.

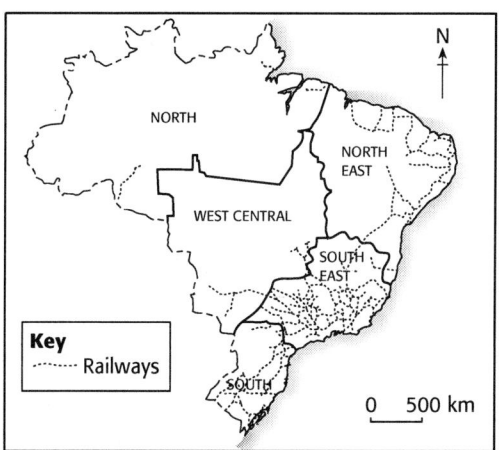

Region of Brazil	Rank
North	
South	
North East	
South East	
West Central	

3   Add together the ranks for each region. As Transport Manager you are looking for the region with the lowest total.

Write the region here: _____

4   Compare your results with the rest of your group. Which region is the best for you to build your factory in? Be prepared to compromise!

Write the region here: _____

5   Now you are going to present your findings. Still working in your group, design a poster explaining where you think the factory should be built. You need to say why you have decided on this area.

Remember to put your company logo on your poster.

6   Show your poster to the other groups. Be prepared to explain why you chose the region you did. Which region did they decide on?

geog.2: 7 Oi Brazil!

Name   Class

Production Manager

You are looking for the region with the highest productivity. One way to measure this is to find out how much each region contributes to Brazil's gross domestic product or GDP.

1   Put the regions in rank order of GDP with the highest number first. Write the rank number for each region in the third column.

Region of Brazil	% of the total GDP it contributes	Rank
North	4.4	
South	17.1	
North East	13.8	
South East	59.4	
West Central	5.3	

2   Now look at the table below. To be efficient you need a good water supply. Put the regions in rank order of the % of homes in urban areas without water supply. Put the region with the lowest % first. Write the rank number for each region in the third column.

Region of Brazil	% of homes in urban areas *without* a water supply	Rank
North	30.9	
South	5.1	
North East	13.9	
South East	4.5	
West Central	17.3	

3   Add the two ranks together. As Production Manager you are looking for the region with the lowest total.

Write the region here: _____

4   Compare your results with the rest of your group. Which region is the best for you to build your factory in? Be prepared to compromise!

Write the region here: _____

5   Now you are going to present your findings. Still working in your group, design a poster explaining where you think the factory should be built. You need to say why you have decided on this area.

Remember to put your company logo on your poster.

6   Show your poster to the other groups. Be prepared to explain why you chose the region you did. Which region did they decide on?

Locating a car plant in Brazil ✱✱

Name   Class

geog.2: 7 Oi Brazil!

Sales Manager

As Sales Manager you are looking for people to sell the cars to when they are finished. So you want a region with a high population density, but with a high income per head.

1   Look at this table. Which region has the highest number of people per square km? Put all the regions in rank order with this region first. Write the rank number for each region in the third column.

Region of Brazil	Average number of people per square km	Rank
North	2.9	
South	39.5	
North East	28.3	
South East	70.1	
West Central	6.1	

2   Do the same with the % of GDP which each region contributes, as this is a sign of wealth. Write the rank number for each region in the third column.

Region of Brazil	% of the total GDP it contributes	Rank
North	4.4	
South	17.1	
North East	13.8	
South East	59.4	
West Central	5.3	

3   Add the two ranks for each region together. As Sales Manager you are looking for the region with the lowest total.

Write the region here: _____

Compare your results with the rest of your group. Which region is the best for you to build your factory in? Be prepared to compromise!

Write the region here: _____

4   Now you are going to present your findings. Still working in your group, design a poster explaining where you think the factory should be built. You need to say why you have decided on this area.

Remember to put your company logo on your poster.

5   Show your poster to the other groups. Be prepared to explain why you chose the region you did. Which region did they decide on?

Oi Brazil!

The assessment opportunities for Oi Brazil! are as follows:

■ The **level-marked assessment** 'How quickly is Brazil developing?' on pages 247-249.

In this assessment, pupils assess Brazil's rate of economic development, and compare it with what has happened in other countries. To do this, they are required to graph data, then work out change in GDP per capita as a percentage. They then write a description of Brazil's changing wealth, and, finally, suggest effective indicators of development other than GDP per capita.

A **feedback form** for the level-marked assessment is provided on page 250.

■ The **scored test** on pages 251-256.

■ Opportunities for interim assessments provided by **geog.2**:

Brazil by rail (an investigation) on pages 235-239 of this file.

Locating a car plant in Brazil (a decision-making exercise, with the opportunity for pupils to work in groups) on pages 240-245 of this file.

Activities 14, 16, 17, 24, 26, 27, 30, 34, 37, and 38 in the *Further suggestions for class and homework* section on pages 154-155 of the *geog.2 teacher's handbook*.

Worksheet B: Contact – right or wrong? for *The lost tribes of Brazil* (a webfile) in *geog.2, Oi Brazil!* on *geog.world*.

■ The **self-assessment form** for the whole Oi Brazil! chapter on page 257.

Oi Brazil!

Name   **Class**   **Date**

How quickly is Brazil developing?

The level at which I am currently working is

so my target level for this assessment is

because

Assessment task

In this assessment, you are going to find out about the economic development of Brazil. You will:

■ draw a graph to show how the wealth of selected countries has changed over time;

■ calculate, as a percentage, the change in wealth for selected countries over time;

■ describe and explain what your results tell you, and suggest other suitable ways of measuring the wealth of a nation.

You are going concentrate on one indicator that is often used to measure development, **GDP per capita**. (Hint: GDP means gross domestic product.) A country's GDP per capita is worked out using this equation:

$$\frac{\text{Total wealth produced in a year}}{\text{Total population}} = \text{GDP per capita (US \$ PPP)}$$

(Hint: PPP or *purchasing power parity* means the GDP is adjusted to allow for the fact that a dollar buys more in some countries than others.)

Before you start work, make sure you understand the task and what you have to do. And look at the **success criteria** on the next page, so that you know how to achieve your target level – or better!

Level 3
- You attempt to draw a graph to show the data in the table.
- You attempt to work out the % change in GDP per capita for some countries.
- You describe how the wealth of Brazil has changed.

Level 4
- You complete a graph to show the data in the table.
- You attempt to work out the % change in GDP per capita for all countries.
- You describe how the wealth of Brazil has changed and relate this to what has happened in other countries.
- You suggest one alternative development indicator.

Level 5
- You draw an appropriate graph to show the data in the table.
- You calculate correctly the % change in GDP per capita for all countries.
- You describe how the wealth of Brazil has changed and give at least one simple reason for this change.
- You relate the change in Brazil's wealth to what has happened in other countries.
- You give simple reasons why GDP per capita is not always the best way to measure development.
- You suggest at least one alternative development indicator.

Level 6
- Your graph is drawn accurately and labelled clearly.
- You calculate correctly the % change in GDP per capita for all countries.
- You describe how the wealth of Brazil has changed and relate this to what has happened in other countries
- You give at least three simple reasons for this change.
- You explain clearly why GDP per capita is not always the best way to measure development.
- You suggest three alternative development indicators.

Level 7
- Your graph is drawn accurately and labelled clearly, with no errors.
- You calculate correctly the % change in GDP per capita for all countries.
- You describe and explain fully how the wealth of Brazil has changed and suggest several reasons for this change.
- You evaluate the use of GDP per capita as a development indicator with reference to at least one named example.
- You suggest three alternative development indicators.

Level 8
- Your graph is drawn accurately and labelled clearly, with no errors.
- You calculate correctly the % change in GDP per capita for all countries.
- You describe and explain fully how the wealth of Brazil has changed and suggest several reasons for this change. In your answer, you consider factors affecting the changing wealth of the other countries.
- You evaluate critically the use of GDP per capita as a development indicator with reference to at least one named example.
- You suggest several alternative development indicators and discuss their use with reference to examples at different levels of economic development.

Exceptional performance

In addition to Level 8...
- You suggest how a combination of measures can be used to measure development, with reference to at least one named example.
- You evaluate critically the sources of evidence provided, and suggest appropriate lines for further enquiry.

Look at the table below. It gives the GDP per capita for ten countries. Figures are given for three different years, so that you can see how the wealth of each country has changed over time.

GDP per capita (US $ PPP) for selected countries

Country	1993	1998	2003	% change 1993-2003
Bangladesh	1290	1361	1900	
Brazil	5500	6625	7600	
Greece	8950	13 943	19 900	
Japan	21 223	23 257	28 000	
India	1240	2077	2900	
Kenya	1400	980	1000	
Mexico	7010	7704	9000	
South Korea	9710	13 478	17 700	
UK	17 063	20 336	27 700	
USA	25 764	29 605	37 800	

1 On a separate sheet of paper, draw a graph to show the information in the table. (Hint: think carefully about the type of graph to use.)
2 Now work out the % change in GDP per capita, for each country, from 1993 to 2003. To do this, use this equation:

$$\frac{\text{GDP per capita for 1993}}{\text{GDP per capita for 2003}} \times 100 = \text{\% change from 1993 to 2003}$$

Write your results in the last column in the table. Then cut out your table and stick it with your graph.

3 Underneath your completed graph and table, describe how Brazil's wealth has changed since 1993. How does this change compare with what has happened in the other countries?
4 Suggest reasons for your answer to question 3.
5 Why do you think that GDP per capita is not always the best way to measure development?
6 Suggest three other ways of measuring development.

Oi Brazil!

Name **Class** **Date**

How quickly is Brazil developing?

Assessment task
An analysis of the changing wealth of Brazil compared to what has happened in nine other countries.

Level awarded:

Teacher's comments:

Targets for improvement:

- Describe ideas in greater detail. ❏
- Suggest more reasons/processes to explain geographical ideas. ❏
- Try to use more geographical words and terms in your writing. ❏
- Try to support your writing with further, researched ideas. ❏
- Improve accuracy and/or presentation skills. ❏
- Use a greater range of presentation styles/techniques in your work. ❏
- Improve personal organisation and homework to raise your achievement level. ❏
- Ask for help about ideas you don't understand. ❏

Student's comments:

Oi Brazil! Test

Name _____ **Class** _____ **Date** _____

1   Brazil is the fifth largest country in the world, but which continent is it in? Tick the correct one from this list.   *[1 mark]*

❏ Asia

❏ Europe

❏ North America

❏ South America

❏ Africa

2   **a** This box tells you about some of the physical features of Brazil – but there are some words missing. Fill in the gaps using the words below.

cooler and wet	Amazon	hot and wet
Highlands	rain	rainforest

The world's second longest river, the River _____, is in the north of Brazil.

Around this is the Amazon _____. The main mountain range in Brazil is

called the Brazilian _____. Brazil has different climate zones. In the north

it is ____ __ _____. The north east can be a difficult place to live because there is

not much _____. In the middle of Brazil it is quite hot all year, with a wet and a

dry season. Towards the south it is ____ __ _____all year.   *[6 marks]*

   b Below are two climate graphs. One shows the climate in the north, in the Amazon rainforest, the other shows the climate in the south, but the labels are missing. Under each graph write either 'North Brazil' or 'South Brazil'.   *[2 marks]*

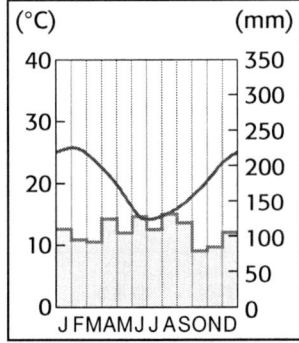

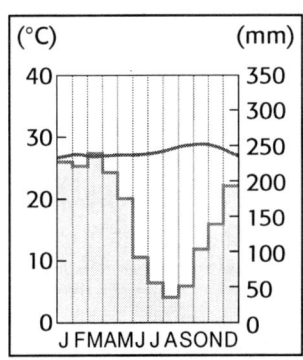

_____   _____

3 Brazil has six main ecosystems. Draw a line from each box to the correct part of the map.
Two have been done for you. *[4 marks]*

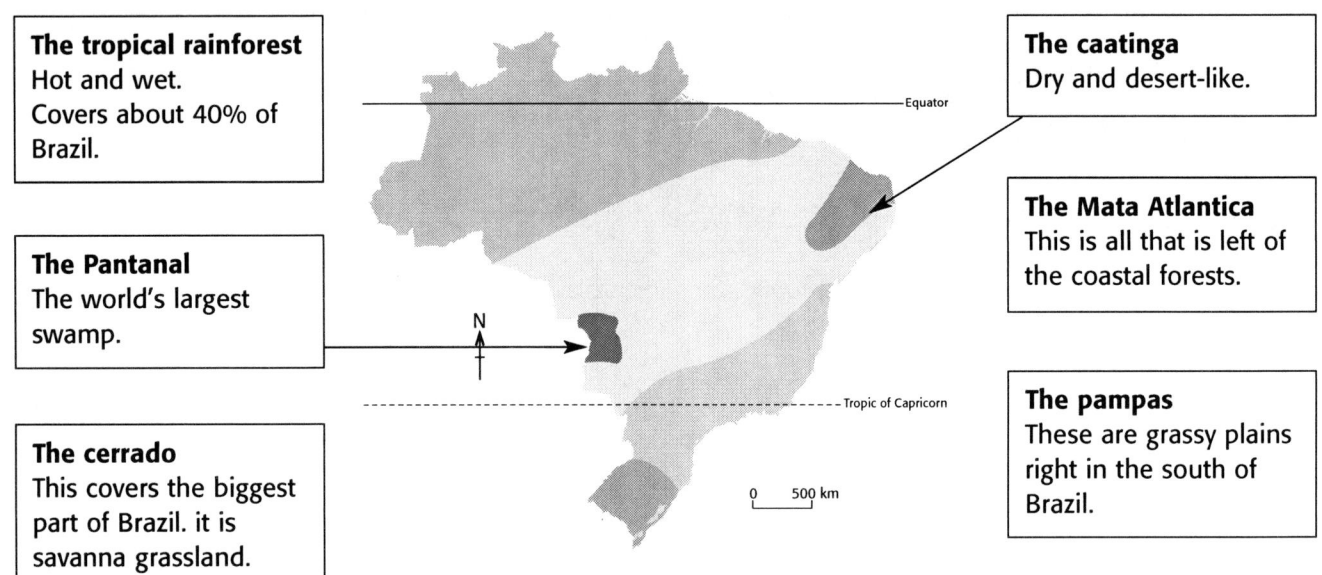

The tropical rainforest
Hot and wet.
Covers about 40% of
Brazil.

The Pantanal
The world's largest
swamp.

The cerrado
This covers the biggest
part of Brazil. it is
savanna grassland.

The caatinga
Dry and desert-like.

The Mata Atlantica
This is all that is left of
the coastal forests.

The pampas
These are grassy plains
right in the south of
Brazil.

Equator

Tropic of Capricorn

N

0   500 km

4 Brazil has lots of natural resources. Put the resources in the box into the correct columns of
the table. *[5 marks]*

| oil | copper | iron | gold | cocoa |
| coal | gas | coffee | diamonds | bananas |

Minerals	Fuels	Crops

5 **a** Brazil's population has grown over time. These boxes tell you what has happened, but
they are not in the right order. Show what order they should go in by putting the correct
number in each circle. *[5 marks]*

( ) In 1500 there were about
5 million people, called
Indios.

( ) In the last 100 years
people from all over the
world have come to Brazil.

( ) In 1700 gold and
diamonds were found and
500 000 Portuguese came
to find their fortunes.

( ) The Portuguese brought
slaves from Africa to work
on their farms.

( ) On 22 April 1500 the
Portuguese arrived and
claimed Brazil.

b Most Brazilians live on or near the coast, where there are ports and large cities, and the weather is pleasant. **Explain** TWO reasons why people would want to live near the coast in Brazil.   *[2 marks]*

_____

_____

_____

_____

6   The population of Brazil varies over the country. You are going to make a choropleth (shaded) map showing population density.

Region	Average number of people per km squared
North	2.9
South	39.5
North East	28.3
South East	70.1
West Central	6.1

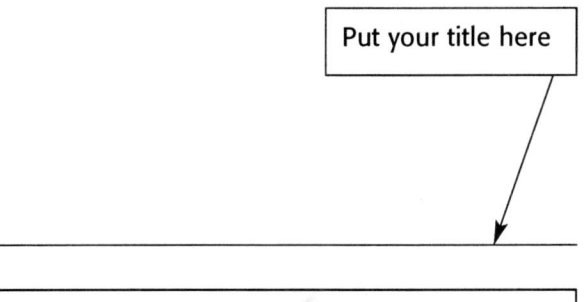

Put your title here

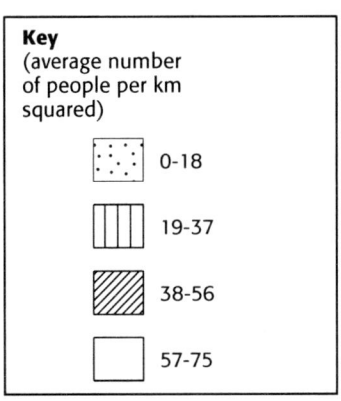

Key
(average number of people per km squared)

0-18
19-37
38-56
57-75

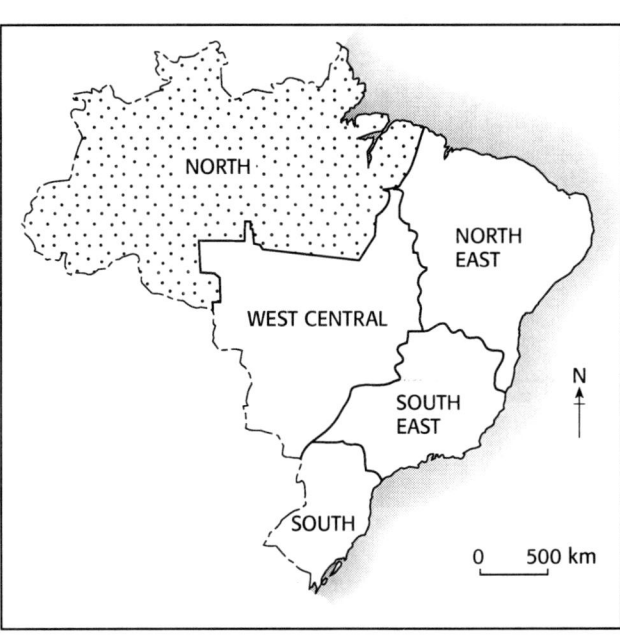

a Complete the key with a sensible choice of shading for the last box.   *[1 mark]*

b Use the information in the table to fill in the regions on the map with the correct shading.   *[4 marks]*

c Write a title at the top of the map.   *[1 mark]*

d Which region is the most densely populated, that is has the most people per square km?

_____   *[1 mark]*

e Which region is the least densely populated, that is has the least people per square km?

_____   *[1 mark]*

7 How developed is Brazil? The table below compares Brazil with two other countries, the USA and Nicaragua.

Indicator of development	Brazil	The USA	Nicaragua
GNP per capita ($US)	3600	27 000	380
Life expectancy (years)	66	76	68
Adult literacy (%)	83	98	34
Daily calories per person	2820	3700	2000

a Put the three countries in order of development (most first)   *[3 marks]*

1._____

2._____

3._____

b The indicators are averages. That means that there are differences in the quality of life for people in Brazil. The poorest people in the cities have a very difficult life, and the richest people in the cities live a luxurious life. Suggest TWO differences in the lives of the richest and poorest people in a Brazilian city.   *[2 marks]*

_____

_____

_____

8 Brazil wants to improve the standard of living for its people and become more developed. It could do this in a variety of ways, like:

▌ selling things to other countries - although often other countries only want to buy cheap natural resources, so Brazil can't make much money;

▌ encouraging tourists - although most of the money from tourists goes to owners of hotel chains, who live in countries like the USA, and local people don't get much profit;

▌ encouraging foreign companies to set up factories in Brazil - although most of the jobs are for people from abroad, and most of the money goes back to the country the company came from;

▌ getting loans from other countries - although they'd have to pay back lots more money in interest;

▌ selling things like timber and minerals from the rainforest - although many people are worried about the effects of destroying the rainforest.

You are going to write out a plan for Brazil to improve its level of development.

Use these hints to help you:

★ Choose one or more from the list above, or make up your own ideas.

★ Explain why you have chosen these ideas.

★ Suggest why this plan is not perfect.

★ Think about the types of people who would like and not like your plan.

★ Think about ways to make the plan more attractive and to solve some of the problems.

★ Consider how things might change over time.

_____

_____

_____

_____

_____

_____

_____

_____

_____

_____

_____

_____

_____

_____

_____

_____

_____

_____

_____

_____ *[12 marks]*

| | Total marks: 50 | Total score: | /50 |

1 1 mark for correct tick.
✓ South America

2 a 1 mark for each correct gap filled.

> The world's second longest river, the River <u>Amazon</u>, is in the north of Brazil. Around this is the Amazon <u>rainforest</u>. The main mountain range in Brazil is called the <u>Brazilian Highlands</u>.
>
> Brazil has different climate zones. In the north it is <u>hot and wet</u>. The north east can be a difficult place to live because there is not much <u>rain</u>. In the middle of Brazil it is quite hot all year, with a wet and a dry season. Towards the south it is <u>cooler and wet</u> all year.

b 1 mark for each correct label.

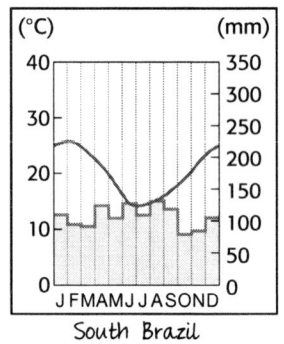

South Brazil

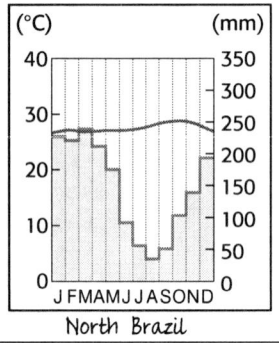

North Brazil

3 See figure below. 1 mark for each correct arrow.

4 ½ mark for each correct word in the table.

Minerals	Fuels	Crops
Copper	Oil	Cocoa
Iron	Gas	Coffee
Diamonds	Coal	Bananas
Gold		

5 a 1 mark for each correct number. In order, 1, 5, 4, 3 and 2.

b 1 mark for each sensible reason (up to maximum of 2) e.g. there are more jobs in the cities; it is easier to grow food due to the pleasant climate.

6 a 1 mark for darker shading in the last box (e.g. cross-hatched).

b 1 mark for each correctly shaded region (maximum of 4).

c 1 mark for a sensible title.

d South East (1 mark).

e North (1 mark).

7 a USA (1 mark). Brazil (1 mark). Nicaragua (1 mark).

b 1 mark per difference (up to maximum of 2) e.g. poor have less education, poor live in shacks and rich live in large houses or apartments.

8 This question is similar to GCSE decision-making exercises and is marked in a similar way:

marks   description

1-2   A plan is suggested with no explanation.

3-4   A plan is suggested with some explanation.

5-6   A plan is suggested with clear explanation.

7-8   A plan is suggested with clear explanation, with consideration of people's views and idea of interaction between the factors.

9-10   A plan is suggested with clear explanation, with consideration of people's views and idea of interaction between the factors. Idea of conflict between people. Awareness of sustainable development.

11-12   A plan is suggested with clear explanation, with consideration of people's views and idea of interaction between the factors. Idea of conflict between people. Awareness of sustainable development. Pupil is aware that people's opinions can be changed, and that the plan will change over time.

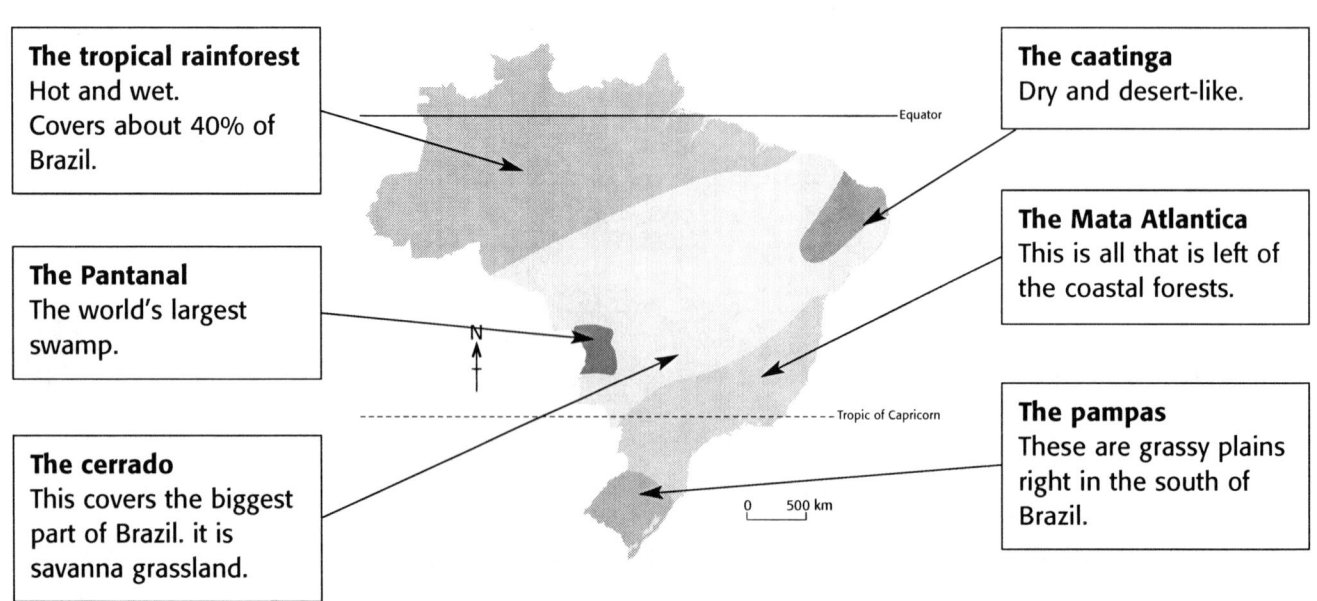

The tropical rainforest
Hot and wet.
Covers about 40% of Brazil.

The Pantanal
The world's largest swamp.

The cerrado
This covers the biggest part of Brazil. it is savanna grassland.

The caatinga
Dry and desert-like.

The Mata Atlantica
This is all that is left of the coastal forests.

The pampas
These are grassy plains right in the south of Brazil.

Equator

Tropic of Capricorn

0   500 km

Oi Brazil!

Name   Class   Date

Now I've reached the end of the Oi Brazil! chapter:

	Yes	Think so	No
◆ I know where Brazil is in the world.			
◆ I can describe Brazil's main physical features, its climate zones and its ecosystems, and can locate these features on a map.			
◆ I know what natural resources are found in Brazil.			
◆ I know why Brazil has such a mix of races.			
◆ I can describe how people are spread around Brazil, and explain why some areas have more people than others, and some fewer.			
◆ I know the top 10 cities in Brazil, and where they are on a map.			
◆ I can describe Brazil's employment structure, and how it has changed over time.			
◆ I know what clues to look for to see how developed a country is, and can describe how developed Brazil is, compared to countries like the UK and India.			
◆ I can describe and explain the inequality in Brazilian society.			
◆ I can describe the differences between Brazil's North East and South East regions.			
◆ I know some of the ways in which Brazil and the rest of the world are interdependent.			
◆ I can explain why Brazil's plans for the future are a threat to the rainforest.			

◆ I know what these terms mean:

GDP ❏   GDP per capita ❏   life expectancy ❏   infant mortality ❏

adult literacy rate ❏   undernourished ❏

The part of this topic that I enjoyed most or found most interesting was:

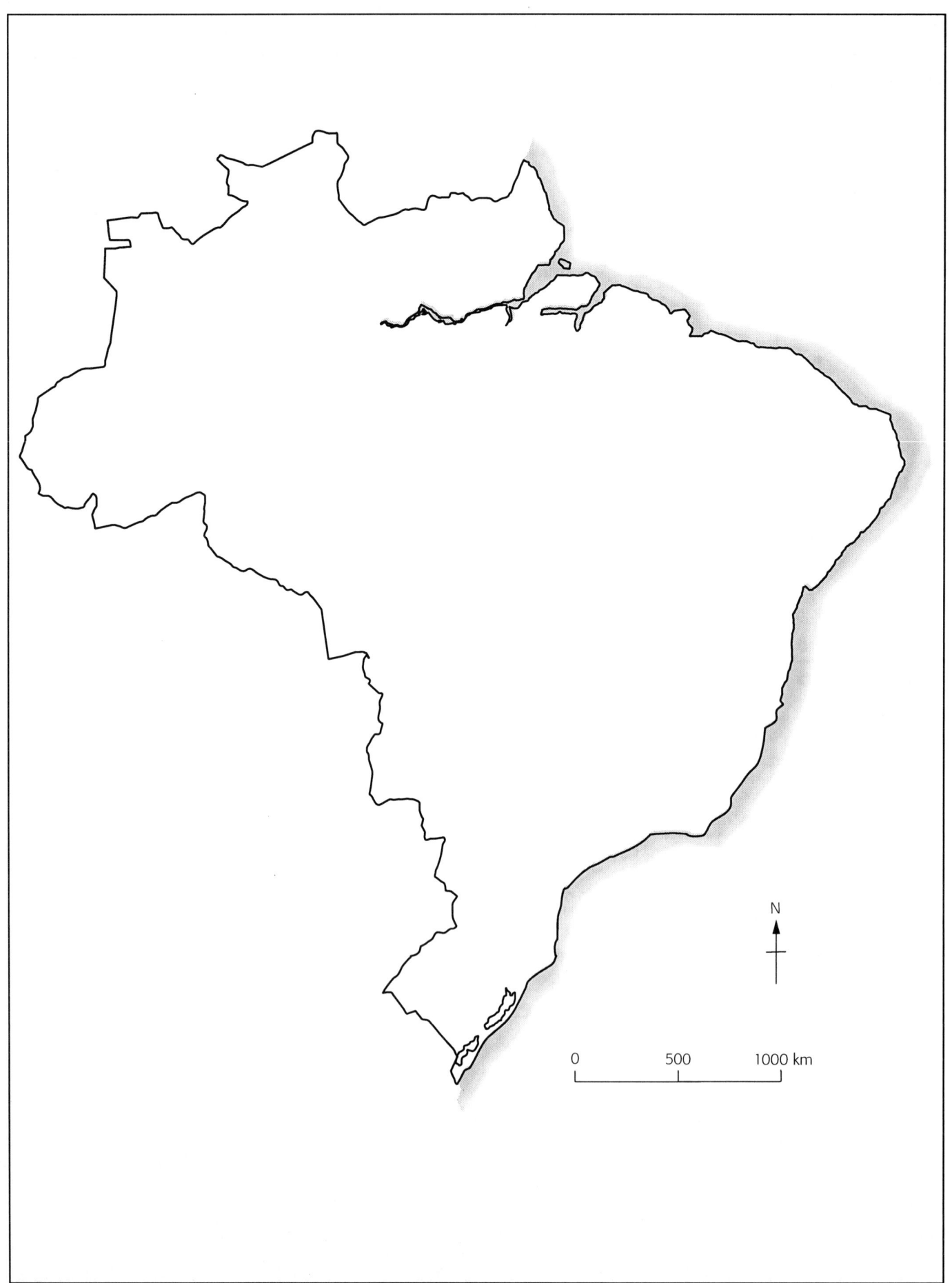

N

| 0 | 500 | 1000 km |

Brazil (political)

0   500   1000 km

N

N

0   1000 km

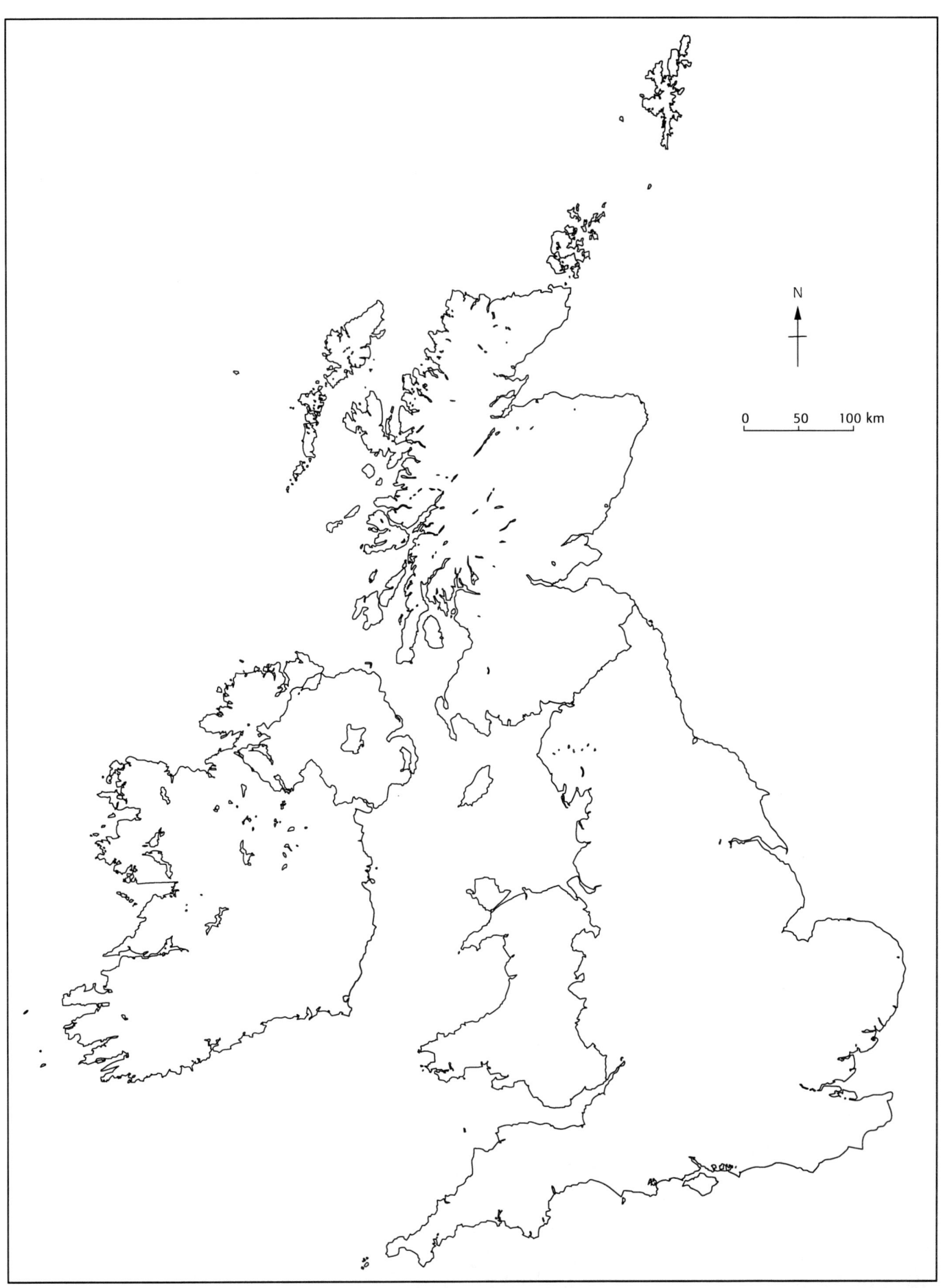

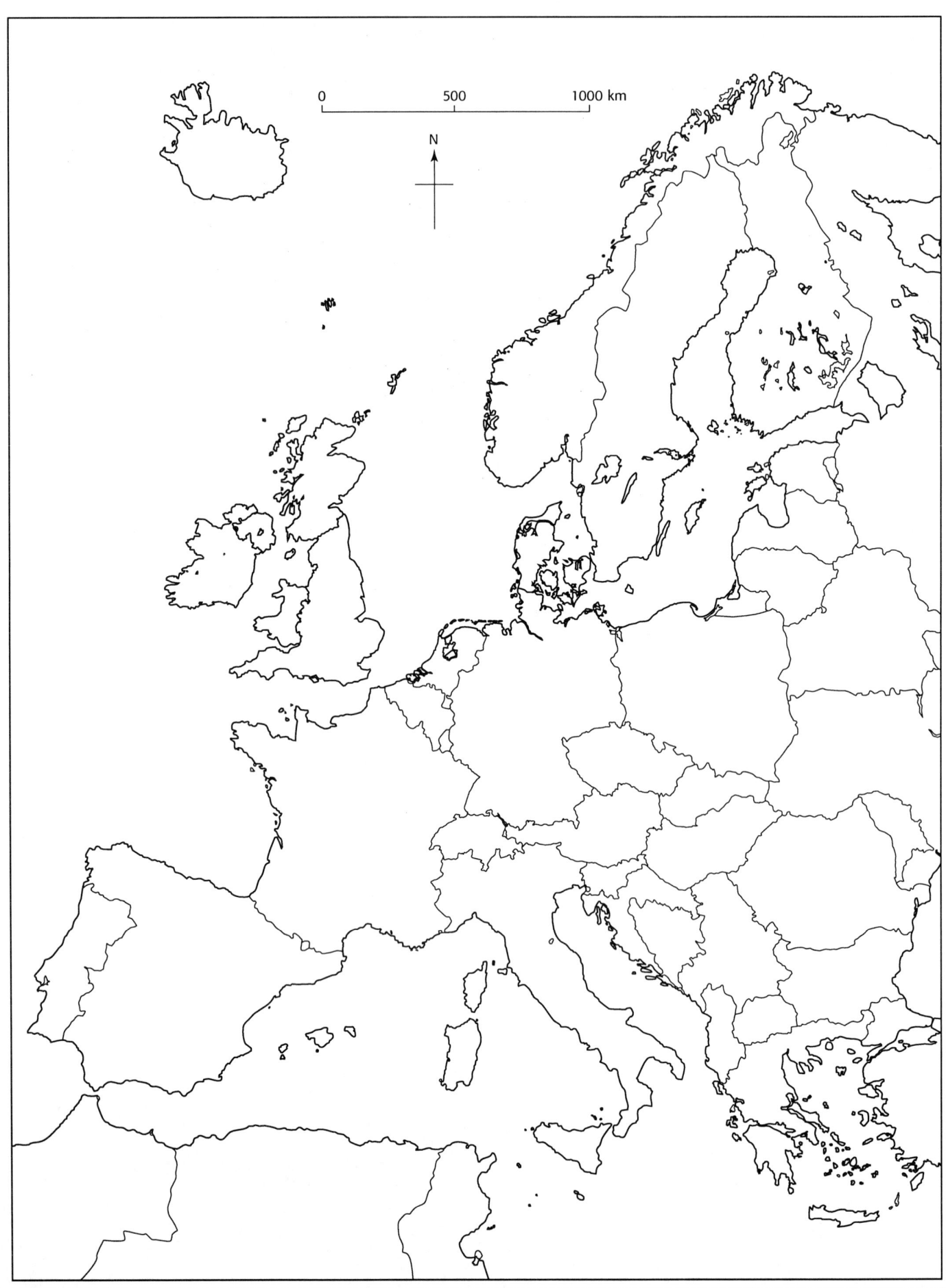

0   500   1000 km

N

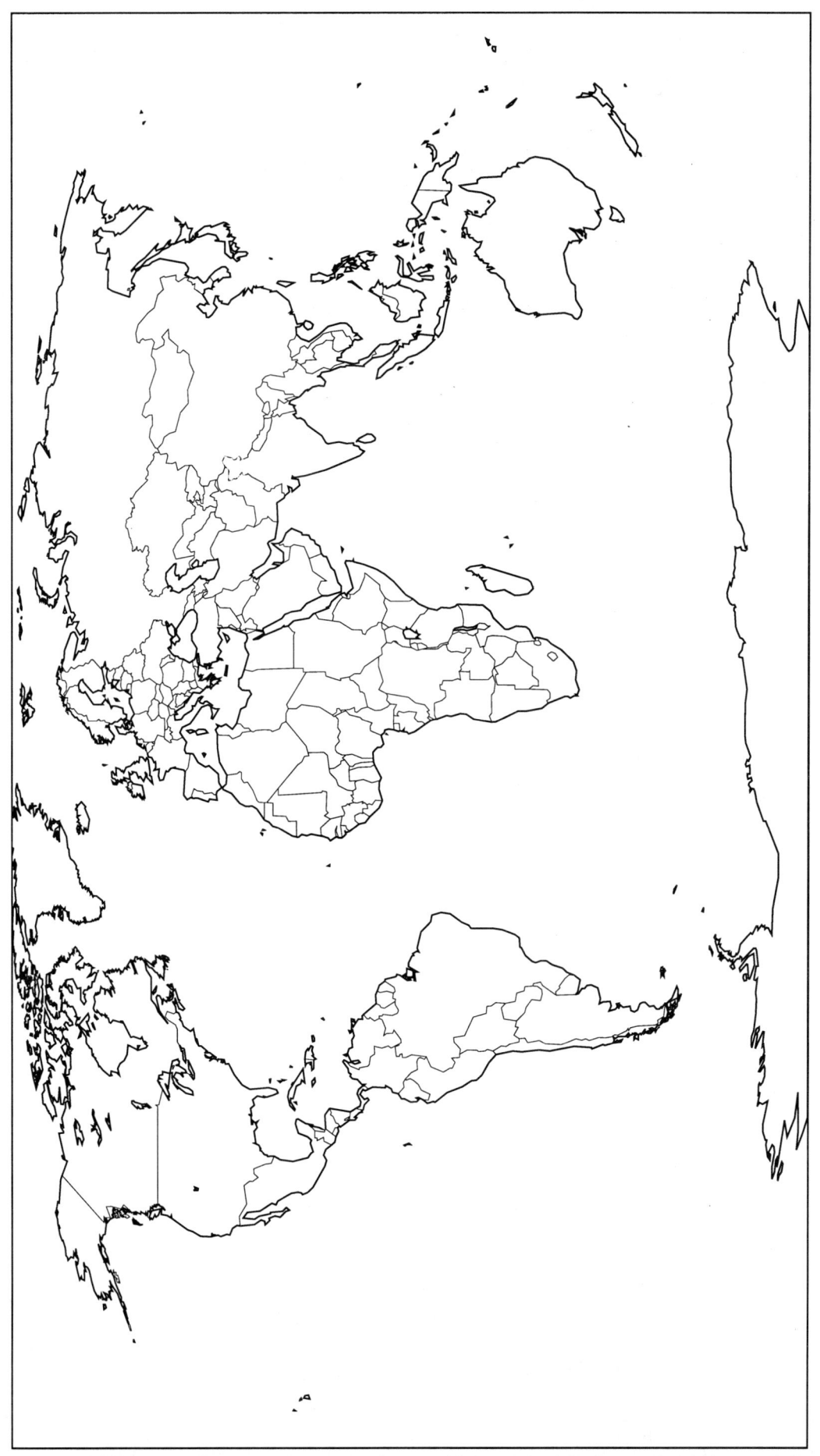

The World – regions to know

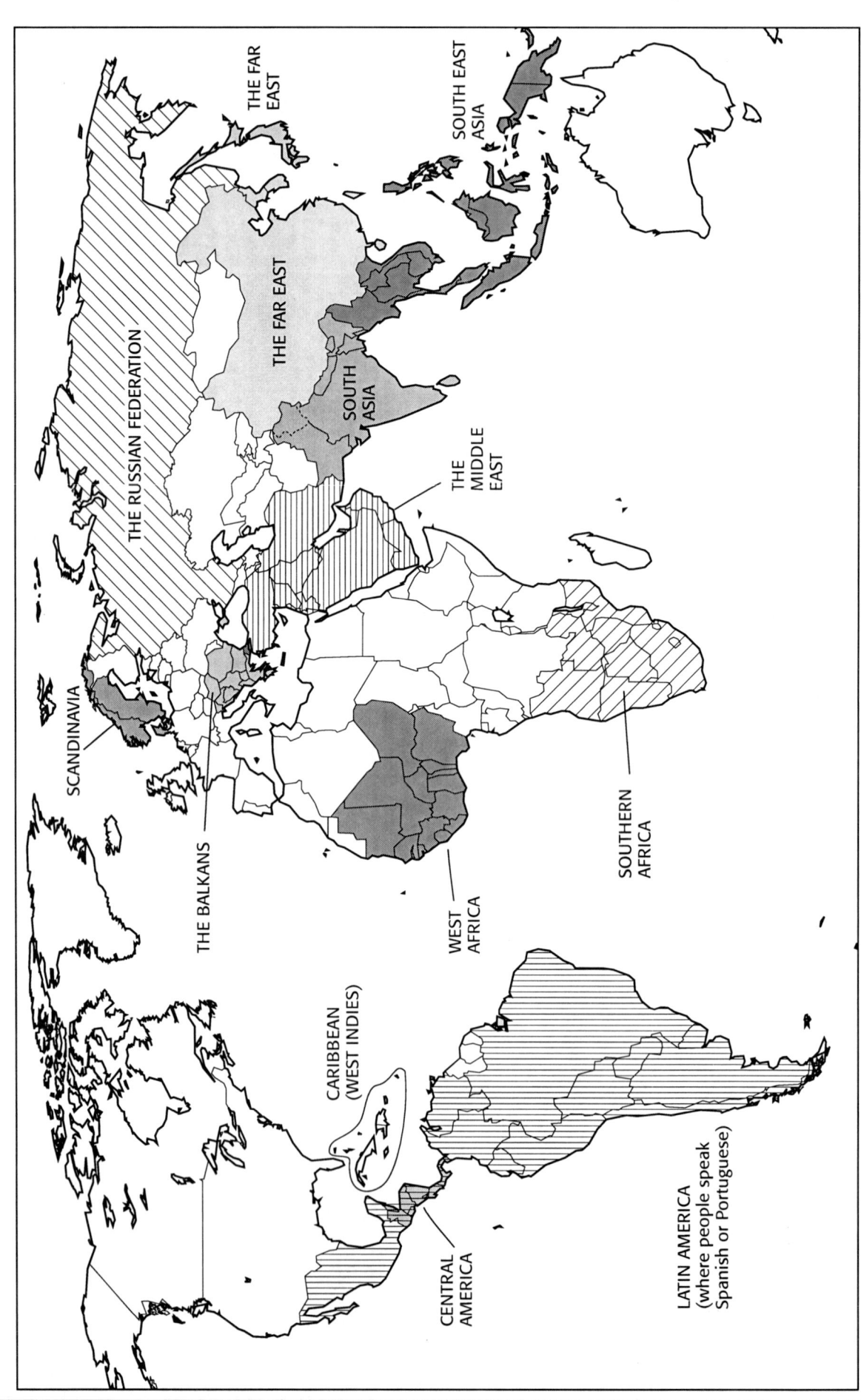

THE FAR EAST

SOUTH EAST ASIA

THE RUSSIAN FEDERATION

THE FAR EAST

SOUTH ASIA

THE MIDDLE EAST

SCANDINAVIA

THE BALKANS

SOUTHERN AFRICA

WEST AFRICA

CARIBBEAN (WEST INDIES)

LATIN AMERICA (where people speak Spanish or Portuguese)

CENTRAL AMERICA